BEVERLY HILLS CONCENTRATION CAMP

BEVERLY HILLS
CONCENTRATION CAMP

A Healing Journey and Memoir

RANDI MAGGID

10/30/2017

Dear Lisa,

It was so great meeting
you and hearing about your
journey. See you real soon

Love Randi Maggid.

P.S.
Enjoy
the
book!

FLYING
SQUIRREL
PUBLISHING

BEVERLY HILLS CONCENTRATION CAMP:
A Healing Journey and Memoir
by Randi Maggid

Published by:
Flying Squirrel Publishing
PMB #804
269 South Beverly Drive
Beverly Hills, CA 90212
USA

Copyright © 2016 Randi Maggid
First Edition
Printed in the United States of America

Cover and Page Design: Elizabeth Barbaglia - www.heldintheheart.com
Cover art: Painting "Savior Soul", Cher Lyn - www.mysticartmedicine.com
Back cover photograph: Gary LeBlanc - leblancphoto@msn.com
Publishing: Warwick Associates - www.warwickassociates.com

Library of Congress Cataloging-in-Publication Data

    Maggid, Randi, author.
      Beverly Hills concentration camp : a healing journey
    and memoir / Randi Maggid. -- First edition.
      pages cm
      LCCN 2015957172
      ISBN 978-0-9969693-0-7
      ISBN 978-0-9969693-1-4
      ISBN 978-0-9969693-2-1

      1. Maggid, Randi. 2. Children of Holocaust survivors
    --United States--Biography. 3. Autobiographies.
    I. Title.

    E184.37.M334A3 2015   940.53'18092
                    QBI15-600227

This book is dedicated to my Mother
with all of my heart
and to the memory of my Father.

Also to Ben, Liana and Adam—
in appreciation, gratitude and with all my love.

May we all let go and heal from the turmoil
of our lineages and set ourselves free.

TABLE OF CONTENTS

(Contents continued)

FORWARD · David Elliott

> *A renowned teacher and healer, David Elliott has helped clients from around the world to heal their deepest fears, blocks and negative beliefs. Reconnecting people with the power of self-love, he shares his gift of clairaudient hearing. He is the author of* The Baptism, Healing *and* The Reluctant Healer.

Randi Maggid (Alix) was raised with a steady stream of the soul-destroying horrors of the Holocaust, as experienced by her mother. After hearing her read at a writers' group that I led, I developed a deep connection to her and an understanding of the events and the players involved in her life, and the effect on families of Holocaust survivors. It was always an adventure when she shared her writing!

Randi also showed up at one of my healing groups and she came to some private sessions, when I found her to be overly fearful. As she explained her family's involvement with the Holocaust, I realized this to be one of the root causes of her fears and her emotional struggle. Through the years I have gotten to know her well and have watched her appetite for growth and evolution flourish. She has worked as hard as anyone I know to deal with her family's heritage and her emotional scars while building a normal life, and that is the fascinating heart of this book.

The book covers a much broader swath of Randi's life than just her mother's lingering memories and, at times, harsh treatment of her daughter. Along with the drama of her upbringing and the challenges of raising her own children, she has injected into her story her lively sense of humor and rich, colorful scenes of an examined life as a mother and wife.

As a healer, writer and artist, I have discovered that one of the most direct routes to healing, especially for highly creative people such as Randi, is to encourage them to express themselves and use their unique gifts. When someone is shut down spiritually or blocking guidance from the spiritual realm, this can be the main cause of illness and unhappiness. Randi's journey and her writing have helped her to become a healed and happy person who enjoys self-love, a spiritual connection and creative expression.

Writing this book has helped her uncover and accept the missing pieces in her life and in her lineage. As she unwinds her story here, her readers will reflect on their own lives and may realize that what happened to their family members generations ago could still be affecting them today.

I have watched Randi wake up and become aware of her gifts and her voice, and I see her as a teacher now, helping people find their way through similar family legacies. The world is a better place by having a person like Randi Maggid in it!

David Elliott
Los Angeles

INTRODUCTION

The waves crashed hard against the pristine sand and six pelicans sailed overhead as I slowed my pace, the daily walking ritual I employed to combat the agony in my body. Gazing at the vast hill behind the beach as it touched the sky, I was uplifted by a euphoric epiphany. I would document the saga of my healing journey, sharing how I opened to creativity and transformed into an empowered and fulfilled woman as I dug my way out of the psychological suffering I had endured, the upbringing from hell—the "Beverly Hills Concentration Camp."

The unaware creator of this saga was my mother, who survived the Nazi death camps only to re-create so much of their essence within our family. While the title is graphic, as hard as I tried to find a different one, none other could more accurately reflect my experience. It's true my experience can never compare with the harsh reality of imprisonment in a concentration camp or with the suffering of any victims of war.

The story begins when I was a little girl in Beverly Hills, California and is told through my memories, my unconscious being the storyteller who reveals my intense private nightmare. My traumas once recalled are released gradually changing me into who I am. In this book I take a risk by showing my truth and accepting the consequences.

The setting is my current life as a wife and mother of two in Los Angeles, my home and the setting where many of my frequent flashbacks (italicized) were triggered.

The central message of the book is that people can heal themselves as I did. When I could no longer keep the person inside separate from the one I showed the world, I was forced to make the choice between staying where I was, caged and afraid, or moving forward to grow and heal. I confronted my fear and landed softly, better, stronger and more eager. This breakthrough to freedom feels as though "the world is my oyster." As a close friend commented, "It's as though the veil has been lifted from your face. Now we can see you!" This book describes the healing paths I followed, those that worked and those that didn't. My success is the result of being open to a variety of alternative healing practices, being diligent in repeating the ones that worked, and the determination to be happy.

The Holocaust survivors' field of influence is vast. I've learned that the negative energies of a trauma suffered by one generation can be passed on to the next. This is called "epigenetic inheritance." In *The Guardian* on Friday August 21, 2015, Helen Thompson wrote, "Genetic changes stemming from the trauma suffered by Holocaust survivors are capable of being passed onto their children, the clearest sign yet that one person's life experience can affect subsequent generations." Based on a genetic study concentrating on 32 Jewish men and women who had been prisoners in Nazi concentration camps, it was discovered that the genes of their children were more likely to have stress disorders compared to other Jews who did not have the same defenselessness. "These gene changes in children could only be attributed to Holocaust exposure in the parents," said Rachel Yehuda, who led the study at Mt. Sinai hospital in New York. There are also studies indicating that this genetic pattern was passed to the grandchildren of Holocaust survivors.

In the healing process, none of us is alone and each of us represents what has not been fully experienced and accepted within our family and history. As I continue in my life's journey after letting go of so much, I hope to no longer be a generational carrier. It ends with me. I am unplugging and changing the trajectory, a relief and a reward for helping create a shift in the lineage. It is not just that I am being healed, but it is also a change in the genetic direction. In fact, the traumas of every generational lineage are many and varied. The universal need for healing is great and offers a vital message of hope for people of all backgrounds.

As a result of the healing work (healing means "becoming whole") I opened psychically, and have visions, perceptions of the past and future, and can increasingly "read" people. I have found a calling as a healer and writer. Others will find their own different and surprising outcomes, fine-tuning their gifts as they release outmoded and painful ways and use their newfound freedom to blossom into new being-ness.

Healers David Elliott, Hyla Cass, MD, Dr. Donald M. Epstein, Loretta Sparks, LMFT, Dr. Grace Syn, Dr. Ruth Ziemba, Dr. Marie Cavanaugh and others have agreed to have their names in my work. I had many chiropractors, guides, teachers and friends who have helped me learn and develop. Using my discretion, I changed the names, places, occupations and some actual events in this book to protect identities. Any similarities to real people are a coincidence. Using aliases to represent some of the characters made truths easier to express. Interested people can go to my website to find a list of practitioners that I worked with in this book along with further information at www.randimaggid.com or www.beverlyhillsconcentrationcamp.com.

1
The Morning

"**A**re you okay?" the African American policewoman asked, responding to my emergency call to the Spanish house when I was 15. Attractive and fit, she wore her hair in a high, tight ponytail.

"Yes. I'm okay."

"Any bumps or bruises?"

"No."

"We know about him," she said. "And I understand. Look, as long as you are under eighteen and your brother hasn't hurt you physically, we can't do anything." She cleared her throat and looked me straight in the eye. "As soon as you turn eighteen, you need to get out of here."

Twenty-five years later, light streamed in through the corners of the olive-colored batik curtains. As I squinted away from the mid-morning Los Angeles sun, stretching my body the full length of the bed, I pointed my toes farther than I thought I could before curling into a fetal position. Holding my luscious Egyptian cotton sheets close inside the soothing womb of my bed just a little longer, I languished under the warm duvet. Distant sounds echoed from the den, the life-giving voices of my family waiting for me to get up.

Dreading this day, I stayed in bed longer, tired of old obligations I didn't want to meet as I acted out the scenes of my daily life. "I need my coffee," I thought.

Imagining the Italian stovetop espresso pot sending its aromatic scent throughout the house, I hoisted myself up. Dressed in my favorite happy-face thermal pajamas, I wobbled along the hardwood floor toward the off-white and granite kitchen. I ground Kauai Blue Mountain coffee beans, filling the pot before setting it atop the blue gas flame. Jack entered the kitchen sneaking a quick bear hug from behind. "Good morning," he said. "What a sunny winter day! Aren't you glad we aren't still living in Chicago? It's got to be 20 below there right now," his very words triggering a flashback to before we were married.

Picked up in a black limo from the Ritz Carlton in Chicago, I was driven to the Chicago Furniture and Gift Show located at the convention center where the annual orgy of people showing their merchandise from all over the world was taking place. Looking to sell their wares, sales reps, business owners and creative staffers were meeting to negotiate and buy and sell, while at the same time looking forward to their annual secret hookups—at least that's what I had heard. Notorious for being extra friendly, many of the attendees seemed to have more on their minds than just sales figures. Lucy and I worked grueling hours standing on our feet all day, introducing our furniture lines to the world and trying to sell them to buyers entering our booth. Even though Lucy was the owner's granddaughter, she worked harder than everyone else.

Entertaining retail and wholesale customers in the evenings, we dined at trendy restaurants with one-word names. Monday night we were at Tomato, a refurbished warehouse, along with the entire Urban Function & Impulse team, 108 stores under their corporate belt. Andrea Sarnoff, the vice-president, was a boisterous and funny woman with big, bright red hair who wore heavy blue eye shadow. She spoke with eloquence only after her third martini. She depended on Harvey Ellison, a dark, handsome man with a handlebar moustache, to make the furniture buys. From time to time I saw Andrea's husband, short, blonde, skinny and fragile, drop by the office dressed in his gym clothes. He always walked out with a white envelope.

"What's in the envelope?" I asked Lucy.

"One can only guess."

Tuesday night we had Northern Italian at the Rose Petal on 5th with Luke and John, two sales reps of one of the largest furniture chains in America. Luke was married, while John was all-American with a strong, hard body, blue eyes and wavy blonde hair. In the powder room Lucy said, "If I was 20 years younger . . . ."

"Ha! Guess what, I am 20 years younger," I said, considering the prospect of a night with John. We had a nice time connecting over dinner. I liked him a lot. I hinted I'd like to see him again.

The next night after work I wanted to do something fun with Lucy. Disappointed because she wanted to sleep, I went back to my hotel room, knocked off my heels and grabbed the phone to call Avi, my friend in Los Angeles.

"I'm bored," I said.

"You should call Jack. I gave you his number when you were there last year."

"I don't feel like calling a guy I don't know."

"Call him now!" Avi said. "He'll show you around Chicago. He's a very nice guy."

"How nice?"

"You won't like him like that!"

"Why not? I thought you said he was a nice guy?"

"He's not your type," Avi said. "He's not me."

"Ha, ha! Fine, I'll call him."

I left a message on Jack's answering machine. "Hi, this is Alix. I'm a friend of Avi. I'm staying at the Ritz Carlton on Michigan Avenue. Maybe we can meet."

Calling me back that evening, he was eager.

"*Would you like to get together tomorrow night?*" *Jack asked.*

"*No, I can't. I'm having dinner with my boss.*"

"*How about Monday?*"

"*I have clients for dinner.*"

"*Tuesday night?*"

"*Oh, that's no good either. Actually, it has to be in the morning,*" *I said.*

The truth was I wanted to check him out before committing to an entire evening. What if better opportunities arose?

"*Meet me at my hotel early for a quick breakfast,*" *I demanded.* "*It's breakfast or nothing!*"

As soon as I hung up, there was a knock at the door. I looked through the peephole. What a surprise! It was John, the adorable sales rep from the night before. Opening the door, I was as giddy as a schoolgirl. Our eyes met seconds before we undressed each other like two kids playing in the park, actors in a scene that seemed all too R rated.

The lights and TV were on as we pounced about the bed, laughing and fumbling. I laid my head on the pillow and looked up at him as he crawled on top of me, entering me sooner than I had expected.

After John left and before I fell asleep, I saw a spirit in my mind's eye, a pirate with long, curly black hair in a loose, white shirt, smiling at me as he stood in a small room lit by candlelight. Since I often saw spirits, the pirate's appearance made me feel so connected and safe that I fell asleep right away, a good thing since Lucy would be knocking on my door early the next morning for work.

Lucy and I were opposites, and a successful, creative team. She modeled herself after Martha Stewart, whereas I was like anyone else. As creative director, I chose the designs that would make a store's new line of furniture or home goods "pop." I was a quiet, curvy, brown-eyed brunette often described as mysterious, while Lucy, the VP of sales, was a tall, green-eyed blonde with pale skin who was as outgoing as she was generous with compliments. Customers couldn't resist our combination—something for everyone. Our simple system was if both of us loved something I had created, it would blow out of the stores. We were better together than apart.

In the morning, there was a knock at the door. It was Jack, Avi's friend.

"Hi! I took the liberty of ordering us coffee, bagels and berries," I told him. "I don't have a lot of time. Let's sit."

Taking a long look at him, I was surprised. He was tall and lean, wearing a woven scarf of black and white piano keys, a perfect wave of gray on the front of his black hair as though God had applied it with the light stroke of a paintbrush. His dark brown eyes were set behind round gold-rimmed glasses, the kind accountants wear. What made him offbeat was his ponytail, a sign he was also creative—an attractive combination. Standing in front of him I felt his energy, a chill running up my spine and the hairs on the back of my neck standing up. It was as if I had known him all my life, all the parts of us connecting in a way I had never before known.

"I'm going to marry this guy," I thought. "He just doesn't know it yet."

We talked as we ate our breakfast by the window, the Chicago skyline stretched out in front of us. Then I noticed the scar under his left eye. "Is that a tattoo?" I asked.

"Motorcycle accident," Jack recounted. "It happened in the south of France when I was eighteen."

Aroused by this information, I began to perspire and wished I had time to learn more about his wild side. If only my work responsibilities weren't tugging on me. "It's late," I said. "Gotta go. Have a great day."

"You too," Jack said.

The next evening, the Chicago Furniture and Gift Show ended at 6:00 pm. Relaxing in my room later, Lucy was finally ready to have some fun.

"What should we do tonight?" she asked.

"I have Ecstasy," I said.

"What? You're joking!"

"*Nope, not joking. Avi gave it to me months ago. I just threw it in my suitcase.*"

Staring at each other, we smiled. Lucy pulled a cold split of dry Chardonnay from the mini bar, uncorked it, and poured us two glasses. We swallowed one white tablet each with the wine.

"*Let's go out,*" *I said.*

The cab dropped us off at the Black and White Sardine Bar. Seated at a blue table, we laughed so hard we almost fell off our black leather bar stools. Waves of happiness ran through me, and my skin was super-sensitive. All I wanted to do was touch myself because it felt so amazing. Hugging my chest so I could run my hands over my own arms again and again, I noticed Lucy doing the same. We both laughed hysterically; then, not wanting to cause a scene, we left.

"*I'm scared,*" *Lucy said.*

"*Everything's fine, let's go back to the hotel,*" *I said. Once we arrived back at the Ritz, we were too energized to sit cooped-up in a hotel room.*

"*What do we do?*" *Lucy asked.* "*What if our customers see us here in the lobby laughing like this?*"

"*Don't worry. I'll call Jack, Avi's friend. He'll take care of us.*" *I phoned Jack from the lobby.*

"*Hi Jack, this is Alix.*"

"*Oh hi, Alix! What's going on?*"

"*Uh, my girlfriend and I just took some Ecstasy. Do you think you could come over?*"

Jack's dream had just come true. "*I'll be right there,*" *he said.*

"*Meet us in the lobby near the fountain.*"

As we waited for Jack, Lucy stared at the large circular light fixture above the fountain, a caravan of gold horse and carriages.

"*They're moving,*" *she said.* "*The horses up there are going fast.*"

Lucy's head was moving in circles as if she were following a race at the track. When Jack entered the lobby, he noticed Lucy staring up. "*What's she doing?*"

"Watching the horses run," I said.

"Oh god, we'd better go," he laughed.

Once outside, we were relieved. Jack hailed a cab.

"Where to?" the cab driver asked.

"Kingston Mines," Jack replied.

Walking into the blues club, we blended into the dancing crowd until we found seats at a table in front of the band. The club smelled like smoke mixed with beer and burgers, a non-appetizing scent, the Ecstasy having made my stomach muscles tight. Laughing and smiling, we were having a great time, the hours seeming like minutes. The lead singer turned away from us and had a chat with his band. Turning back around, he looked at Lucy and said into his microphone, "The band and I are wondering what you are thinking about."

Lucy turned red while the audience laughed, and the band continued to play, intermittently flirting with Lucy. Hungry as the Ecstasy wore off, we had beer, cheeseburgers and fries with lots of catsup.

"Let's go to The Green Mill next," Jack suggested as we rode away in a cab.

Once inside The Green Mill, Jack pointed out all the secret rooms where Al Capone and his mafia friends used to hang out. It was a small and elegant jazz club, with green velvet curtains and white tablecloths. We listened to music while polishing off a bottle of Cabernet and a fruit and cheese plate. Afterward, Jack escorted us back to the Ritz, gave us hugs and watched Lucy and me take the elevator up.

The next morning I almost didn't recognize myself, sticky, sickly and pale, drained of life, my cheeks sore from all the smiling. How could I have smiled so much last night and feel so terrible today? Getting back into bed, I slept until 4:00 pm when Jack called.

"How about staying for the weekend?" he asked.

After changing my flight I took a cab to the Michigan Grand, the Art Deco-style high-rise where Jack lived. The large silver elevator was filled with stylish executives coming back from work; their scent was a mélange of colognes and perfumes making my nostrils itch as I ascended to the fortieth floor.

Jack greeted me at the door and said, "Hi! Come in and relax while I get dinner ready."

I sat on the couch and kicked off my shoes. Jack brought out two wine glasses and placed them on the dining table. He pulled open the shades to reveal an expansive city view. As I stared out, Jack uncorked a bottle of Merlot.

"Something smells amazing," I noticed.

"It's my homemade Bolognese sauce."

Jack disappeared into the kitchen. The sounds of pots and pans and dishes clanking made me hungrier. Comfortable as if I were at home, I relished the moment. "Nice that he cooks," I thought. "I certainly can't!"

"Sit down," he said as he filled our wine glasses.

He went back into the kitchen and came out carrying two steaming bowls of spaghetti Bolognese and set them on the table. We ate enjoying every bite, a most romantic night with everything fitting together just right.

As I finished my second espresso, the flashback faded and my hungry family wanted breakfast.

I cooked up bacon and eggs for Jack, Lola, Aidan and myself. Aidan just seven and a half years old was melancholy after yesterday's fishing trip with our neighbor Barry's family. He had walked through the door with a mischievous smile on his sunburnt face and his chestnut hair was a mess. "Look! I caught a fish!" He filled the bathtub with water thinking that's what we do with the fish we catch. We play with it. But, when he went into the kitchen to retrieve the fish he saw Jack cleaning it in the sink! Aidan was destroyed. Hearing him sob, Lola, ten years old, compact and strong, walked out of her bedroom wearing a pink tutu, colorful sparkly make-up and a princess tiara atop her long brown hair. She teetered between consoling Aidan and making fun of him, pushing his buttons as she saw fit. "Come on…you knew we were going to eat that fish, didn't you?" she coaxed with a smile.

Aidan turned red with anger before yelling at the top of his lungs, "I did not! I even named my fish Finneas!"

"Dad told you to throw it back in the ocean! You threw the first fish back," Lola badgered.

As Aidan's tears flowed, Lola knew she had gone too far. "I'm sorry about your fish," she said, and she gave Aidan a big hug.

When we all sat down to dinner, a grilled Finneas was presented on a white oval plate accented by lemon wedges in the center of the wood table. As Aidan chewed, he felt a weird combination of delight and remorse realizing he was at the top of the food chain.

The next morning there was little discussion of Finneas's demise. Aidan seemed to have recovered. After breakfast, we loaded ourselves into the SUV. The day was bright, sunny and breezy as I glanced up at the blue sky, breathing in the sharp aroma of the tall eucalyptus trees. It was just a short walk down to the beach, the place I loved most. My rustic neighborhood was safe for me because it was far enough from Beverly Hills where I grew up, and just a forty-minute drive to visit my mother in Los Angeles. Contemplating this trip, I sat in the driver's seat with a heavy heart.

"Do we have everything?" I yelled. "Did everyone bring a snack? Lola! Did you let the dog out to pee?"

"Yes, Mom!"

Everything seemed okay, but inside I was uneasy. My emotions swelled, and I remained clueless as to what to do about it. So, taking a deep breath, I buried them. Turning on the ignition, I headed away from the beach. As I drove, crows, squirrels and dogs were arranged beautifully within the neighborhoods as though God had just doodled them in with colored pencils.

As I entered the freeway, Jack, sitting in the passenger seat, was pointing to the left, his thumb cocked back as if he were shooting a revolver— his way of signaling me toward the carpool lane.

I said, "I do know where the carpool lane is, Jack."

Jack's shenanigans reminded me of one of our many long-distance phone calls, this one when I was on a business trip in Paris. As I think back, Jack was persuasive.

"Move in with me!" he said.

"What?"

"I want you to move in with me."

"We just met! Let me have time to think."

Jack sent me plane tickets to Chicago and came to California often. For the first time in a decade, I asked my mother for her opinion.

"I like a guy who lives so far away. He wants me to move there. What should I do?"

"Tek a chanz," she said. "Vat du u hev to looz?"

Securing a new job with a furniture company in Chicago, I moved in with Jack. Working and living in the city for two years was totally exciting, especially since Jack had many diverse friends and colleagues. He met people easily, and could change his accent to match where a person was from, speaking with a polished Boston or New York inflection. Having spent some time in Israel during his youth, his Israeli accent and knowledge of Hebrew were perfect. I even wondered if he was a Mossad agent since he traveled so much. We married a year later when I was 30 and Jack was 31.

When Yitzhak Rabin became Prime Minister and signed a peace agreement with Jordan, Jack thought it was a good time to move to Israel and persuaded me to move there. Up for an adventure, I quit my job and packed my bags. Lola and Aidan were both born in Jerusalem. Having kids in Israel was exquisite, since everyone cherished pregnant women, treating them like royalty.

Missing the California lifestyle, eventually I persuaded Jack to move. We settled near the beach where upon I had my mid-life crisis at 40, a time of coming to terms with the fact that no matter how much I exercised, my twenty-five-year-old body was gone for good.

In the car, Jack cued up the Abbey Road CD from his music compilation, declaring "Aidan and Lola need to recognize the Beatles' greatest hits, otherwise what kind of parents would we be?"

Jack sang out loud, "Here comes the sun . . . da da da da. Here comes the sun."

"I am not enjoying this," I thought. My head felt like two large cymbals were smashing my ears together. I tried to block out the music while tuning into the kids' backseat conversation.

"Mom? What happened to the Beatles?" Aidan yelled.

"How did John Lennon die?" Lola squawked.

They asked questions quicker than I could spew answers. Suddenly, a ball hit me in the back of the head.

My eyes on the road, I became aware I was responsible for everyone in the car, everyone out of the car, and my mother who was not even near the car. "Okay, I am handling this. No problem juggling it all," I thought.

I felt in control and yet I had an unexplainable energy in my psyche creating an uncomfortable, chaotic stew. My back stiffened with determination as the volume inside the car seemed louder. "Octopus's Garden" reverberated through my ears, throbbing in my head. As if I were a castle made of cards, if the wind blew the wrong way, I thought I could lose it.

Exiting the freeway, gazing left as I made a left turn onto Robertson Boulevard, I felt a shift in my neck—a loud popping sound as though something had snapped. "Ouch!"

Needle-like pains scattered through my head like bullets firing from machine guns. My body went limp. The street melted into a muted grayish-brown until everything went black.

"Wake up! Wake up!" Jack screamed. Opening my eyes, I saw the steering wheel spinning away. Heading toward the back of a red Budweiser truck, I straightened the wheel with a firm grip.

"Hit the brakes!" Jack yelled.

Sitting up and forcing my foot down hard, I stopped an inch away from impact. Tears streamed from my eyes as I rubbed the left side of my neck.

"Are you okay?" Jack asked.

"I don't know."

As I turned my head gingerly back and forth, the pain dissipated. I continued on my way.

When we reached my mother's apartment building, we found her sitting on a gray wooden bench in the garden. The black, beige and mustard façade of the building loomed upward behind her like a hovering mechanical bumblebee reminiscent of the Kaiju films that show a monster attacking a major Japanese city.

Dressed casually in black pants, a pale yellow short-sleeved cotton shirt and comfortable white orthopedic shoes, my mother at 82 was oddly color-coordinated with the building behind her. Her hair was short and simple. She had no extraneous accessories like a hat, sunglasses or even a purse; a pant pocket was all she needed to carry her keys and folded-up dollar bills. There was an air of ease about her as if she were Dorothy Hamill about to free-form ice skate around the garden before moving into an impressive pirouette.

Cautious of her brittle hip, my mother held tight to the door handle as she climbed into the car with a grunt. We drove on Fairfax toward Canter's deli, and pulled into the parking lot, which was lined with dark gray pigeons that seemed to be standing in line for leftovers. We walked past the black and white mural of Jewish life in America, 1841 to 1985, painted on the side of the building. Appreciating the landmark artwork, I looked down at the old, grayish chewing gum stuck to the sidewalk. As I thought about how long that gum had been there, my mind riffled back over thirty years to when my mother ran things.

Taking on new responsibilities, my mother managed rental units. Often on the weekend when she had appointments, my mother left me at home with Billy, twelve years my senior. Billy was tall and slender, dirty blonde curls falling past his shoulders. Popular, he had a sweet face and hazel eyes. Captain of the Beverly High basketball team, he was popular with the girls while pushing decent grades. One day when I was about seven my mother stopped letting Billy watch me. Never explaining why, she now forced me to spend drawn-out afternoons in silence, tagging along behind her.

Arriving in front of an apartment building an hour early one morning, my mother and I waited in the car. Four hours went by. We didn't talk much. Breaking the monotony, I played on a nearby lawn and jumped over the cracks in the sidewalk until my stomach began to ache.

"I'm hungry," I said.

"You hev to vait."

"Why?"

"Somevon iz comink," she said, "To see de apartment. I hev to open de door."

"Can't you call and see why he's so late?"

"No."

"I'm starving . . . can we get something to eat, please?"

"Vait here," she said. "Maybe he vill com."

I watched my mother leave and walk up the street toward the bustling boulevard, wishing she had taken me with her. Uneasy about being left alone waiting for a stranger, I had a sinking feeling in my stomach. Never had I gotten used to this loneliness that made me wonder why I had ever been born. Sitting very still, tears falling behind my thick brown bifocals, I stared down at my white tights tucked into my black patent leather shoes. That day I wore a heavy jumper over a long-sleeved turtleneck, an outfit much too warm for a day spent in a hot car.

"I wish I had someone to play with," I thought. "I wish I had a daddy."

Returning to the car, my mother handed me a brown paper bag. Relieved I was about to eat, I licked my lips and reached into the bag. Touching something cold and round, I pulled out a light green head of cabbage.

"Cabbage?" I asked. "You brought me a cabbage?"

"Yes."

"I don't eat this!" I yelled. "Kids don't like cabbage, especially not raw cabbage!"

"Datz vat dere iz," she said.

Having not eaten all day, I gnawed at the cabbage like a hungry rabbit, ignoring its putrid flavor. My mother stared with sadistic satisfaction, understanding she was the only one who could set me free. Spending the next few hours stuck in the car with my cabbage head, I thought about what it would be like to be eating a hot, gooey slice of cheese pizza.

The neighborhood around Canter's had changed since my mother moved there fifteen years ago. New restaurants, art galleries and hip clothing stores replaced some of the older Jewish establishments. The street was in transition, a fact that made me feel old. Pushing through the heavy glass and metal door into the deli, I smelled dill pickles, salted meats and assorted baked goods. It was as though the white-gloved hand in the old Warner Brothers cartoons had tapped me on the shoulder, leading me to the freshly baked apple pie cooling on the windowsill. We stood in the midst of a mélange of smells, voices and people, the restaurant so crowded it was as if we were at the airport trying to find our gate on Thanksgiving, the busiest flying day of the year.

I sensed my mother's nervous energy shift to high. Waiting in line for food was unbearable to her. Gone were the days when she had to wait for a bowl of sawdust water with a potato peel, her daily meal in Auschwitz.

When I was younger, she would ignore the restaurant hostess and bolt past her with me in tow, choosing the best booth and sitting down. Not understanding the role of a hostess, my mother treated her as if she were invisible. When I was lucky, the hostess would ignore the situation. When I wasn't so lucky, she would run after us, making a scene.

The Canter's hostess wore blue stretch pants with orange Crocs and white tube socks. Over her pants she wore an extra-large T-shirt with an image of a woman's face taking a big bite out of an oversized pastrami sandwich. "Come this way," she said.

We followed her to a corner booth with mauve, faux-leather seats and a brown Formica table. A waitress with short black hair appeared, tossing a plate of bagel chips as if she were throwing dice at a craps table. "I'm Shirley," she said with a low, raspy voice, an obvious tell of a smoker. As she deciphered her order pad through her tiny gold metal reading glasses, she clicked the top of her pen, gripping it with the expertise of a welder.

"Soup to start, honey?"

"Chicken soup with rice for everyone, please," I said.

Jack added, "And I'll have the complete Thanksgiving dinner."

"I'll bring some pickles," Shirley said.

Lola and Aidan slurped the chicken soup as though it connected them to the rest of the universe—the glue that binds us. As I watched my mother survey the lunch orders, I sucked in my resentment toward her, my anxiety hidden beneath a smile.

As I ate lunch, I stared at my mother and began to daydream, seeing myself many years earlier at Nate 'n Al's, a deli in Beverly Hills, my hometown.

Sitting in a booth facing my mother, I was eight years old. I was sad, having said the wrong thing to a classmate who no longer wanted to be my friend. Wishing that someone in my family could explain how to behave, I made mistakes, learning by trial and error with no one to guide me.

"Mom, what should I be when I grow up?"

She looked at me in a familiar way. She had honed an expression over the years that encompassed intelligence and concern, her face still and serious, her dark eyes staring straight. She drew me in and gave me hope of an oncoming omnipotent answer. Unfortunately, the expression was only a shell; like a large hollow chocolate turkey, you bite into the chocolate expecting something exquisite, and instead you get bupkis.

"Mom, what do think I should be when I grow up?" I asked again.

"Vat iz you takin' for d'lunch?" she asked.

"You never answer me! Why do you always change the subject?"

My words bounced back like the red rubber handball I played with at recess. It didn't matter how hard I hit the handball because it always came back with the same force. If only my mother were like the Zoltan fortune-telling machine in the movie "Big," I would put in a dollar and have my mother's head light up before telling me everything I needed to know about life. With my luck, the machine wouldn't work. I'd kick it over and over again until my foot broke.

"Vat is you takin for d'lunch?" she asked again.

"Beef dip on a Kaiser roll with au jus," I replied.

I struggled with food most of my life, unable to discriminate meals from snacks and healthy from junk.

"Da stomak dozin know vat time it iz," my mother would always say as she tried to serve me another meal too soon after I had already eaten. Plates of food were available, left out on the breakfast or dining room table so that I could pick at it all day long.

My life revolved around food, the only subject my mother wanted to discuss, creating my love/hate relationship with it. If I was lonely, I had the cake. If I was sad, I had the pastrami. If I earned good grades, I had the pastry. If I earned bad grades, I had more pastry. If I ate a lot, I was good girl. If I didn't, I was rebellious. If I went on a diet, I was a problem child.

Offering a serious nod, my mother approved when I ordered a glutinous, sugary, high-cholesterol meal at any deli: pastrami on rye with French fries, Dr. Brown's black cherry soda and a slice of my favorite chocolate mocha seven-layer cake. Conflicted because I wanted approval for me, not just for what I ate, I compartmentalized that disappointment, and my mother, apparently, was never aware anything was wrong. The price tag of overeating for this approval was becoming fat.

My mother always enjoyed watching me eat, until a certain point when her face changed to a long stare, her breath exhaling into a long sigh. At that point, she was no longer with me, but with them, her family that had been killed in the Holocaust. When I thought of her in striped pajamas, skinny, eyes bugged out like the victims in the documentaries, I tensed, unable to comprehend the reality, my mind often blocking it out unwilling to consider what she saw, what was done to her, or the reasons the Nazis chose to keep her alive.

The one spared from death in her immediate family, she had worked in an ammunition factory that made bullets used to kill her own people. She was unaware of what was happening outside the gates while she was inside Auschwitz. Her survivor guilt manifested itself as selflessness, not wanting to spend money because she was worthless. Treated as though she were less than a dog during WWII, she believed it.

Being awoken and marched outside naked in the snow until someone dropped dead was a nightly occurrence, along with prisoners forced to hold their arms up. Whoever dropped his arms first was shot. Only then could they go back to sleep. This horror created something foreign in my mother, a parasite that feeds on negative beliefs causing fear and depression. In my own processing, I wondered why my mother had no physical reminder of this past, the tattoo branded into every prisoner's skin.

"Mom, why don't you have a number on your arm?"

"I dunno," she said.

She skimmed on the information she would divulge. She either blocked it out or was unable to express it. Did she receive special treatment? Was she a domestic slave for a commandant? Was she destined for the gas chamber and then the war ended?

Understandably, everything she remembered before the war was perfection. Anything after the war was stale chopped liver and leftovers, including me.

Grinds at the bottom of the coffee mug, soon to become compost, not good enough to drink. "How could she possibly love me if I feel this way?"

"Look at my report card!" I said proudly. "Almost all A's."
My mother was silent.
"Aren't you glad?" I asked.
"You did dat for yerself, not for me."
"I thought you would be happy. Some of my friends get $50 for each A."
"I don ker vat dey do."
"You don't care how I do in school?"
"No."

Shirley, the waitress, placed the Canter's check on the table after I had finished off the meal with a second cup of coffee. After the bill was paid, I drove the family to Pacific Park where the kids climbed "dinosaur" rocks and rode Razor scooters. The tall grass cooled my bare feet as a breeze blew over me while I appreciated the moment, and thanked the universe for allowing me to be so fortunate as to afford Lola and Aidan the luxury of just being children.

Marveling at their pure spirits, I wanted to give them everything I had lacked growing up. Acting as a filter between them and the world, I saw my role as a gauge that regulated the flow of information, allowing the "good" to enter when my mother was warm and generous, while preventing the "bad" when my mother's strange behavior and traumatic memories could be triggered.

We went to my mother's house after the park, where I organized her pillbox and surveyed the refrigerator to make sure she had food. Taking care of my children while taking care of my mother was difficult to balance, giving them all I could while allowing their independence. I was conscious of the family dynamic at all times, paying special attention to mood changes and shifts in energy. When something seemed off, I packed up the kids and went home.

My mother's living room couch was brought over from the Spanish house when she moved. As I relaxed on the couch, I remembered its original color was royal blue velvet when it was purchased in the 1960s from Glabman's, the "in" furniture store back in the day. The couch made a grand and stylish statement and remained the focus of my mother's living room, even in its reupholstered sage green. Lola disappeared into the bedroom.

"Look what I found!"

She had discovered a photo album in the antique nightstand. Her big brown eyes filled with anticipation as she plopped down next to me, with an eagerness that made me cringe. The prospect of looking at old family photos was torture because considering the future was what had so far kept me sane. Lola balanced the photo album on her thighs with bent knees, her bare feet flat on the couch cushion as she leaned back.

"I'll turn the pages," she said.

As I watched her view the past, my forehead perspired more with each turn of every cardboard page. "How would Lola ever understand?" I thought. If only I had a magic wand to change my history, I would present her with a different story.

"Look Mom," Lola said, "You are smiling here. Mommy, look how cute and little you are!"

Lola was delighted as if she had just opened a fresh box of See's chocolates, the sweet scent begging for indulgence. She was enthusiastic about me. Someone caring about my life was not a common occurrence. Life was always about someone else.

"Wow, look at your brother!" Lola said. "He's so much older than you!"

"Yes he is," I answered. Anxiety rose within me as I swallowed it down.

Chin creeping forward, I peered over the edge of the album. Allan, my oldest brother, sixteen years older than me, was standing proudly with his waist-length brown hair and a toothy grin. He was a boisterous, large man with a presence that couldn't be ignored. Remembering that time in 1972 when I was eight, I was thrilled he was visiting from university. He played, tickled and spun me around. On that visit, he brought home a dog, a black lab and Irish setter mix.

> *"Wow, a dog!"*
> *"He is for you," Allan said.*
> *"Me?"*
> *"I can't take care of a dog," he said.*
> *"What's his name?"*
> *"Munkuss."*
> *"Munkuss? What kind of a name is that?"*
> *After a moment of silence, Allan cleared his throat. "Munkuss was named after an American Indian Chief," he said.*
> *"Really? An Indian Chief?"*
> *It was as though the Queen of England had knighted that black hairy dog. Believing Allan, I never considered he might be making up the story.*

Lola giggled as she continued viewing earlier photos of me at six years old, jumping on the grass in front of a white plastic bathtub wearing only a blue sailor hat with white trim. "Where were my clothes?" I wondered.

Bothered my being so exposed was "cute," I was uneasy in a way I couldn't quite understand. "Lola, it's time to go," I said.

Lola went back into the bedroom to return the photo album to the antique nightstand. Following behind her, I sat down on the round magenta velvet loveseat in the corner of the room. After a few seconds, my mind went back in time, the room expanding until I saw the same loveseat in the Spanish house.

> *Through an open window, I could see the large leafy tree. Scanning to*

the right, I saw myself rummaging, like Lola had, through that same wooden nightstand. Kneeling down on the beige carpet, I looked through my mother's old papers and memorabilia. Noticing a small black and white photo of my father, I picked it up and placed it flat in the palm of my hand like a tiny diamond. Taking a long look, I scrutinized his handsome face and remembered his bright blue eyes as if the photo had been in color. Tears brimmed over in my eyes as I remembered the doctor in the long white coat at the hospital looking down at me when I was four and a half years old. "Your dad won't be coming back for a long time," he said.

Taking the doctor's words literally, I waited for my father for a long time. Imagining him pulling up the driveway and then into the garage, I waited outside every evening until dark. "When is daddy coming home?" I asked.

"I dunno, maybe zoon," my mother answered.

The moment I saw the little black and white photo when I was eight, I became conscious my daddy was dead, my chest caving in as my life changed forever. Loss and betrayal soaked into my tiny heart from the shock that my father had died in 1969, and my family watched me wait for him until 1972. Maybe my mother didn't know any other way to deal with my loss. No one had explained to her that her family had been killed while she was waiting for them to save her in Auschwitz.

Exhausted, we drove home from my mother's, looking forward to Bone, our Beagle waiting by the door leading us to the treat drawer, followed by a pizza delivery, and kicking back in front of the TV.

As we pulled into the driveway, I noticed our garage door was worn and needing a new coat of paint.

Out of habit, I hung out by the garage waiting for my father to return. Reddish-brown storage spaces lined the interior, scattered cobwebs stuck to the corners. Designed to keep things from falling, wire was strung across the sidewalls. When my father was alive, the garage was filled with toys, beach chairs, bicycles, tools, paint cans and footstools. One day sometime after I had discovered he had passed, the electric garage door opener stopped working. Never repaired, the garage door had to be opened and closed manually, and then, the door broke off its right hinge. Struggling for years to stay connected to that one hinge, the door finally collapsed.

"For vat do ve neet a new garashe dor?" my mother asked.

"Because everyone can see our stuff."

"Forgit aboudit!"

I didn't understand why she was so stubborn about something that she could easily have fixed. Within weeks, everything in the garage was stolen right down to the slippery oil stains on the cement floor. Stripped down to its bare bones, the garage was now a vessel used only for my mother and brothers to drive in and out.

"Vat ken you do?" my mother said. "Dis iz da laben." (This is life.)

Her voice trailed off as though it was easier to die than to call a repairman.

The antithesis of the garage was the adjacent flower-filled, sunlit street, which reminded me happiness might still exist outside our house.

Did you ever drive down a well-kept street and see that one house? It catches your eye because it must have been lovely in its heyday, but now has overgrown bushes and a dried-up lawn. Trees and plants, dead and alive, were woven together, covering the stained glass windows and decorative wrought iron railings. As the years went by, our "90210" address became more like that broken garage door—an eyesore, too weak to go on.

Soon after the garage door fell, my mother drove her car the wrong way down a one-way street in the middle of the Beverly Hills. Afraid to try again, she gave up driving. She also stopped getting her hair done properly, cutting it herself, short and uneven with dull scissors, a walking billboard that read, "Something happened to me."

"You look like a lesbian," Billy said. "Why did you cut your hair so short?"

"I like it dis vay," she said. Billy sounded like a parent to my mother that day, her behavior sometimes that of a stubborn child, a part of her having never grown up.

"Jack, let's get a repair man to make sure the garage door is working properly. Maybe you can give it a new coat of paint?"

"Sure."

"Goodnight everyone," I said. "I've had it." Kissing everyone on the forehead, I went to bed.

The next morning, I woke up with a sharp pain that scared the hell out of me.

"Jack!" I cried.

"Yeah."

"Something is wrong."

2
Heal Me

The debilitating pain didn't stop me from driving my car as I refused to depend on Jack who worked long hours, having started his own company. Without turning my neck or lifting my left arm, I managed by swiveling my torso at the waist and leaning my right arm on the wheel.

I parked the car on Olympic in Beverly Hills and slithered out feet first, bumping against the car door to close it, my feet staggering up the sidewalk to a mirrored building with automatic entry doors. The lobby was devoid of flowers or furniture. The elevator had mirrored walls reminding me I hadn't brushed my hair or put on make-up. Disgusted, I looked down, where at least my shoes looked nice.

The redheaded receptionist for the orthopedist looked at her appointment book with her cat-like green eyes. "Fill out these forms," she said, "and don't forget to give me your driver's license and insurance card!"

Keeping my body still helped me avoid the sharp stings shooting up my neck. After I filled out the forms, I noticed a woman leaning over a walker, an old man with salt and pepper hair, and a boy on crutches making his way around the room. A handsome actor from "The Young and the Restless" was sitting two seats away; his body appeared much thinner than it did on television.

"Alix Wiseman," the receptionist announced. "The doctor will see you now. "

Following her, I noticed her jeans were nestled into high-heeled black boots and her black cashmere sweater was tucked into her Gucci jeans.

Sitting on an examining table on the white parchment cover, I felt as though I was about to be rolled up like a cut-up chicken at the butcher. Cold and smelling of disinfectant, the air in the room irritated my sinuses. "Let's Call the Whole Thing Off" played in my head.

After a knock and a click, the door swung open and Dr. Michelle Mitchell walked in—tall, thin and clear-skinned, with large, black-framed glasses. As if she were a runway model, her jet-black, straight hair was pulled back into a high bun. Her body was slight in her loose white coat and her retro-blue eye shadow was odd at best, a look most women couldn't pull off.

"Hello!" she said, smiling. "I'm Doctor Mitchell. How are you this morning?"

"Not good. I'm frightened. I can't move my neck or use my left arm."

Dr. Mitchell looked up, her expression serious. "You'll need x-rays. Call this number to make an appointment." She ripped a page off her notepad and handed it to me.

"I'm giving you a prescription for Vicodin to help with pain and Soma to reduce inflammation."

"Do you think I could get a cortisone shot?" I asked, hoping to manage my own care.

"That's always a good option to try before surgery."

"Surgery? I don't need surgery."

"We'll see," she said, wearing a brilliant smile.

As I drove home on the 405 South with my neck bent to my left, tears rolled down my cheeks. I stopped at Walgreens to fill the prescriptions and took the pills at the water fountain. Thirty minutes later, I felt wonderful.

"What a relief," I thought. "Thank God for pills!"

The next day, Megan, one of my best friends called. Our kids were in pre-school together.

"How ya' doin'?" Megan asked.

"I'm in terrible pain unless the Vicodin kicks in."

"You should try Network Spinal Analysis (NSA) with Dr. Ruth."

"What is it?"

"She uses light touches on your back to release emotional and physical tension, some of which can be very old. These sessions are called entrainments and each time improve the spine and promote further healing."

"It's not going to work on me," I said. "Light touches are a waste of time. I need a deep massage!"

"It's great. I promise. I do it once a week to stay open."

At dinner, I asked Jack what he thought about NSA. He was skeptical.

"Sounds like a cult," he said. "What is it? Something like est?"

"I don't know, but at this point I am willing to try anything!"

I made an appointment with Dr. Ruth Ziemba, or Dr. Ruth as she preferred. She was petit and pretty with shoulder length auburn hair and hazel eyes. She touched my back as I rested facedown on the massage table. Soft music filtered in through the speakers—"Shakti Shanti"—creating what felt like a safe and spiritual environment. Windows faced the Santa Monica mountains, and a breeze was blowing in from the sea. She evaluated the shape, position, tension and tone of my spine before touching my back. Cradled like a baby, I felt a sort of magical energy move inside my body.

"We are done," she said.

"We are?"

"Yes, how do you feel?"

"Fine I guess. I'm relaxed. But I still have this sharp pain in my lower back on the left side."

"Turn over please." Dr. Ruth held her hand on my painful place, pressing down. While accessing my spinal defense patterns, she commented, "Oh, yes."

After the session as I was about to leave the waiting room Dr. Ruth asked, "Was there some event that happened in your past that could have caused this tension in your lower back?"

"I don't know," I answered. This question triggered thoughts of all the things that had happened to me. As I drove home afterwards, a sudden and fierce emotion erupted from my toes to my fingertips. Pulling over to the side of the road, I screamed at the top of my lungs. Then I cried for a while, until, vulnerable and exhausted, I felt as though God had lifted a layer of turmoil. In this new space, I knew that I was coming closer to a truth— something terrible had happened to me.

I wanted Jack to understand the power of NSA, so I pestered him until he agreed to go with me. Jack went in first, stretched himself out on the table and had a peaceful, enjoyable experience. He slid his legs off to the side of the table and sat up with a Cheshire-cat grin as though four naked women had just massaged him.

"How are you feeling?" Dr. Ruth asked.

"Great!" Then he said, "Alix isn't doing well though. The neck pain is worse, and I'm worried."

Dr. Ruth called me in.

"How are you?" she asked.

"The pain is so piercing sometimes it's hard to breathe." Preferring the pain of childbirth to what I had been experiencing, I prayed it would end.

"Lie down. Let's see if we can alleviate this."

I followed Dr. Ruth's rhythm internally, conscious of how she moved my ankles and touched my back, evaluating the shape, position, and tone of my spine. I felt relief afterward. As I was about to leave, Dr. Ruth introduced me to Dr. Marie Cavanaugh. She was an attractive tall, slim brunette with blue eyes and a firm handshake. "I will be in Italy for the next six months, Dr. Ruth said. "I am referring my clients to Dr. Marie."

That night I took Vicodin and went to sleep. At 4:01 am I woke up in pain, got up, walked into the den, picked up a yellow legal pad and starting writing—the beginning of a habit of writing daily in my journal.

Journal Entry #1, October 15, 2008 4:01 am

Again your piercing pain has awoken me. Congratulations, you have lodged yourself into my neck. You are strangling me as I await your secret. Please let it out. Before I woke up, I dreamt that I was a baby and it was wonderful: sexual and euphoric. Peeking upward with my new little eyes, my stiff arms and legs jolting back and forth, I wanted to get up, but my back was glued down and shadows of people were all around me. Happy and sweaty, I was pleasant and cool.

After writing I went back into the bedroom and snuggled down next to Jack, wondering if God was reminding me there were some good times, and I had been born with pure intention and endless possibilities.

The next morning, I washed my Vicodin down with espresso as usual, a nauseating combination. Eating some cereal, I tried to calm my acidic stomach.

After Jack and the kids left that morning, I sifted through that week's mail. A yellow flyer advertising a "neck release," a type of massage at Shapeshift Pilates caught my eye. I made an appointment and met Harvey, the masseur, at 3:00 pm. A tall, slim man with shiny blue eyes and silver hair, he glowed as though having drunk juice from an endless fountain of cold-pressed fresh greens.

Supported by Harvey's hands, I was face up on the table, my head hanging off the edge. As he pressed his fingers into the soft spaces between the discs of my neck and upper back, my mind saw a black hole that after a minute turned into blue and white crystals. Magically, the crystals changed into pillow-like clouds scattering silver confetti. Ecstatic as the pain disappeared, I held onto positive thoughts.

By dinnertime, the pain had returned. Needing more Vicodin to achieve the same soothing effect as I had with Harvey, I swallowed one with a half more. The Vicodin took the edge off the pain, but neither that nor the anti-inflammatory medication could cure me. Like a walking zombie bird, I pecked on bits of Vicodin to be able to drive my kids to school and drive 90-minutes to Beverly Hills to get x-rayed the next day, trying to balance the pain and the Vicodin, careful not to let either component get out of control.

Returning to Dr. Mitchell's office a few days later, I felt as though tiny, yellow guppies were swimming through my bloodstream, a high accompanied by nervous tension that made me feel like I was going crazy. Even my family noticed I was acting "weird."

Dr. Mitchell put the x-rays up on the light box. Pointing with her index finger, she said, "Your disc is bulging out and hitting this nerve."

"So when can I get the shot?" I asked.

"The shot is too dangerous. The nerve could get damaged."

In disbelief, I saw my world land in the garbage disposal and disappear in a loud grind.

"You'll need to see Dr. Baxter, the orthopedic specialist."

Walking across the green lobby, I went to see Dr. Rick Baxter.

"Hello," he said. "I understand that you are in some pain."

Scanning my x-rays as though they were bar codes at the supermarket, he said, "We need to make an incision, remove the damaged disc, and replace it with a metal one."

"I need to think about this," I said.

"If we don't operate immediately, you will lose the use of your left arm." Handing me his card, he looked into my eyes, emphasizing his point; he then glided toward the door as if on wheels.

It was early evening when I left the building, disheveled, hungry and exhausted. Hobbling along the sidewalk in my low-heeled Cole Haans, I thought, "Nobody is going to cut me open. Spinal surgeries only lead to more surgeries! Everybody knows that!"

My body stiffened in the cold wind as I got into the car and decided to head for Dr. Marie's office. She was the NSA practitioner Dr. Ruth had recommended and I had been to her office a few times. As though on autopilot, I took side streets toward the freeway. I held tight to the wheel maintaining a straight, tense back as I entered the freeway and relaxed cruising in the middle lane. After a few moments, everything went black.

I became aware of myself in a few blinks, my eyes opening wide, as though an unknown force had intervened. I was on the freeway! Panicking, my memories came flooding back like a huge ocean wave. Was it stress that caused the blackout? Maybe it was the Vicodin. Something, however, was protecting me from death.

I exited the freeway and drove until I neared my destination. I stepped hard on the brake, making a loud screech in front of Dr. Marie's office. Grabbing my x-rays, I slammed the car door with my hip and jogged up to and through the office door that opened onto a large treatment room smelling of lavender and sage. Dr. Marie was startled and asked, "What's going on?"

"Look at these x-rays!" I said. "They want to operate or I will lose all the feeling in my left arm!"

"Your body can figure it out," she said.

"How?"

"Go home and let your body talk," she said. "I'm sure with a good night's sleep, everything will become clearer."

The next morning, after I chased my Vicodin tablet with a second espresso, I felt like a vampire with something other than blood running through my veins, one of the walking dead blindly foraging for pills. "How long can I last like this?" I wondered. Having always believed in a higher power, I prayed to God for my life back.

Just then, the phone rang. "Alix, it's Parisa from Shapeshift Pilates. I told my chiropractor about your neck. She wants you to call her. Her name is Dr. Grace Syn. I'll text you her cell number."

That afternoon, I took two-and-a-half Vicodin with a half-glass of white wine and felt good enough to put together a butter lettuce and pear-walnut salad sprinkled with honey goat cheese and balsamic vinaigrette, with roast chicken and garlic mashed potatoes. The Vicodin made me feel like I could do it all and be the woman I wanted to be, because now there was absolutely nothing wrong with me. Taking another two-and-a-half tablets with chamomile tea, I went to sleep right after I tucked in the kids.

The next morning, Dr. Marie showed me how to do Somato-Respiratory Integration (SRI), which is a set of breathing exercises designed to connect isolated traumas and memories locked away in the body. One hand on my chest and one on my stomach, I lifted each section, my breath moving deeply, in and out.

After a few minutes, a black eight ball, the kind on a pool table, appeared in my mind's eye, floating in mid-air. I imagined that the ball contained all my stress; the energy of my mother, her past and her lack of mothering; my brothers, and Lucy, the woman with whom I worked for over twenty years.

My job at Urban Function & Impulse came easily as I had a good eye for what people wanted. Using my instincts, I learned the idiosyncrasies of each area of the country as related to purchasing and home décor habits. My involvement increased sales as I had spruced up collections sent to rural areas, giving them options one might only find in the city, such as dark streamlined modern museum looks as opposed to chunky country.

Having worked for Urban Function & Impulse for six years brought me to the point where I quit and moved to Chicago to be with Jack. Loving the combination of design and business, I found a better job in the same industry and continued working with Lucy on certain projects.

Lucy's unusual drinking habits weren't noticeable, until she married Brian Michaels, the tile and marble man. They eloped, as though she had gotten herself pregnant and was in need of a "shotgun" wedding (impossible since she was past menopause). This desperate attempt at a third wedding did not have the desired Cinderella effect.

First meeting Brian in high school, she fell in love with his bright blue eyes and tall, tan physique. Her father wouldn't let them date. Brian just wasn't good enough for his little girl. The pain of not dating the boy she loved was almost as bad as the time her father had beaten her black and blue in public after she had drunk from the "colored" water fountain in Birmingham, Alabama, an event that fueled her desire to become an inner city school teacher.

Soon after her marriage to Brian, alcohol ruled her, facilitating the façade of her perfect, but crumbling marriage. She smelled like tequila at noon. Calling me in the wee hours of the night to complain about her husband, her work and her parents, she drained my energy while increasing my pain.

"He left an open bottle of Jack Daniels on the table before he went to bed," Lucy said.

"So?"

"He did it to get at me, to get me to drink, to bring out the worst in me. Everything is his fault. He planned it," Lucy said.

"Maybe he just forgot to put the cap back on the bottle?" I challenged.

"No! He's out to get me," she said. "He knows I have a problem."

Listening to her blame everyone else, I heard her sipping a drink, ice cubes cracking against a glass. It tied me up in knots she was drinking in the middle of the night while she was talking to me—a conflict I didn't need.

The black eight ball in my mind grew larger, rolling like tumbleweeds with memories, spinning faster and faster as I anticipated an explosion. The ball, instead, turned into a mere puff of smoke.

"All done," Dr. Marie said. "Whenever you are ready, you can get up from the table."

"That's weird."

"What?"

"Nothing happened. I was expecting to remember something. There was this ball that spun and disappeared."

"It's a release of energy. You don't always need to know what it is that clears because your body does, she said.

A text from Parisa gave me Dr. Grace's number. I made an appointment with her.

The Vicodin was wearing off and my eyes were watering. I shivered while perspiring, trying to appear normal while my left ear was stuck to my left shoulder, the C5 disc piercing my spinal nerve. As I sat in the waiting room sucking in the screams of pain, I felt like I was being stabbed in the upper back with a dull kitchen knife. The waiting room was clean and crisp, with five blue chairs against the wall and inspirational photographs of people holding hands and cute polar bears on glaciers. A quick-paced, determined set of heels came down the tiled hallway. A petite, attractive, big-breasted and small-waisted Korean woman approached. Dressed elegantly, she wore black heels, black slacks and a black button-down blouse with long sleeves as transparent as her sheer black pantyhose. Her calm, clear, almond-shaped brown eyes exuded a powerful energy that I accepted as reassurance.

"Hello," she said. "I'm Dr. Grace Syn. You can call me Dr. Grace—everyone does."

I held my right arm out to hold her hand. "I can't lift my other arm," I complained.

Dr. Grace led me into a small examining room where she viewed the x-rays I had brought.

"I'd like to take my own x-rays," she announced. "Put on this gown and meet me across the hall."

Slipping into the blue gown, open in the back, I held the thin fabric together with my right hand, being careful not to expose my rear, and tiptoed into the ice-cold x-ray room.

"Do you see that long white board with the three vertical lines?" Dr. Grace asked. "Please stand in front of it comfortably as you perceive 'center.' Keep your head straight as I take six views of your spine. Turn to left. Hold. Turn to the right."

Anxious afterward, I stood still and silent until she said, "Okay, all done. Can you come back tomorrow with your husband? I'd like to go over everything with both of you so I can answer any questions directly. It's better if you're both on board."

"Sure. See you then."

The next afternoon, Jack and I went to Dr. Grace's office, where my X-rays were up on the light board.

"This is your neck," she said, "and to the right is a normal neck."

"Mine is bent the wrong way!"

"Yes, your neck is stuck forward 1 ¾" in front of your spine," she explained. "A normal neck curve from should be 45 degrees. You are at negative 6.5 degrees—that's a 117% loss of normal curvature!" The cervical vertebrae that are stuck going the wrong way are forcing the disc to bulge, pressing on the nerve."

"Why didn't the orthopedist tell me my neck was bent the wrong way?"

"A surgeon looks for a reason to operate. You have a mechanical problem that we can reverse."

"Really? How long will that take?"

"Every case is different, but yours may take between a year and a half to two years. You need to be compliant with all my recommendations in order to achieve the desired results. Are you willing to try?"

"Yes, let's do it," I said. "Anything to avoid surgery!"

Jack nodded in agreement.

3

Black Dawn

As I was getting the kids ready for school the next morning, I remembered what my mother had once told me about the war.

> *"Dey took d little vons from d school in Ozerkov. Dey tell mine moder dat dey vould be pickin radishiz. Dey took mine little broder, four years old. Mine moder came home beaten, hair fes black, svollen."* (They took the little children from school in Ozerkov at the beginning of WWII saying they would be picking radishes. They took my four- year-old brother from my mother. She came home with her face beaten, black and swollen.)

After the war, my mother understood that secretly killing the youngest Jewish children had been the first stage of implementation for the Nazi killing machine, the "final solution" to the Jewish problem.

Showered and dressed, I drank my espresso with Vicodin, before dropping Aidan and Lola off at school and heading down the hill to Dr. Grace's. Unique homes surrounded by forest-like foliage, the ocean views behind them were breathtaking. Hard to appreciate my picturesque neighborhood, probably the effects of too much Vicodin, I thought the scenery dark and bleak.

After I completed twenty minutes of warm-up exercises which included neck traction and hip movement in a "wobble" chair to nourish my spinal discs, spinal muscles and improve my flexibility, I relaxed face-up on the chiropractic table. Dr. Grace then adjusted me.

"Have you been taking your Omega three's?" she asked.

"Yes."

"How many?"

"Four, three times a day."

"And the natural pain supplement?"

"Yes."

The natural pain supplement contained cumin, cayenne, turmeric, burdock, oregano and ginger. I imagined myself making a marinade of crushed up supplements mixed with olive oil, lemon and garlic and brushing it on chicken before roasting.

"I still have to take the Vicodin," I said. "It's not a choice."

"Just do what you can do. Turn to the right," she said.

Dr. Grace adjusted me with precision, using speed and leverage. She explained, "It's not about brute force; it's specificity that gets the job done." The release was so intense I cried.

"Tell me what you're experiencing," she asked.

"Just thinking of my brother, Allan. He was such an ass, so abusive, loud, screaming. I don't know why I am thinking about it right now."

"It's ok to cry. Just let it out. Many people do experience an emotional release after an adjustment along with a physical release. You know many modalities can help you deal with the past. I can suggest some later if you'd like."

"Maybe when I feel better."

After the adjustment I relaxed and then remembered playing outside our house when I was six years old.

A tall, slender woman walked up, dressed in an elegant, black linen dress.

Like Audrey Hepburn in "Breakfast at Tiffany's," she wore fashionable black sunglasses and a large, wide-brimmed black hat.

"May I take your picture?" the woman asked.

"All right."

She took pictures of me and of our house. I went inside to tell my mom.

"It's those people again," she screamed. Horrified, my mother ran outside to look for the woman.

With incessant phone calls, people had been pressuring my mother to sell her property in Hollywood. She begged them to leave her alone; the woman in black trying to scare her into submission by taking my photo, my mother's fear of the Nazis was reignited. She was probably afraid that they would take everything, even her family, as the Nazis had done.

Dr. Grace finished giving me the adjustment. "I'm going to complete the process with my own checks and balances," she explained. "Please stand up and march in place with your eyes closed." As I marched, she added, "This ensures that every misalignment detected on your spine was corrected."

"Why do I close my eyes?"

"We are taking the visual field out of the equation so your body won't compensate. I then check that your nervous system is communicating with your muscle system properly, and that you have the correct center of balance."

She then clicked my neck and chest with an activator instrument and said, "I use this activator if your posture is still a bit off. This is called a standing 'mirror image' correction." Your body is placed in a mirror opposite of your posture imbalance. I click on your neck and chest area to "control-alt-delete" the bad posture pattern so the nerve system and muscle system hold."

"Great job! You are balanced and done for today!" She gave me a quick hug and said, "Have a marvelous day!"

Aidan and Lola were eating green grapes and string cheese that afternoon while doing homework on our rustic wood dining table when later the phone rang. It was Leslie.

"How are you?" Leslie asked.

"I'm okay, been better. My upper back and shoulders hurt. It's always something!"

"Oh no," Leslie said. "I'm sorry."

Leslie and I had been friends since high school. She was married with two boys almost the same age as my kids. A hippie at heart, she was also a child of a Holocaust survivor, and that made it easy for us to understand each other.

"Listen," Leslie said. "I got this email. There's this guy who helps people unlock blocks. I thought maybe he could help you. I'll email you the flyer. If it resonates, let's go! We could grab some drinks and dinner beforehand."

"Okay, I'll check it out," I said. "How can I tell if this healer guy is the real deal or a con artist? Then again, what do I have to lose?"

Decorated with blue and white shooting stars, the flyer seemed "New Age" and reminded me of a trip I had taken to Sedona with a girlfriend, Stella, years ago, when we discovered crystals, red rocks and vortices.

I met new people in Sedona and learned about energy, chakras and spiritual things about which I was completely unfamiliar. Interested in all they had to say, I annoyed Stella.

"They're shysters," she said. "They just want to sell you something."

Leslie and I met for a short, pleasant meal over a bottle of California chardonnay. Mixing the alcohol with Vicodin was risky, but I wouldn't have to drive for hours. Happy to be socializing, I was also uneasy, on the edge of something and I didn't know what.

After dinner, she and I walked over to the old Spanish-style building where the presentation by healer David Elliott would take place. We checked in, took off our shoes and grabbed yoga mats.

The spacious, wood-floored room was filled with people of all ages sitting in a circle on their mats. I noticed many had brought personal items such as fuzzy white rugs, stones, crystals, oils and feathers. I simply stared and breathed, my lungs fragile and my muscles stiff. Everyone seemed to be glowing, happy and eager, as though they had a wild secret. Nervous, I felt like an oddball—jealous, caged and miserable.

Leslie and I sat on opposite sides of the circle. Shaky, I fished through my purse for Vicodin. A handsome man entered the room. Younger than I thought he would be, the healer walked across the floor, sat down on a colorful, woven rug surrounded by little bottles, rocks and trinkets, and lit a small candle.

"Hello," he said with a Southern accent.

"Wow, he's kind of cute," I thought. "This could be interesting." Suddenly, he looked down at the ground as though I had yelled my thoughts out loud.

"I am not going to look up right now," he said. "I can't." He was blushing. He had obviously heard my thoughts.

After a few minutes of going around the circle and asking each person to state their names and why they came, he seemed ultra-sensitive and confident of his psychic gift. He came across as able to hear and intuit on a high level. I was amazed.

It was Leslie's turn. "I like to be in control," she told him.

"She does," I thought.

He looked up in my direction and then at her. "Tell me more about why you need to be in control. What would happen if you weren't?"

"Complete chaos!"

When it was my turn, I kept my answer short and sweet. "Hi I'm Alix. My friend Leslie brought me here."

I wished I could run out the door. Terrified to be seen for who I was, I thought I would be unable to divulge much in front of the group.

David began to teach us an ancient two-stage, yoga-based breathwork process called Pranayama. "I'm going to give each of you a set of ocean stones to take home and to hold while you are breathing," he said. "They will help ground you during the breathwork."

"Breathe though your mouth. Breathe into the lower belly, then into the high chest and let it out," he instructed.

I tried to focus on the breathing, soon forgetting about the people in the room, my problems and my pills. When we stopped, I could feel something different, something wonderful, a shift. I felt better and wanted more! Everyone should be doing this breathwork," I thought. I now had a direction. On the way out, I came up to David.

On an intuitive level he understood me. I didn't explain anything. I asked him only, "What do I do?"

He stared at me for a few seconds before speaking. "You are holding generations of pain on your shoulders, the energy of female martyrs. Breathe into that place and ask it to give you the answer."

"Okay." I thought, "What the heck is he talking about?"

He gave me a big hug before I walked away. "Be careful driving home," he yelled after me a second later.

Light-headed and on a natural high from the breathwork, I walked to the corner of the room and purchased two of Elliott's breathwork discs from an exotic-looking Sri Lankan woman dressed in orange and green silks.

Leslie and I walked to the parking garage, said good-bye and got into our cars. I drove away as though flying with intense energy. Soon, I was on the 101-freeway heading toward the 110 going sixty-five miles an hour. My cell phone rang. It was Leslie. I pushed the speaker button.

"Alix, I see you—you are driving on the freeway at night with your lights off! Got to go, I'm merging onto the 405!"

I made it home forty minutes later to relieve the babysitter. Jack was out of town and the kids were asleep. In my bed, I tossed and turned like a zombie fresh out of the pod in "Invasion of the Body Snatchers." The pain in my shoulders was unbearable. I was too tired to read, too awake to sleep and too uncomfortable to watch television. Through the darkness, I crept into the bathroom and found my Vicodin, my hands cupped under the faucet collecting water for the three tablets I swallowed before sitting down on the cold tile floor.

Eventually I stood up, found the light switch and stared at myself in the mirror. Looking drained, tired, old and ugly, I saw that the sockets of my eyes were sunken in like little caves, and the skin underneath shiny and almost black. My legs gave out from under me as I rolled down to the floor. I managed to scoot over to the shaggy blue rug, putting my head in my hands and waiting for the pills to save me, unsure of how much time had passed.

I brought to mind what the healer had told me about the pain of martyrs weighing on my shoulders. Swollen with emotion, pain pumped up inside of me as though I were a balloon about to burst. I staggered like a drunk to put the new breathwork disc into the player, turning off the light before lying down on the carpeted floor under two warm blankets. The pain throbbed as though I were a drum being beaten by a tribesman. Listening to the instructions on the disc and the soothing sounds in the background, I breathed into my stomach, into my upper chest and then let it all release. Repeating the pattern, I felt transported.

I thought of my ancestors killed in the Holocaust. I began to feel connected to them as though they were right next to me. Suddenly, ice-cold air blew into my face.

"What the heck," I thought, sitting up. "Where is that coming from?"

There were no open windows and the room was warm. As ludicrous as it may sound, the cold breath came from the other side, from spirits letting me know they were present. All of a sudden, I spiraled into a state of mind I would never forget. I had always had this psychic gift and now it was time for me to accept it. Fear dissolved within, as I remained calm and open to whatever might happen next if I communicated with the other side.

"I am so sorry for what happened to all of you," I said. "You haven't been forgotten."

As I mumbled "I'm sorry" over and over again, tears poured down my face onto my shoulders while I breathed into my stomach, up into my chest, and blew it all out.

"I'm sorry," I said again. "But it wasn't my fault! I can't suffer like this anymore! Please help me!"

As though I were watching Orson Wells in "Citizen Kane" while in deep pain, I saw a face, a black and white image of a wrinkled old woman, smiling and toothless. I sensed that she was my great-grandmother and wanted to hold onto her image. She faded and was replaced by an old man with a cane, a burlesque dancer, and my pirate with long black curls down to his mid-back wearing a long, loose white shirt backlit by candlelight as though he were in a Rembrandt painting. My pirate then turned into a young couple kissing. Images went on and on as I watched people emerge as though I were watching them on a movie screen. At first I thought I was looking at my ancestors, but how could I be sure? Was I looking at my own past lives? Was this a window to another universe?

Relaxing deeper, I watched the sun rise out of the sea, the brightest and most magical vision I had ever seen. Staring into this sun, like I was high on "magic" mushrooms, high on my own breath, I stared with my eyes closed for what seemed like hours. Never had I felt so good, so warm and so nourished spiritually. I felt I would never be the same.

I woke up the next morning and looked out the glass doors, the whole world brighter and my shoulders lighter as though a weight had been lifted. Able to distinguish old green leaves from newer ones as I walked along the hiking trail across the road, I was in awe of having literally "seen the light." As though someone had turned up the volume on all six of my senses, I was given a wonderful gift signifying my connection to nature as well as to God, the Source, a higher power or whatever it was.

I told Leslie about what happened. "Oh wow!" she said. "That's what I learned in that six-week course I took on Spiritual Psychology. You have reached a place that everyone in the class aspires to!"

"Really?"

"That's not fair! I've been trying to get there for the past twenty years. You must have some kind of psychic thing going on," she said. "You should really develop that."

A week later, I went to see Dr. Marie and told her about what happened. With raised eyebrows, she pulled out Donny Epstein's *12 Stages of Healing* and flipped through it. Epstein is the founder of Network Spinal Analysis (NSA).

"This is where you are," she said. She pointed to a chapter called "Stage 10, The Ascent." She read out loud.

"Although not the highest stage of healing, it is the most sought-after by NSA believers. Ascent is the stage that mystics, gurus, and other religious leaders from both eastern and western traditions have long spoken about. This state of consciousness has similar aspects to *nirvikalpa samadhi* in Hinduism, *knana samadhi nvdanta* in Zen, and the stage of effortless insight culminating in nirvana in Buddhism. Sri Aurobindo called it "the Overmind" and among Kabbalists, this state is parallel to *chesed-chomach*. Chesed is the highest idea, which can be understood in an intellectual way. Chomach is the vital energizing element in existence. Christian mystics call it Christ Consciousness, while transpersonal psychologists sometimes refer to it as "transpersonal integration." (Donald M. Epstein, D.C. with Nathaniel Altman, *The 12 Stages of Healing: A Network Approach to Healing* (New World Library), Pg. 165)

"They talk more about this universal vision in depth in the Kabbalah," Dr.

Marie continued.

"Really?"

"Check out a book called *Connecting to God*. It will explain all of this."

"How could I have reached this spiritual place before figuring out how to release the pain in my neck?"

"You have tasted it," Dr. Marie said, "and you still have a few things to clear up before you can stay there."

At a bookstore the following day, I found *Connecting to God* in the religion section, and the glowing sun on the cover confirmed that my vision, the ascent, was indeed a universal spiritual destination.

4

Sitting Shiva

Bone and I walked along the wide country road in my neighborhood as I was thinking about writing a book. I pictured the book and people reading it with intense interest when a hummingbird flew toward me, hovering above, madly fluttering its fast-moving wings. Stunned, I stared up at the small creature, watching it stare right back.

"Oh my gosh," I thought. Time stood still for those few moments, and I sensed the hummingbird was a sign that I was on the right path as I felt the bird pouring positive energy over me. And then, quick as a wink, he flew off. I've learned over the years to be watchful for these messengers who would come at interesting and critical times.

Healing my pain became a path of desperation. Instead of jumping into surgery as had been suggested by the Beverly Hills orthopedic team, I opted for figuring out my own natural solutions. Journaling every morning was invaluable, as the words coming through me in a stream of consciousness led to great personal revelations.

As I walked home, the pain in my lower back was embedded deep, a hard chunk of blocked energy holding painful secrets of long ago. A lighter layer, an oval-shaped soreness stretched from my breastbone up to my throat, just one of the troublesome sensations that were a part of my everyday life.

When I arrived home I checked my emails, clicking on the first one, an invitation to join David Elliott's writers' group, the timing uncanny. The group was made up of creative individuals who were encouraged to express themselves through short stories, poetry or song in an atmosphere of safety and love.

Although I wrote a lot to prepare for the first 6 p.m. conference call of the writers' group, I couldn't bring myself to read my work out loud, for fear that I wasn't good enough. As usual, something was blocking my progress and my potential, and I thought in despair I would never make it at anything. With my cell phone speaker on loud while I listened to others read, I went outside to get some fresh air and walked to the edge of my hill overlooking the ocean. Watching the orange sunset, I took in a refreshing breath, calming myself.

Intuition told me what was holding me back from expressing myself was somehow connected to the pains in my body, and an awareness I was in a life not fully lived.

After the writers' group conference call, I had difficulty sucking air into my lungs, my muscles ached and my back was stiff. Walking home like only Herman Munster could, I was exhausted. Lying down on my bed, I took a nap. Waking up an hour later, I had hot, soupy pain above my coccyx. Sliding toward the edge of the bed, I leaned my hand on the nightstand to gain enough leverage to stand. Energy was moving out of two places: just above my coccyx and from the left side of my sacrum, in two streams flowing upward toward my neck. Overflowing with this fast moving energy, nauseous and out of sorts, I was terrified. "Something's coming up!" I thought with dread.

Tense and nervous, I held in my fear as the stiffness lingered and became worse after dinner. After serving leftovers from the night before, I stood washing dishes when I had an emotional "burp."

"What's wrong," Jack asked, as I cried over the soapy dish I was rinsing.

"Mom, are you okay?" Lola asked. "What's wrong?"

"Nothing!"

"Why are you crying?" Aidan asked.

"I don't know. Please just let me just finish the dishes!"

When everyone went to bed, I lay down to breathe. As I focused on my breath, the night slipped away. Going further into myself, I saw balls of energy and different shades of light. Everything went black as if the shutter on a camera closed, transporting me to another place.

Pushing open an elegant mahogany swinging door, I looked into a room filled with flowers in purples, lavenders, whites and pinks. I smelled their scents, appreciating the sunlight falling over them as it shone through the window above, creating a mystical glow, almost a divine light. At first, I didn't recognize this place, but then I saw it was my kitchen in the house where I grew up.

I turned to see the dining room crowned by a spectacular crystal chandelier. "Was there going to be a party here? Will Daddy finally be coming home?" I asked myself, all of four years old.

The scenes I remembered were those from my father's shiva. In the Jewish tradition, family members and close friends sit shiva for seven days after a loved one passes. They come with wholesome food to pray, talk and eat while mourning together and sharing stories.

This "party" for my dad was a turning point in my life. Alone on that strange day, still wearing a diaper, white lace-up shoes and a pink dress, I moved around the shiva unnoticed, walking in and out of the house through the swinging screen door and winding around people's legs in silence. This perception of invisibility grew throughout my childhood until I no longer felt special, a fact that my mother confirmed at my daughter Lola's seventh birthday party.

We had hired live musicians and kiddie entertainment, and served delectable Greek fare. My girlfriend brought Harry, her four-month-old baby boy. My girlfriends and I gawked and cooed over his sweet face. My mother stared at the baby for a few seconds.

"How meny childrin you hef?" she asked.

"This is my third," Lynn said.

"People should never hef a tird child," my mother said. "Iz zo much verk!"

Lynn stared at my mother in disbelief.

"You become a slev (slave)!" she said. "Who needs det?"

Shaking her head from side to side, it was as though my mother thought Lynn should just shove that football-sized baby right back inside. Clear to me, at that moment, was that my mother never wanted me, her third child.

The morning after, I remembered Lola's party, I awoke wearing my usual badge of pain at my coccyx once again, energy moving from the left side of my sacrum up my spine to my neck. Dizzy and out of sorts, I went to meditate. "Please God, what's going on with me?"

Stiff and on the verge of tears, I continued the breathwork. A swinging door emerged before everything went black, the camera shutter in my mind closing once more. When it opened a few seconds later, I returned to the room full of flowers.

In the kitchen on the morning of the shiva, as though a magnifying glass was highlighting the details, I saw an alcove of weathered red brick surrounding the white General Electric stove. The kitchen floor was a mosaic of small white pentagons. The breakfast room was filled with sunlight beaming in through the screens, with what seemed like gold dust flickering in the air. In the dining room, I noticed lifelike plastic fruits, golden statues, European paintings and sheer window curtains. Pristine white linen tablecloths were laid on the dining table and credenza.

In the den, I marveled at the cherry-wood walls and shelves filled with books. Staring at the rust-colored couch, I remembered times I had slept there. Long, bronze doorbell chimes accented the front door. Fixating on them, my mind blurred as the four in the middle were broken off, and the cherry-wood door was now smashed and hanging off one hinge, with large splinters sticking out.

Echoes of Allan's raspy voice screaming in German at the top of his lungs was the gruesome reliving my nightmares were made of. I hid in the dark corners of the house, scared to death, like a Jew in WWII Poland hiding from the enemy. My mother recreated that concentration camp atmosphere in our home. Of course, my reality was not literally as horrid as the real thing. My home life was a mere echo of the past, with no concern for my best interests and controlled by an abusive figure who victimized me as if it were normal, as if my life were of no consequence. It would be five more years before I reached out to my mother for help. Begging to be sent away to boarding school or to live with another family, I watched my mother, a prisoner in her own world, remain silent and stiff-lipped as I suffered.

I walked through the dining room to the breakfast room, noticed a small hallway and remembered that it was a hallway to the bedrooms. I continued through, recognizing my mother's cedar closet, the smell of mothballs and the fur coats that my father had bought her. Across from the closet was a staircase leading down to the basement where my older brother Billy stored things.

Down the hall was a decorative wood desk, a drawer with a crystal knob and a beige dial-up phone with a curly cord. I had a moment of heightened awareness and love of my father, remembering that I used to sit next to him and listen to him talk on the phone, even though I didn't understand Polish.

Three bedrooms spanned out from the hall in my vision, as I saw myself wearing a long ruffled nightgown. My eyes blurred as I became younger and my outfit changed into the pink dress I wore at the shiva. Peeking into Allan's bedroom, I saw my brothers sitting there, lethargic. Wondering why they were so

sad with a house full of people and yummy goodies, I wanted them to play with
me. I wanted my daddy to play with me.

I didn't know then that I would never again see my father walk through
the swinging doors of the dining room. When he died, he was a contractor
and property owner in Los Angeles, having come to the United States after
WWII with nothing. He took many odd jobs, from butchering meat in New
York to cutting bathing suit material for Catalina Swimwear in California.

The journey that brought him to the US was long and convoluted. He
had married and had a baby in the Lodz ghetto. The last time he saw his first
family was when they got off the train together at Auschwitz.

In Auschwitz, my father's job was to shine shoes and iron shirts for a
high-ranking Nazi officer who took a liking to him. Helping my dad to stay
alive, the officer would sneak pieces of crusty bread and jam to him in his
military boots. He got the job by saying he was a tailor even though he wasn't.
He learned what he needed as he went along, his nerve helping him to stay
alive.

After the war ended, some of those who remained alive returned to their
hometowns in hopes of finding someone familiar. The green Polish countryside
in the summer of 1945 was a sharp contrast to the death and decay of the
concentration and work camps from which they had been liberated. Instead
of finding old friends and extended family, they found that others, non-Jews,
inhabited their homes, occupations, towns and villages. Life went on as usual,
but without any Jews. They were all gone. The nightmare that was technically
over because the war ended would never be over for them.

My father met my mother after the war. She was all alone, young and
beautiful in Ozerkov, the Polish village where she was born. She had attended
school only until the fourth grade, when her family was forced to move to
their first ghetto. Jews were rounded up and forced to live in squalor, their
possessions and property stolen before being systematically starved in

designated neighborhoods kept under siege.

At the end of the war, my mother was eighteen years old. She was one of the fortunate ones who survived, perhaps because she was pretty and strong. She spent what should have been her high school years as a teenage slave, making bullets for the Nazis. Returning to Ozerkov hoping to find family members, she met my father through mutual friends. They married in Poland before settling in Germany, where they lived for two years and had a son, Allan. Times were hard in postwar Germany, fueling their decision to move to America. When they arrived by ship at Ellis Island, their names were so difficult to spell and pronounce, that they were significantly changed and shortened by US Immigration officials.

After living briefly in Chicago, they finally settled in Boyle Heights, Los Angeles, which in those days was a thriving Jewish community consisting mostly of European immigrants. Billy was born there six years later, and by the time I was born, my family had moved to Beverly Hills, as my father was earning a good living.

Always working, making deals on the phone, and going to building sites, my father was so busy that he didn't take care of himself. He insisted on finishing a building in the pouring rain, and his simple cold turned to pneumonia. Many Holocaust survivors were reluctant to see doctors because the Nazi doctors were notorious for experimenting on Jews and murdering instead of helping them. By the time he went to a doctor, it was too late.

5

Peter Pan

"4-Year-Old Peter Pan Puzzles Firemen" headlined the front page of the *Beverly Hills Post* in 1969, the year my father died.

At that time, I spotted the old gray ladder in my backyard leaning against the wall next to the big leafy tree in front of my mother's bedroom. I rubbed my tiny hands along the sides of the ladder. "Rough like the sandpaper in Billy's toolbox," I thought.

I looked up. "It goes up to the sun. I wonder what it's like up there?"

Fearless, I began my barefoot ascent. Stretching my arms up, I grabbed on, pulled myself up to the first step, and kept going until I reached the top rung. Now eye-level with the rooftop, I stood on my tippy toes looking at the roofs across the street and the white flowers on the magnolia trees. Looking down, I was scared.

A three-foot gap between the top of the ladder and the roof stopped me. My eyes widened as I grabbed the terra cotta roof tile in front of me with both hands before flinging my right leg over the tile. Pulling myself onto the roof, I rolled onto my back, smiling and squinting at the sun. Standing up, I rubbed my toes on the tiny pieces of weathered tar underneath my feet.

"Not as soft as the carpet in the house," I thought.

Prancing across the rooftop to the side of the house, I touched the red bristles on the bottlebrush tree. Spinning in circles until I was dizzy, I thought, "The birds are bigger up here."

I walked to the edge of the house peering over the side to see the long way down. I sat down like a little Buddha, peacefully looking out, a breeze coming at me like a magical, warm hug.

A siren in the distance was getting louder. I heard car doors slamming shut, and men yelling. I wondered what was happening. A yellow metal ladder rose over the roof and a man in a dark blue uniform appeared.

"Are you okay?" he asked. "Are you hurt?"

I started to cry.

"Everything will be fine,'" he said. "I'm a fireman. My friends and I are going to help you down." He picked me up and handed me to another fireman, who held me tight as he climbed down, then handed me over to my mother.

"Oh!" she cried shrilly. "Vat vuz you doo-ink up dehre?"

"You're a lucky little girl," one of the officers said. "The neighbor across the street saw you on the roof."

"How did she do it?" he asked. "How could a four-year-old have made such a climb? What are you, Peter Pan?"

My mother was silent.

After the men left, everything went back to normal. My mother peeled a banana and held it out to me, then pinned me into a corner with the banana touching the tip of my nose.

"Iz already opind," she said. "Eat it."

"No!" I screamed.

"Vat do I do vit it? Eat it!"

Tired of being harassed with pre-peeled bananas I didn't want, I ran out of the room.

Soon I was called to the table for lunch, which was chicken soup, cucumber *slices, a bologna sandwich, a tuna sandwich and assorted European cookies. After all that, I was put down for a nap in the bedroom my mother and I shared. She laid a satiny, burnt-orange blanket on top of me. Snuggling under it, I gazed out the window at the big tree, with its thick trunk and long branches that spread out like arms. The tree was its own universe and I was somehow part of it. I stared at my tree listening to the chirping birds and fell asleep.*

The Beverly Hills Post *article "4-Year-Old Peter Pan Puzzles Firemen" created a buzz in the neighborhood. Billy thought my fifteen minutes of fame was awesome. He was getting a lot of attention from girls at school wanting to meet me.*

My mother's friends, other Holocaust survivors, were concerned. They spoke with each other in a mixture of Yiddish, Polish and broken English about my ordeal.

"It ken happin," my mother said about my pilgrimage to the roof. Then she shut down and offered a cold silent stare.

"Vat kind of niz Jewish geerl climbs?" Frieda asked. "Vat kind of moder let's her 'maidele' climb azoy?" (What kind of mother lets her little girl climb like that?)

"Git a small bicycle," Mr. Pinkus Yaroslavsky suggested. He was the well-respected elder spokesman of the group of Polish survivors. "Shi neets somtink to do!"

I sat in the backseat of the blue Pontiac GTO convertible my father bought Allan in 1968 when it was the hottest American car on the market. My mother drove away from our house with the top down. At the Beverly Hills bike shop, she bought me a pink tricycle.

My light brown pigtails were attached to my head like two taxidermic birds as I spent most days peddling up and down the block from the alley to the corner. The fast ride on the sidewalk was exhilarating, especially on a hot, sunny day when the sprinklers were on and spraying the sidewalk. I peddled fast trying to escape the water and got drenched instead, always finding a warm, grassy spot to sit and dry off. As I became more daring, I challenged myself to ride down the high slope in front of the garage. If I missed the tricky left turn at the bottom, I careened into the street.

Inside the house, I didn't have many toys or games, a lack due to my mother having had nothing during WWII, along with the struggles she had making it in America. She spent little on extras, the same sort of attitude toward money that baby boomers inherited because their parents lived through the Depression.

Unfortunately, when my mother's friends wanted to buy me a present, my mother acted as though she were the one having to pay for it.

"She duzen neet anytink!"

Not allowed to receive gifts, I was punished for who I was, an idea difficult to overcome as an adult. I wished she were more like other moms, interested in my friends, my schoolwork and fashion, rather than making me feel like I was just another churned-out model of humiliation produced a generation after WWII.

One day, my mother brought home some dolls. She laid them out on the magenta velvet love seat in the bedroom. The dolls were made of hard glazed porcelain, heavy and scary looking creatures with ghost-white skin and bright red lips. Their long black hair looked so real, I thought it was human hair. Afraid the dolls might come to life, I fled the room.

"What are those?" I asked.

"Dalz," she said.

"Who are they for?"

"You."

"Me? They don't look anything like the doll on TV that I showed you. I wanted the soft, rubbery life-like doll. Her hair grows when you turn the knob on her back. I showed it to you at Thrifty's. These dolls look like the Talky Tina doll from the Twilight Zone that kills the dad."

The dolls were so scary I hid them in the back of her closet.

Coincidentally, Jack, Aidan and Lola were watching the annual Twilight Zone Marathon, black and white reruns from 1959-1964, as I was cleaning out my closet that afternoon. All dusty and standing on a stepladder, I pulled out the cherished glazed handprint I had made in 1969. I placed it on my bedroom table and thought back to the time when I made the handprint, painting the hand part yellow and the background cobalt blue. Pressing my little hand into the soft red clay in kindergarten class, I engraved the year 1969 on the lower right hand corner with a sharp pencil.

"My father died in 1969," I reflected. "That means the last time I held his hand, my hand was the size of this handprint." Tying together these facts, I held my breath, my stomach tightening. I forgot there was somewhere I had to be.

"You better jump in the shower," Jack said. "We are supposed to be at the Horowitz's in an hour!"

"Okay, I'm going in."

"Aidan! Lola! Start getting ready to go," Jack yelled.

At the Horowitz's in Malibu for Rosh Hashanah, the Jewish New Year, we chatted while sitting on the cream-colored couch overlooking the sea. The air was cool and crisp as we enjoyed appetizers of fresh vegetables, chips and hot spinach and artichoke dip.

We had met Marcie and Jim when our kids were in preschool. Marcie reminded me of a mannequin. She wore her pencil straight red hair in a bob and dressed only in modern lines. Jim was an avid runner who, at 62, still had a full head of thick black hair. Even though we lived an hour away, Lola was best friends with their daughter, Veronique, a stunning mixture of her parents.

Marcie said, "I ran into an old neighbor of mine just the other day while I was shopping. She used to live right around the corner with her husband and four girls. Now they live in Westwood. You might know her, Jackie Katz? She went to your high school."

"What was her maiden name?" I asked.

"It was something with 'stein' at the end."

"Not Lipstein!"

"Yes, that's it."

"Oh yes, I remember her WELL," I said. "She was in my kindergarten class. She was the one who ruined my life!"

The kindergarten classroom was decorated in olive green, brown and beige, with a hint of primary colors. With a private courtyard where we played outside, the class was separate from the big kids. Finger painting was one of my favorite activities. I loved that mushy-gushy texture of the paint between my fingers and the smooth, translucent way the colors spread out as I moved my hands around the shiny paper. We sat with our desks facing one another, forming two rows creating a rectangle. Making small talk and giggling, the girl sitting next to me was Jackie Lipstein. She had white, freckled skin and long, stringy, dirty-blonde hair that looked as though she never washed it. Her cheeks were bright red as if her mom had drawn red circles on her face with lipstick before school.

"Do you want to say something really super-nice to the teacher?" Jackie asked.

"Sure I do!" I answered.

Mrs. Roberts, our teacher, could have been a fashion model in a magazine. She had long, thick blonde hair and sometimes dressed in white boots, a white skirt and matching white blazer.

"What should I say to her?"

"Say f*** you!"

What does that mean?"

"It's really nice," Jackie said. "Mrs. Roberts will like it if you say it."

"Okay," I said.

Approaching our desks, Mrs. Roberts was checking on our finger painting progress when she looked at me.

"F*** you!" I yelled.

With the biggest, brightest smile on my face, I waited to receive the teacher's praise. The class gasped. Everything was silent. I froze and reaped the doom of what I though was a good deed.

Mrs. Roberts went from beautiful 1960s bombshell to bounty hunter. She reached across the desk, grabbed my ear and dragged me into the dark coatroom. She pushed me against the wall and then down on a chair, her face was an angry red. Having meant to do something nice, I was crushed.

"You are never to say that word again," she demanded. "Only dirty old men say such things. Who taught you that word?"

I didn't want to rat on Jackie Lipstein. If I did, all of the kids would hate me.

"My brother says it at home," I said.

"Sit in the coatroom for the rest of the day and think about what you have done!"

Stationary for a few moments, I thought about it and came to a conclusion: never, ever, trust Jackie Lipstein while you are finger painting!

Family was over for the Passover holiday meal later that week. Somewhere between the gefilte fish and the matzo ball soup, Billy pulled out a letter.

"We got this in the mail today," he said, "from Mrs. Roberts."

Dear Mrs. Resnick,

This letter is to inform you that Alix used harsh language in class today. She explained that she learned this language from her brother at home. We advise you to put a stop to this.
Sincerely,
Irma Roberts

Everyone at the table roared with laughter.

"Alix, what did you do?" Billy asked.

"It was Jackie Lipstein!" I screamed. "She told me to say it. I didn't know it

was a bad word."

"Why did you blame me?"

"Because I didn't know what to do."

The brisket was served. No one ever mentioned the incident again.

"I can't believe that Jackie Katz did that," Marcie said.

"I can!" Marcie's husband Jim chimed in. "She hasn't changed a bit, gallivanting around town. Last month I saw her at the airport when I was on my way to that meeting in Geneva. She was dressed in white faux fur and fish net stockings, looking for her gate with a group of young musicians."

"Time for dinner," Marcie announced. A beautiful spread of holiday foods were served.

"So I have this new doctor," Marcie said. "She's just ten minutes away in the Palisades. I feel so much better now!"

"How did you feel before?"

"Tired, run-down and depressed. And I couldn't lose weight."

"That sounds like me. Last week I almost considered anti-depressants because one of these stupid drug commercials came on TV."

I took the cue and called Marcie's doctor the next morning.

Dr. Hyla Cass, a doctor of integrative psychiatry, greeted me at the front door of her home office. Warmer than I imagined she would be, she was blonde, attractive and petite. She smiled as she sat in front of her computer asking me numerous questions no doctor before had ever asked. Her goal was to make me feel better and solve my issues. After evaluating my body and chemistry, she would prescribe natural supplements to restore balance.

"Tell me about your family," she asked.

"Well, my mother is a Holocaust survivor, and my father was also. He died when I was four. My two older brothers are nuts, and my mother made me live with them both."

"That's a double dose of stress. You appear to have both Post Traumatic

Stress Disorder (PTSD) from being the child of Holocaust survivors as well as having PTSD from your own family trauma, she pointed out.

"Really? I never thought of that!"

"EFT can help," she said. "It's been used to achieve great results with war veterans."

Emotional Freedom Technique (EFT) was a way of tapping on pressure points to rewire circuits in your brain, so whatever was bothering you has less of an emotional charge. I found a practitioner only a few minutes from my house. I saw this coincidence as a sign from Spirit.

Loretta was a hip, warm and friendly, with stylish white hair and extra-thick, burgundy-colored reading glasses. A great listener, she shared much of herself in our sessions.

"How is everything?" she asked.

"Something strange happened to me yesterday."

"Go on."

"I saw my mother just before she arrived at my house. I was meditating and saw her face hovering above mine."

"Has this ever happened before?"

"I've been seeing spirits ever since I was little. Human images from different time periods sometimes show up, especially during breathwork or other meditation, some smiling, some serious, all making a connection. Sometimes I have a strong intuition someone is with me. I've seen whitish spirits, like ghosts, I guess, once or twice. I always wondered why they were appearing to me, of all people."

"What do you do when you see them?"

"Nothing. If I told anyone, they would probably think I was crazy. Am I crazy?"

"No, I don't think you're crazy. You have an awareness that you are able to tap into. Some people see, hear and feel things that others don't, and you are one of those people. There are different levels of it."

"I have this memory that has been bothering me, too. When I think about it, I feel like the ground is falling from underneath me."

"Tell me."

When I was seven, our family was invited to Pearl's wedding in Philadelphia. Tzella, Pearl's mother, was born in the same village as my mother. Engaged to an Israeli man named Yossi, Pearl had fallen in love and wanted to tie the knot fast.

Reluctant about Yossi, Pearl's parents decided to go along with her wishes even though they suspected he drank too much. After all, an opportunity like this didn't often present itself to a girl who stayed home most evenings eating dinner on a tray while watching "All in the Family".

"Oh, so niz det she iz getting married," my mother said. "You vill come vit me."

"Why can't I stay home with Billy?" I asked.

"No, you are comink vit me. You are goink to be d flower girl at d veddink."

Giddy with excitement during the flight to Philadelphia, I pictured myself dressed in creamy colors, wearing fancy makeup, having my hair done up in curls, and the guests watching me lead the procession as I, the center of attention, tossed rose petals from a white basket. Never in my life had anyone asked me to do anything so wonderful! For the first time since my father had passed, I mattered.

Mo, short for Moishe, picked us up at the airport. Born in Poland near the same village as my mother, he married Tzella immediately after the war. I stared out the car window listening to Mo and my mother yap in Yiddish. When they didn't want me to understand, they would switch to Polish.

I could tell from the car window there was nothing in Philadelphia, besides the Liberty Bell, except dingy, brownish brick buildings partially covered in snow. When I arrived at the light-blue Craftsman-style house, I ran to the front yard to touch snow for the first time. Tzella brought me a saucepan from the kitchen so I could fill it with snow and bring it inside. I sat on the living room floor while the adults drank schnapps and discussed which friends and relatives were still alive. I played with the snow until it melted. My fingers were red and numb.

The next morning, I laid my party dress on the bed, put my shoes on the floor next to dress, and picked out a matching barrette for my hair that also matched my brown bifocals.

"I am going to look so pretty!" I thought.

Entering the room, my mother began preparing her clothes as well.

"Look how beautiful my dress is mom! I can't wait to wear it! I can't wait to be the flower girl!"

"You not goink to be de flower girl," my mother said.

"What? Why not?"

"Dey asked de husband's sister's daughter," she said.

"Why did you tell me I was going to be the flower girl?"

"I jus taught so."

"They never asked you?

"No."

Tears formed in my eyes, my face turning red. "You liar!" I cried.

"Iz notink! Juz get yourself redy! Forgit aboudit!"

Hating my mother, I cried.

"Juz get drest, vipe your ice (eyes). Don tink aboudit zo much."

Still upset during the wedding, I hated being there. Never again would I return to the blue house. Never again would I be so naive as to believe anything my mother told me.

"It's the lies, Loretta, that unground me! Why was I always lied to? She would promise me things I never asked for like the Bat Mitzvah and the Sweet Sixteen party that never came, getting my hopes up and then destroying me, never lifting a finger to fulfill those promises. It shouldn't matter she was lied to as a child. Why did she have to do it to me?"

"I don't know. Do you have any other thoughts as to her reasons?"

"Well, I know that she hates any type of confrontation. She says whatever she has to say to make things seem fine."

"I understand. Now, let's try this. Think about the moment you were getting ready for the wedding. Your mother comes in and tells you a different little girl is going to be the flower girl. How do you feel?" Loretta asked.

"Like shit!"

"Good, now stay with that sensation. Now follow my tapping and repeat after me."

Loretta had me tap the side of my right hand with my fingertips while repeating, "I deeply and profoundly love and accept myself."

Then I tapped between my eyes, the side of my eye, under my eyes, under my nose and the crease in my chin.

"How do you feel now?"

"Lighter."

Repeating this exercise a few times, the pain associated with the image lessened until it was simply a memory. Later, I was able to go deep when I thought of another promise my mother made to me when I was a child.

I remembered the magnificent, long string of pearls my grandmother wore, as she stood next to my grandfather in a black and white 1920s photo that stood on the mantle in our living roon. My mother longed for those days in Poland with her parents. Her father was young, handsome, nervous and serious. Her mother was stunning and elegant wearing a feathered hat, with an air of anticipation and excitement in her eyes.

The pearls hung low around her mother's neck, reaching her navel. A symbol of a different time, a happy moment when there was much to look forward to, the pearls were a thread of possibility.

"I von buy you pearlz like deez," my mother had said, staring at the photo of

her parents she displayed in our living room. Her words blew out of her mouth as though everything was going to be okay, a moment of instant gratification, and a quick fix to her guilt about my lack of mothering. She would seem like a hero, a good mother, when in fact she was leaving me with my intestines tied up in knots and my stomach swollen. Wondering how anything would ever be made right, I prayed and plotted, considered and planned possible escape routes.

After my mother's eighty-sixth birthday, she spoke of the pearls more often, as though she wanted to give me something before it was too late, something her mother didn't have a chance to give her.

"Why don't you just buy a pearl necklace at Tannenbaum's on Pico?" I asked my mother. "I'll drive you! You can pick it out and wear it before giving it to me."

"I'm not ready," my mother said. "Someday."

Someday meant never. A material item I didn't need, but wanted, the pearl necklace on a spiritual level might have brought me joy as I found meaning in the spaces between each pearl, just like those who chant Torah find meaning in the spaces between each written word. Needing to hold onto something, I wanted the pearls for an emotional connection to the past, a history that was more than a chapter in a book or a scene in a movie, an heirloom that could be passed down, my connection to generations before me.
Buying new pearls would not be the same as wearing the original ones my grandmother wore, but maybe they would give me a similar feeling.

"Why don't you buy yourself the pearls," Jack said. "You'd be doing your mother a favor!"

"I'm not buying myself pearls, Jack. Besides, I like rare black pearls. Hint! Hint!"

"Your mom needs completion with this pearl thing, Alix." Jack said. "Just buy the necklace and show it to her. Then give it back to the jeweler before the thirty-day return policy is up!"

6

Cigarette Butts

Pilates was making my back strong and flexible without straining. It complemented the work I was doing with Dr. Ruth and Dr. Grace. Using many modalities at once sped up my healing progress.

A boisterous single mom with wavy blonde hair and freckles on her tan skin, Tess was my Tuesday and Thursday morning Pilates partner. During our morning workouts on the reformer machine, we talked incessantly. This morning, however, Tess was droopy, quiet and deep in thought.

"Are you feeling okay?" I asked.

"I haven't had a cigarette in five days," she said.

"That's fantastic. What's the occasion?"

"A new prescription medication. You take it for three months. It was just approved by the FDA."

"It's great that you are quitting!" I said.

"I'm miserable, though!" she exploded. "I'm starving and I'm fat! All I want are carbs!"

"Maybe you should take a detox bath."

As I continued my leg lifts, I was grateful that cigarettes were never one of my vices, a reaction to having grown up with Allan who was a disgusting smoker.

Allan was lying in bed watching TV, smoking. He used a large salad bowl for an ashtray. Cigarette cartons were stacked next to his bed with a layer of ashes resting on top, creating a stale stench. His large stomach stuck up like a jiggly mountain peak. I pushed my index finger into his stomach and watched it disappear, wanting to see how far it could possibly go in.

"What the hell are you doing?" he asked.

"I just wanted to touch it," I said. "It's so mushy!"

"You bitch! You think you know it all at fourteen, don't you? Well, I know you will always be fat," he yelled. "Now get out of my room!"

Not only did I have a reaction to cigarettes, but I also had a reaction to the food also my mother used to control me. There were as many uses for the sweet as there were for the savory. I had the impression that she used food in different ways to manage the outcomes of certain situations, but I have yet to figure that out. Somehow no matter what atmosphere was created there was a food that soothed.

Pressuring us to gorge on food, my mother was doing her mom job as she saw it. As a Holocaust survivor, her behavior was unreasonable, but not irrational. Every morning she walked to Bene's European Bakery on Third Street and purchased a fresh batch of soft, sweet, doughy goodness: cheese and pecan Danish, rugelach, Napoleons, and croissants, which she delivered to our breakfast table. Waking up to the smell of baked goods every morning, I ate at least two or three with my tea or coffee. Getting fatter than most other tenth graders at Beverly High, I asked my mother if she would take me to a doctor. Wanting to figure out what to eat in order to lose weight, I begged my mother to make an appointment, until she agreed.

At the pediatrician's office, a nurse led me to an examining room where an obese female doctor was reclining in a high-backed chair. Her short brown hair was in a Beatles-style bowl cut. When she stood up, I saw she was so large she had to wear wide orthopedic shoes for comfort. She was the biggest woman I had ever seen.

"Hi," I said.

"Hello," she said. "What can I do for you?"

"Uh, well. I would like to lose weight and I don't know which foods to eat."

She laughed and said, "Okay, I think I can help."

In the car while my mom drove us home, I read the healthy meal plan that the obese doctor had given me. Learning that one Danish from Bene's held an entire day's worth of calories, about 1,400, while offering minimal nutritional value, I was shocked.

"Wow," I thought. "This is what my mom is giving me to eat every morning? What am I doing to myself?"

Eating Danish was heaven to my now overweight mother, who had once been starved for seven years. Food was the most important thing in the world to her now, and maybe the only thing that really mattered.

Plates and plates of tasty treats were always available on the breakfast and dining room tables. When the plates remained partially full, she left them out because someone might get a bite later.

"Doos iz allis essen?" (Is that all you're eating?) If you weren't eating, you were doing something wrong.

No matter how I tried not to eat when I wasn't hungry, I was worn down, so I surrendered by grabbing rolled veal or a slice of Jarlsberg cheese. My dilemma was how to make my mother happy by overstuffing myself while, at the same time, trying to make myself happy by eating differently and looking better. I began to follow the sensible food chart that the obese doctor had given me as if it were gospel.

Cooking my own dinners, I bypassed whatever my mother made by broiling my own fish, chicken or steak and adding fresh veggies and a salad. After six months, I had lost weight and looked very different. Lean and tan, I looked great in a bikini. Noticing that heads turned as I walked by, I had renewed confidence that doing the opposite of what my mother told me was the best way to live.

Nonetheless, staying trim was an everyday struggle, while my mother watched me like a hawk, waiting for a moment when she could sabotage my progress. Still struggling to eat normal amounts of healthy food, I was scrutinized for my food choices well into adulthood. She pressured me at every meal, creating battles of Q & A.

"Vat you eatink?"

"A turkey sandwich."

"Oh, very goot. un heving salat?"

"Yes."

"Un did ju hev breakfast?"

"Yes."

"Vat you taking?"

"Scrambled eggs."

"Only d'eggs? Vas dat enuf?"

"Yes. Plenty."

"Na, tek more bred."

"No."

"I dun understen how you cannot hev bred. Tek dis piece, is goot!"

"No thank you, it doesn't make me feel well."

"How bout a slice of da chocolate kek?"

"No thank you."

"Na tek it!" she demanded.

Standing up to her constant questions wore me down. When I had a weak moment, she would stick a slice of cake, a bar of chocolate, or some challah toast in front of me, and after I ate it I felt horrible, as if I had let the devil win.

The next summer, I was fortunately re-learning and healing from many of the psychological and edible triggers that kept me stuck. Attending my first "Gate," a weekend workshop of Network Spinal Analysis (NSA) and Somato Respiratory Integration (SRI) in Colorado with 200 others, I was able to connect, integrate and release these emotions. My body was lighter and I became enthusiastic about my ability to heal myself.

Dr. Marie insisted I come to her office for the next few days in order to prolong and deepen these positive effects. While I was on the massage table, she touched my heels, ankles, neck and sides. A wave of energy ran through me, my body moved like a snake, releasing tension, while I saw swirls of orange and red turn to black in my mind. Then an image emerged.

I was dressed in a lime green sweater when I was eight years old standing expressionless, my shoulder-length, dark brown hair parted on the side. My left eyeball was rolling around, allowing my eye to cross toward my nose. Aware of how odd I looked, I was desperate and alone as I sat still and silent, a negative energy holding me back, keeping me afraid.

"Dr. Marie, I just had the strangest vision of myself. I was a little girl."

"Lay back, close your eyes and see the little girl again," she said.

"Okay, I see her."

"Talk to her. Say 'I'm sorry for neglecting you in this way.'"

Tears streamed down my face as I watched my adult self speak to my inner child, filling a void where a loved one should have been. I understood the universe had given me this unique opportunity, a moment in which I could heal the hurt that had been hidden for so long. Moving closer to her, I smiled and reached out with open arms, hugging, holding and soothing her for a long while.

"Everything will be okay now," I said.

By loving a part of me that had been abandoned since my father died,

I had opened a new door, moving me closer to wholeness. A new sense of worth, a respect for life, love and God and miracles warmed me over. Elated, I went to the beach and walked along the sand, free and relieved, a rare moment when my pain disappeared.

The next morning, I woke up with a burning sensation in my lower back, and my chest was uncomfortable, too. As I tried to feel my way through it, there was a pattern to my pain. When I felt great, my subconscious decided it was time to toss me another curve ball, attempting to confuse me, slipping in a dark, overpowering and oppressive perception. Always at the pinnacle of when I was most serene and happy, my body presented me with something new to clear out.

Journaling that morning with my Vicodin and coffee, I wrote a poem, a clear picture of how I felt that day— a new type of expression.

Journal Entry (March 15, 2008)
It's been a while since I felt so dark and creepy
Bricks on my feet and pushed down deep
No air no light
Just darkness in sight
Please, God in heaven, open your gates
And let me get beyond this fate
To the other side
Where the air is fresh
Where the water is blue
And all I can see are images of you

Reading the poem out loud a few times, another painful memory emerged. It took place at a childhood birthday party in Beverly Hills.

The twins were popular girls at school; skinny and well-manicured, with shoulder length, wavy brown hair. Polite and entitled, they were typical of many girls in school. Dressed in matching green floral party dresses with white trim, with skirts that poofed out as they spun, they wore white patent-leather shoes, a perfect match to their dresses.

As I sat in their huge living room at their birthday party, I watched the twins open their birthday gift from me. It was wrapped in cream-colored paper adorned with brown teddy bears wearing pink and blue sweaters, with a pink bow on top. They pulled off the bow and the wrapping paper, exposing a shiny silver box stuffed with pink tissue paper. Excited with anticipation, their faces suddenly dropped as they looked down at identical ruffle-sleeved, high-necked nightgowns, one decorated with green apples and the other with red apples.

"Oh, we have these," Jenny said.

Annoyed, as if they had wasted precious party time on me, they ran off. Humiliated, my heart dropped to my stomach and then to my feet as I remembered the conversation I had with my mother.

"Mom, do you promise to buy the twins a great present?"

"Of curse," my mother answered.

"Will you buy a board game or a Barbie?"

"I know vat to buy," my mother said.

"Promise?"

"Yez."

Promises didn't mean much to my mother as in the example of her wanting to buy me a pearl necklace like my grandmother had. My mother had listened to her parents' stories of what life would be like when the war was over. Those promises kept her alive and able to endure hardships in hopes of returning to her family home in Poland, attending school, and celebrating the Jewish holidays with her family.

As I sat on the couch watching the twins through my brown bifocal glasses, I pretended their reaction to the gift didn't matter, and my mother's broken promises counted for nothing.

When I close my eyes and imagine the twins now, I see two spoiled little brats in the remake of "The Shining" when wide-eyed Jack Nicholson smiles in that evil, crazy way as his wife stares terrified at the twins. Chalk-white, long-haired little girls with black lips stare without speaking, wearing their long nightgowns, while pools of blood pour into the hallway.

My mother probably chose warm nightgowns for the twins because they were luxuries she never had as a child. In the concentration camp, she had worn only a paper-thin gown, even when it was snowing.

She even made me wear undershirts, as if I were living in a Hasidic shtetl (village) in Poland, while ignoring the fact that I was growing so much and my boobs stuck out.

"Why don't you wear a bra?" one girl snapped.

"Can I touch them?" one boy asked.

"NO!"

"I need a bra! Now!" I screamed at my mother. "Take me to Lerner's. If you don't buy me one, I'm not going back to school."

Crying and screaming like a lunatic was the only way I was going to get what I needed. My mother ignored me when I needed her most. Stress shot through my stomach and erupted on my acne-scarred face. Weeks passed until she bought me my first a bra, a thick, almost industrial thing, the grandma kind. Not having seen lingerie for my age before, I trusted that the saleswoman and my mother were steering me in the right direction.

Just as my first bra signaled a turning point in my life, a trip to Las Vegas turned out to be a milestone, too.

Not trusting anyone to watch me at home, my mother schlepped me to Las Vegas for a rare weekend with her good friend, Eva Friedman. A widow with a thick Polish accent that sounded like my mother's, she lived in a comfortable high-rise condo decorated with hanging plants, overstuffed contemporary-style couches and white wicker end tables. Dressed in colorful printed blouses over white slacks and white leather loafers, she wore lots of make-up. Compared to my mother who only wore a little lipstick on occasion, Eva appeared like a clown. Her auburn hair was curled tight, especially on Thursdays when she had her weekly hair appointment at Freddy's on Third.

We shared a hotel room that first night in Las Vegas. In the morning, room service delivered our breakfast, which was a big deal for me. Sitting at a nice table in front of the TV, I ate my bacon and scrambled eggs as if I were special. Funny how we ate bacon even though Jews weren't supposed to. Not trusting God after the war, my mother never considered staying kosher.

They dropped me off at Eva's daughter's home later that day so they could visit the casinos and see a live show. "Hi Alix," Laurie said. "It's so nice to meet you. We are going to have lots of fun."

Laurie's husband was part of a famous comedy team that performed in Las Vegas and he was a regular on late night TV talk shows. They had four children ranging in age from four to twelve. Stirring a huge pot of soup on the stove, Laurie pulled out a beef bone with a pair of tongs. The bone looked to me like a human brain. I felt queasy.

"Can I offer you some of this soup?" she asked.

"Uh, no thanks."

"How about a turkey sandwich with macaroni and cheese and ice cream for dessert?"

"Yes, please!" I said.

Laurie was a tall, beautiful woman, with dark-blonde hair pulled back in a ponytail. Her husband was at least twice her age, which made me wonder, at first, if he was her dad. I sensed the love between them, a powerful electric surge I had never before witnessed. Their connection to their children was my first introduction into what it meant to be part of a healthy, loving family. They were genuine and pleasant with each other, smiling across the dinner table, telling jokes.

"I must have been born to the wrong family," I thought. "Someone must have made a mistake up there in heaven."

After dinner, Laurie doted on me. I was used to being either ignored or treated like a thick thorn stuck in someone's foot so I wasn't sure how to react. Responding to a sense of ease in Laurie's house, this was the moment when I decided to mentally separate myself from my family — my first step toward independence.

"Come see all the toys we have," she said, pointing to a mountain of toys stacked in the corner of the den. Grabbing a big, fuzzy, brown teddy bear, I hugged it close, never wanting to let go.

"Would you like to keep that teddy bear," Laurie asked.

"Really? I've never had a teddy bear."

"It's yours," she said.

Eva and my mother came by the next morning to pick me up on the way to the airport.

"Leaf da bear," my mother said.

"It's mine!"

"You don neet a bear."

"I want her to have it," Laurie said. "I insist, please."

"Okay, tank you."

7
Flower Essence

I walked out of a late afternoon Pilates class confident my new sports bra had enough support and looked across the brick courtyard toward Tara's Garden, a new flower essence chakra-clearing shop. Maxx, a tall and lean dad from class told me he had taken his twenty-two-year-old daughter, Cheyenne, to the shop two nights ago to meet a healer named Neda upon his wife Julie's recommendation.

"I wanted to find out why Cheyenne is so attracted to large, muscular Latin men," Maxx explained. "She's a petite, blue-eyed blonde who will only date Latin athletes. She gets attached and then switches to the next."

"At least she's not posting about how they were in bed," I said. "I read that a girl at Duke University rated sex with thirteen athletes on a bar graph as part of a mock master's thesis that went viral."

"Seriously, Alix, I still don't understand my daughter's attraction to Latin men."

"Well, just look at Alex Rodriguez. He's gorgeous, muscular and tan, with baby blue eyes! He's got a lot of blonde superstars drooling. The question should be, why wouldn't she be attracted?"

"Neda said Cheyenne's attraction stems from a past life. She had been a poor young girl from El Salvador who died a virgin."

"She sure is making up for it," I laughed.

Thinking about Maxx's predicament, I remembered walking Lola to her acting class earlier that morning.

We took a short cut through the shopping mall when I spotted the Frederick's of Hollywood sign on a storefront. "Isn't this store on Hollywood Boulevard?" I thought. "What's it doing here? It's like having a strip club next door!"

I hoped Lola wouldn't notice the display of intimate lingerie, eye-popping creations which would bring up one of those uncomfortable moments when my ten-year-old asks questions for which I would need a glass of wine. Walking past a voluptuous mannequin wearing a maroon, push-up thong-teddy with matching sling-back stilettos, Lola looked up and stared.

"I don't get it?" she said. "Who needs fancy underwear like that? You're just going to sleep in it or wear it under your clothes. It doesn't even look comfortable."

"Different people like different things," I answered.

"Mom, guess what! One of the Jonas brothers was dating Miley Cyrus! She even wrote a song about him, mom! But they broke up, and now he's dating Hilary Duff."

Relieved that Lola had forgotten about the underwear, I watched her scurry off to class.

The Frederick's of Hollywood window display made me think of pornography even though it was simply an attempt to attract lingerie customers. Walking fast past the window, I did not want to expose my daughter to something she was not ready to handle. When I was her age, my mother was careless about the negative images I saw, while at the same time, censoring healthy ones. When a couple kissing was on the television screen, she grimaced and changed the channel as though it were wrong to express healthy love. Her reaction was the consequence of Nazi domination and the way they treated the Jews as less than human, a twisted expression of power and love of humanity.

Censoring sexually explicit films and placing parental blocks on porn channels, I steered both my children toward healthy relationships; the best example being the one between Jack and me.

Maxx said, "It's getting late. Julie probably has dinner waiting for me."

Watching him sprint up the street to her car, I thought about Neda, curious if she might have something to offer me. I walked into her shop and looked past the sign that read "Free Chakra Readings" to see a voluptuous brunette woman with long wavy hair dressed in loose jeans and a purple embroidered blouse.

I said, "Hi! Are you Neda? My friend Maxx came here a few days ago with his daughter Cheyenne."

"Oh, yes, I remember them," the woman said. "And you are?

"Alix."

"Would you like a chakra reading, Alix?"

"Sure!"

Neda swung a glass sphere in front of me. "Your second chakra is stuck," she said. "You have issues with self-worth, sexuality, self-criticism and guilt."

Walking over to a shelf stacked with colorful, liquid-filled bottles, Neda selected a few. As I watched her, a clenching in my stomach stretched up to my throat, sensitivity so intense I began to cry.

"Let it all release while I mix your remedy," she said. She measured the liquids and poured them into what she told me was a bourbon base.

I wiped my wet face and looked up. Neda stared at me, as though about to press the nuclear missile button in Dr. Strangelove's control room, and she dropped a bomb.

"Do you think you might have been molested?" she said.

"No I was not! Of all the terrible things done to me, that didn't happen! If I had been molested, I would know it, wouldn't I? I don't remember anything."

She was silent as she wrapped the small glass bottle in parchment paper and tied it with a curly lavender ribbon as though it was a gift, which I guess it was.

"Take six drops of this remedy under your tongue, three times a day."

This was the second time I had an inner sense that I had been molested, a coincidence I couldn't ignore, the possibility making me sick. I cried off and on for the next few hours, wanting to crawl into a hole and throw up.

At home, I took the drops as Neda had recommended and felt more at ease in my body and mind as I went through my days. Unsure if it was a placebo or if it was indeed working, the fact I felt better was all that mattered.

The next few days were filled with strange dreams swimming into my brain in an unorganized kaleidoscope. Confused and insecure, I continued the healing modalities that had moved me forward. I continued NSA and SRI, and continued with corrective chiropractic care, acupuncture and massage, and practiced Emotional Freedom Technique (EFT), Pilates and breathwork meditation all in a ritualistic manner as if it were my career choice to be a Professional Person Being Healed. During all this, I continued taking Vicodin, and Neda's drops.

Haunted night and day by a nameless villain, I wondered if there was any truth to Neda's proclamation someone had molested me. Preparing myself like a prizefighter to face the possibility, I made an appointment with David Elliot, the clairaudient breathwork healer; I told him about Neda and her comment.

"I don't remember anyone ever touching me like that," I said. With tears streaming down my face, as though I were out of my body, I felt like I was an imposter discussing someone else.

"Journal about the problem," he said. "Keep searching!"

"Search where?"

"Ask for answers before you do the breathwork. You will remember."

"Even if I could remember, why would I want to?"

"Okay, it's time to breathe," he said.

As I relaxed, my back on the massage table, composing myself for what I hoped would be a breakthrough, I breathed and focused inward.

"Do you have any idea who might have done this to you?" he asked.

"No, not really. Maybe it was my oldest brother, Allan."

"Tell me about him?"

"He was loud and scary. Terrified of him, I never knew if he was going to be normal, silly or violent. Sometimes he acted like a toddler in a grown man's body, eyes popping out like Marty Feldman's, blood vessels bursting while he made silly baby sounds."

"I don't think it's him," David said. "He masturbated about you, but I don't think he ever touched you."

"Ew!" I thought. A crude way to put it, David didn't mince words.

Relieved and disgusted at the same time, I continued to do the breathwork. Then, I squirmed.

"What are you thinking right now?" David asked.

"I have another brother, Billy, but it can't be him."

"Why not?"

"Because, it just can't be! He was the quiet one everyone thought was so good and responsible, the one who my mother asked to take care of everything when my father had died. It's him, isn't it?"

"Did your mother leave you alone with him?"

"Yes, all the time. Allan was away at law school. Billy was the only one home."

Refusing to believe it could have been Billy, I couldn't remember specific details, yet was guided by an intuition I was on the right track.

"Wait!" I said. "I just remembered something else. One of the first times I saw Dr. Ruth, the NSA practioner, I had an incredible release. Afterward, I had a sensation that something terrible had happened to me."

"What happened?" David asked.

Thinking back, I told David what I could remember from that day in her office.

"I was lying on her massage table face down as she was ending our session."

"How are you feeling now?" Dr. Ruth asked me.

"Great except for the one pain that never leaves."

"Show me where," she said.

I pointed to the spot on the left side of my sacrum. Dr. Ruth put her hand there and pressed into it, then pulled her hand back as if she'd just touched a hot stove.

Dr. Ruth looked at me as though she perceived something I didn't, she let the matter go.

"Go back and see her," David said. "She can help you remember. Remind her what you just told me."

Teary-eyed, swollen with emotion, I anticipated these next steps, ready and willing to learn more.

I decided Jack, Lola, Aidan and I would go to Dr. Ruth for an entrainment. Jack was also eager to learn what I would discover. After the kids and Jack had their entrainments and felt wonderful, I went in alone.

"Tell me what's going on," Dr. Ruth said.

"I'm ready!" I said. "I know there's more to remember now. Two other healers helped me understand the emotional release I had when I saw you last."

"Remind me what happened," she said.

"You touched my lower back. Later you asked if anything had happened to me that may have caused the pain. I didn't know what you were talking about. On the drive home afterward I cried and had a feeling something bad had happened to me. "

"Relax," she said. "Lie down on your stomach, and close your eyes." As she touched my neck and back, a white light shone in my third eye, an opening sensation.

I saw a younger version of my body at about seven years old emerge from the background wearing a silvery-grey tank top and a black skirt, an outfit my mother had bought for herself. I didn't have a head.

"I saw myself without a head, like I had been decapitated," I said. "There wasn't even any blood! It was so weird. What does it mean?"

"Your mind is giving you clues," Dr. Ruth said. "You'll put it all together."

Jack, Lola, Aidan and I went out to lunch at a farm-to-table restaurant on Abbot Kinney Street where I soon forgot my problems while indulging in a savory meal. Confident in their loving support, I was grateful and proud of them and myself on many levels. Open with my husband and children about my healing process, they became accustomed, interested and supportive, wanting to participate in breathwork and NSA, encouraged by the fact that I was improving. During this healing process Dr. Ruth, while accepting my spine and nervous system, made certain conclusions and recognized certain patterns. As my spine became healthier afterward, it appeared that old traumatic memories disappeared and those wounds then became gifts.

As I went deeper into my healing modalities over the next few weeks, two distinct sides of myself became apparent. One side was everything I had repressed since I was four years old, while the other side was the real me, my higher self, coming forth from behind a barrier.

I returned to Neda's store. I wanted her to help me deal with my new reality.

"Maybe you can make me a new remedy," I asked. "It's like I am walking around carrying two different people."

"That's huge," she said. "What else?"

"Well, there is a strange soreness near my pelvis," I said. "I went for a check-up, and my gynecologist said nothing is wrong."

"How about if I give you a polarity massage to help integrate the two sides of you?"

She led me into a lavender-and sage-scented massage room overlooking an Asian-style courtyard lush with cherry blossoms. Removing my clothes, I hopped on the massage table. Neda began the treatment. I was apprehensive about meshing the two sides, fearful of the unknown.

"Relax," Neda said. "Go deep inside yourself."

"The soreness in my pelvis is getting larger," I whispered. "It's the size of a football."

Finding the football-sized pain place with her hand, Neda used a light touch with her curled fingers.

"Old memories are stored here," she said. "I am seeing a Teddy bear. What does that mean to you?" (Her ability to read things accurately was impressive. She was among the better healers I had consulted.)

An image appeared.

In my mother's large bedroom, I sat on the bed alone holding my Teddy bear, the one that Laurie had given me in Las Vegas when I stayed with their family for a night. Happy to have a friend, I told Teddy about my day.

Hearing my mother's heavy footsteps, I jumped as she entered the room wearing a knee-length dress printed with tiny lavender and blue flowers.

"Gimme dat!" she screamed.

She snatched the Teddy bear out of my arms, and held it high up so that I couldn't grab it back.

"What are you doing?" I screamed.

Tough and stoic as though she had every right, she began to rip my brown bear to shreds with her bare hands—the white stuffing flew everywhere.

"Please stop!" I cried. "You are killing my bear!"

"Goot!" she said.

I whispered, "A senseless act of cruelty," the phrase I so often heard my mother say when talking about the Nazis.

She killed my best friend, the only creature I loved. She wanted to tear me apart, dim my last light, and squash me like a worthless cockroach. Wishing she had killed me instead of my bear, I wanted to be free, to escape the bondage of my Beverly Hills home. I wished the truth behind the pink concrete walls that hid her secrets would be revealed.

I sat on the bed in a cloud of white stuffing and brown fuzzy fur, helpless and grief-stricken. I sobbed. A small red rubber ball appeared within the stuffing. I held it in my hands.

"It's Teddy's heart," I thought.

Neda's massage room took on a new energy as I explained my vision and the teddy bear.

"You must imagine a wonderful new Teddy bear," she said. "Think of the best bear you have ever seen."

"First, I am going to kick my mother out of the room and lock the door behind her!" I said. "Okay, now I am imagining a brand-new, bulletproof version of my Teddy bear!"

"Go to the little girl and give her that new Teddy bear," Neda instructed.

"As you are holding onto this beautiful moment, imagine your tailbone stretching long down into the earth, making roots," Neda said. "And, have a magical rest of your day."

The next morning, I awoke with intense, sharp jabs in my lower back. Holding onto the mattress with my left hand and Jack's shoulder with my right, I propelled myself out of bed. I wobbled into the den at 5:45 a.m. My muscles were cold and stiff as I turned on the breathwork disc and burrowed between two Mexican blankets. Sending my breath toward the excruciating pain, I searched for a new portal in the front of my body. Relaxing into a rhythm, I saw in my mind's eye the pain place transform into what resembled a slimy piece of liver. I dissected the liver with the pointedness of my breath creating a tiny opening that spread; a white light shone through and the space became a place of ease within the large, black, stuck mass. A new relationship with my body was born. For the first time, I no longer had the same old pain. "If you can change your mind, you can change your life," said William James, the father of American Psychology.

8
The Car

One day I stumbled into unexpected luck. Through a once-in-a-lifetime promotion, I had the chance to lease a luxurious Dakar Beige Audi at a price even I could afford. I ignored the fact that I hated the limited edition color everyone else seemed to adore.

I picked Lola up from acting class and drove south along the 405 from Century City. Fiddling with the dashboard gadgets, I plugged Lola's iPod into the docking station. We listened to "My Humps" by the Black Eyed Peas before I pushed the Bluetooth button to dial my mom.

"Halo?" my mother answered.

"Hi. I'm talking to you from my new car."

"Mazel Tov! Vat color is da car?"

"It's a combination of taupe with hints of gold like Coco, the Weimaraner dog we used to have."

"Oh!" my mother exclaimed. "Iz like de Bonneville, de first car I hed. Da Tata drove it before dat." (Your father drove it before that.)

I pondered my mother's words about the new car being the same color as the Pontiac Bonneville. The next day after I did breathwork, I was driving home when I recalled sitting in the back seat of the Bonneville with my brothers when I was four, as my parents spoke Yiddish up front. As I thought about this image, I felt as though I were driving that old gold Bonneville instead of the Audi.

"Oh shit, I am driving a gold car. I hate gold. I don't even wear gold jewelry unless it's white gold. It just isn't me. It's an old lady car and I am not old yet. This is a car my mother would have driven!"

Horrified, I began sweating. I despised the lavish beige leather interior accented with exquisite wood inlay.

"Am I losing my mind?" I thought. "How could I have leased this car? Why didn't I insist on a convertible? I love those old convertibles. Am I having a midlife crisis?"

As I headed into the driveway and parked, I felt like a child, crying because I chose a piece of hard candy at Thrifty's Drug Store when I could have had a Three Musketeers—a wrong decision, the difference between life and death. I walked through the front door like a spoiled child facing Jack, my face beet red.

"I hate that car!"

"What?" Jack asked.

Lola and Aidan looked at me, foreheads wrinkled, trying to figure me out.

"I'm not driving it, ever. It's yours!" I said.

I planted the key in the palm of Jack's hand and curled his fingers around the key. "Here! I'll drive the other car until we can get a convertible."

"A convertible?"

"Yes, I'm not getting any younger. If I wait three years, I will be too old."

"Why didn't you say you wanted a convertible?"

"Temporary insanity."

"Seriously?"

"Get rid of that car!"

The devil had entered my body, turning me into a nervous bitch.

"What do you mean get rid of it? We signed a contract."

"If you love me, you will fix this!" I yelled.

9
Feeding Frenzy

Sivan's family and ours were going to Disneyland together for the day. Sivan was a talented Canadian clothing designer, and when she and her husband and kids arrived at our house, she handed nine-year-old Lola a big white box with a purple bow.

"Open it!" Sivan said.

Lola opened the box and lifted the white tissue paper inside. "Wow!" she exclaimed. "It's new clothes!"

White cotton pants with a pink frill on the bottom, and an elegant halter-top accented with a pink satin sash that tied in back.

"That's beautiful on you," I said. "I can picture a fashion model wearing it while vacationing in Marbella. It's adorable and sophisticated. I want one!"

"Can I wear it today, please?" Lola asked.

"We are leaving for Disneyland in twenty minutes," Jack warned.

"Can I wear my new present, Mom?" Lola asked.

"Sure."

The kids were thrilled to be enjoying Disneyland on this warm sunny California day. After taking a break from the rides, we entered the GE Theater to watch a video of appliance innovations since the 1950s. The audience was invited to try the computer technology. As I looked for an available computer, Lola ran off ahead of me. Finally, I found her working on a computer on the second floor—she looked striking in her new outfit. I walked up to her and watched her work. When I glanced up, I noticed a man, 50ish, with shoulder-length, stringy brown hair, was videotaping her.

"This weirdo is filming my kid!" I thought. I stuck my head in front of his camera. He jumped back, turned around and disappeared. I was sick to my stomach. I couldn't leave my beautiful young daughter alone for a minute! I felt protective of her, and I recollected when I, at her age, could have used some protection from the creepiness around me.

My father brought home a beautiful GE black-and-white television, and ceremoniously rolled it into Allan's room. The first-born male and parental favorite, Allan received the best of everything. The center of our home life, his room was where we ate dinner while watching "All in the Family."

Ten years later, Allan's room was a smoky dump, with dingy yellow walls and a mattress and box spring lying on the floor against the wall. The dresser drawers were etched with graffiti, ashtrays overflowing with cigarette butts and ashes were strewn everywhere. Spreading sweet-smelling, clean sheets on top of that stinky mattress, my mother reminded me of Nurse Ratchet in "One Flew over the Cuckoo's Nest," acting as though everything were normal.

When the two large windows in the room were wide open, I could see the ivy hedge that separated our house from the Plotnick's next door, and a flat dirt path that went down the entire side of the house like a moat around a castle. Skipping along the path like a fairy princess when I was seven years old, I was in an imaginary world filled with bees and butterflies, fairies and angels. Closing the wrought iron gate behind me, I walked across the lawn and up the steps into our house.

"Anyone home?" I said out loud.

No answer. I stepped into Allan's room, and snooping around, I noticed the edge of a magazine poking out from under the mattress. I lifted it up and discovered several magazines with pictures of naked people on the covers. Never having seen anything like that, I pulled some out, sat down on the carpet and looked. Shocked by what the men were doing to the women, I froze. I saw penises being pushed into big, round rear ends, and thought the women were being tortured and ripped apart. I saw their horrid expressions as men stuck their penises into the women's mouths—violent, scary and confusing images that made me wish I were anywhere else. I trembled, afraid someone might see me so I stuffed everything back under the mattress.

Allan was evil and disgusting. Nauseated from the smell of cigarettes and musty magazines, I ran out of the room, trying to forget the porno-cigarette-smelling nightmare that was my life.

Never would I have imagined that as an adult, a writer, a healer, a friend, a wife and a mom I would still be carrying the negative energy of what I saw in those magazines. Finally, connecting with and releasing that energy, I am now able to face the shock so rooted in my psyche.

I acknowledged the forces that contributed to what I came to understand was my brother's porn addiction, the wartime trauma experienced by our parents channeled directly to their children. My brother suffered from a lack of nurture, not receiving comfort and connection to others when he was very young. These factors may well have created his relationship and addiction issues. Allan and Billy were the effect of our parent's angst; as a result, I was fortunate to have been the youngest, ignored except where food was concerned.

When she cleaned Allan's room, my mother must have seen what I saw—those hardcore porn images piled high under the mattress, so expertly covered with fresh, clean sheets. I wondered how she could have allowed those images in her house, and how she could have allowed them to be so easily discovered by me.

The content of the porn magazines, so shocking to me, may not have been shocking to her. Raised with abuse, desensitized and punished for no reason, women, like my mother, were herded to factories as slave labor in inhumane conditions. Never discussing what happened during the war with me, her silence was loud, sending a message that the horror was unimaginable. One of the privileged few, she was forced to walk several miles a day, barefoot in the snow on an empty stomach, toward a long workday in the ammunition factory, her body and mind numb. She preferred to be barefoot as it was less painful than wearing the oversized wooden clogs provided by her captors, more than likely worn by prisoners previously killed. Her emotional trauma during these formative years would never be repaired, and one of the ways she overcompensated was with food.

Her actions stemmed from the insanity of what the Nazis had done to her. Some Nazi guards were pedophiles who kept children submissive. They abused those lucky enough to have been kept alive, especially if they were attractive. Beautiful at fifteen when she was in Auschwitz, my mother was one of those abused prisoners. She may not remember what happened, but the scars remain. As I was growing up, my mother screamed often in the middle of the night, the sounds of being raped echoing through the house while she was asleep, never remembering in the morning.

Whenever I walked by a bakery, I thought of the relationship I had with challah toast. The braided challah, made with eggs, was the Jewish Sabbath-and-holiday bread. My mother bought extra loaves on Fridays and froze them so we could eat it all week.

Jack once asked my mother, "Were you ever happy even for a moment during the war?"

"Yes, vonce ven dey gave us a round bread. Ve each got a quarter piece of da bred before ve hed to valk to verk in Czechoslovakia, in da ammunitions factory."

Black Lipton tea with challah toast topped with loads of butter consoled me through elementary school as I tried to deal with the complexities of living with my family. I sat in the breakfast room eating two or three or more tasty slices at a time. I forgot anything was wrong. My mother had a strong connection to baked goods, as her grandmother owned a bakery in Poland and was responsible for all the bread, noodles and pastries in her village. After school, all the kids ran to the bakery window to stare at the goodies. Because my mother had all that taken away from her, she overcompensated and taught me to do the same, a fact that dragged me into an unhealthy state.

Unable to take a deep breath when I was 42 years old, I found myself forty pounds overweight. The Channel 2 News that morning reported shortness of breath as a cardiac symptom in women. Wondering why I was gaining so much weight, and concerned about heart trouble, I visited some of my healers.

"You are carrying that extra weight for protection," David Elliot told me.

Not understanding the need to protect myself, nor why I carried around that extra layer of belly fat, I felt as big as a bear about to hibernate.

To Loretta, the Emotional Freedom Technique (EFT) practitioner, I said, "I am getting heavier and can't seem to lose the weight. Do you think we can tap the pressure points on this?"

"EFT can be very effective with cravings, but emotional eating takes time to ferret out the root causes and release them. Some people just need to be educated on nutrition and calories. So if you eat a cookie, it's got a certain number of calories. Just do the math," Loretta said.

Never having counted calories before, I didn't plan to start. My mother certainly didn't teach me about calories when she brought home the daily Danishes.

Didi, the blonde, blue-eyed trainer I recently hired, tried to help me. "If you exercise a lot, you can eat anything you want," she said.

Her method of sneaking in exercise throughout the day, while insisting

I allow myself a slice of pizza or two, was not working. Worried that my lack of success might somehow ruin her coaching reputation, she gave me a wristwatch that monitored my steps, heartbeat, blood pressure and calories. She treated me as though I were the bionic woman whose data needed to be stored for future investigation.

"I think you should try taking lithium," she said. "If you can't get any, eat at least a dozen or more tomatoes, three times a day. The lithium will get into your system that way."

"I'll think about it," I said, as I visualized crossing her off my healer list.

I listened to the disc "Think and Get Slim" narrated by Ester Hicks, an American inspirational speaker and author who channels Abraham, a group of spirits (non-physical entities). They delivered a message of joy that focused on being in vibration with weight loss, a message of thinking the next best feeling thought, while eating whatever I wanted. This didn't work. In fact, I gained another ten pounds.

Wanting to look in the mirror and smile because I liked what I saw regardless of my age and what had happened in the past, I followed the advice of Abraham through Ester Hicks CDs and books and connected to my source by listing a rampage of appreciation. This changed my energy allowing in more of what I wanted. On a yellow legal pad, I wrote down things for which I was grateful.

"I appreciate all the things I enjoy in my life. I appreciate my income. I appreciate the lamb chops I had for dinner last night. I appreciate my family. I appreciate my big, round, voluptuous body. I appreciate the sun. I appreciate the warmth that surrounds me." I began losing weight slowly after shifting to positive thoughts became automatic.

(For the reader interested in Abraham-Hicks, I have a summary of their teachings in the back of the book.)

10

Remembering

While Jack was away on a two-week business trip, I managed my days on autopilot, solemn and constricted, a life without enjoyment. One day, I went down the hill to rent movies from the video store in hopes of putting myself in a better mood. Attracted by the DVD cover of an exotic woman peering out of a dark corner, I chose an Italian film entitled "Don't Tell" about an Italian woman who woke up every night with recurring, terrifying dreams. She decided to uncover the meaning of her dreams by visiting her brother in the United States. While there, she discovered her father had sexually abused them both when they were children. Her mother knew about it all along. She managed to free herself from the beast inside her heart.

By accessing her repressed memories and reliving those moments, the woman remembered more before running away, feeling dirty, guilty, sinful and unworthy of love, as though she were to blame. After serious soul searching and tears, she forgave herself and was able to recover. She returned home to her boyfriend ready to heal and connect with the love that awaited her.

In the days that followed watching the movie, I was bloated, uncomfortable and depressed. I cried at odd times, unable to connect the tears to anything specific. Finally, a voice inside told me that the film was the cause. To get my mind off my emotions, I went to work on my book at a coffee shop.

I sat at a Starbucks near my kids' school where I worked on my writing, armed with a medium double Americano coffee with two-percent foam by my side, so strong my stomach turned. I took a sip and looked up to see a young man reading the book "Star Wars Republic Commando," his nose glued to the page. He sensed my gaze and looked up.

I focused on his brilliant light-blue eyes, noticing they appeared as weary as they did genuine. He had pale skin, coarse, brown hair in a military cut, and a goatee. Rough around the edges, the kind of guy you wouldn't want to mess with unless he was your friend. He wore a white T-shirt with a scar peeking out from his sleeve.

"Hi," he said. "Are you a teacher or something?"

"No, a writer working on a book. I'm Alix."

"Levi," he said in a resonant voice, giving me a chill.

"Cool name. That's biblical isn't it? The Levis are one of the Jewish tribes."

"That may be true, but I'm Irish Catholic. My mom, bless her heart, named me after her favorite blue jeans. What's your book about?"

"It's a work in progress," I said. "Probably a memoir. So far, it's about healing an injury, WWII, mental illness and a deli. The character I'm working on now is manic-depressive."

Levi stood up and took a seat at my table. I watched his firm body and the outline of his muscles as he leaned in, probably closer than he should have, an intimate distance. His leg touched mine beneath the table and I could smell his aftershave. I looked at his scar peeking out his left sleeve; wishing I could touch it. Strange thoughts popped into my mind, thoughts that I hadn't had in years. I wondered how old he was.

"I know about manic-depression," he said.

"Tell me."

"In second grade at age seven, I was given Ritalin for ADHD. The pills made me feel terrible so I traded them with my friend Johnny at lunch for a chocolate snack-pack pudding cup. Johnny was in my class and he liked the way the Ritalin made him feel."

"What about that scar on your arm?" I asked. "Were you in an accident?"

"Nah, I used to cut when I was fifteen."

"That's weird, because Lola, my twelve-year-old daughter tells me that everyone in middle school is cutting."

"Well, I'm sure not everyone!"

"So, you cut with a razor blade?"

"Nope. A pocket knife."

"Why?"

"Cutting made me feel. Katie and James, my two best friends who were dating each other, cut too. It was an emotional release for us because we were so depressed—suicidal in fact."

Surprised and grateful that Levi, who just met me, would exchange such intimate details out of the blue, I pressed on.

"What were Katie and James like?"

"Katie was seventeen, petite, pale and small-chested. She dyed her hair every shade from blonde to rainbow. She had a long Mohawk and piercings in her ears, tongue and belly button. She had scars from cutting all over her upper thighs.

"James was the same age as Katie. He was tall, tan-skinned and athletic, with two piercings on his left eyebrow. He was Italian."

"Depression can be brutal! How did you handle it?"

"We took a lot of Ecstasy. One night when James was out of town on a university tour, Katie and I got wasted on X, weed and liquor. All I remember was waking up, naked, cuddled next to her. I knew we must have had sex; that was the only time we slept together."

"Did you love her?"

"Yes. As soon I met her, I thought we were soulmates. We complemented each other, liking the same music—The Doors, The Misfits and The Clash. We also had similar childhood traumas, with messed-up fathers and some sexual abuse."

"So you understood each other."

"Yeah."

Levi's eyes began to water, and I could feel his deep emotional pain come up. Taking a moment to compose himself, he cleared his throat.

"The next night when James came back, I told him that Katie and I had slept together. That's when he beat me. I stood there and took it, not fighting back, not telling him to stop. In fact, I half-expected and half-wanted him to beat me to death. He was closer to me than any other person had ever been, a brother. I betrayed him. I deserved it. Dragging myself out of that house, bloody and sore, I walked down the street to a friend, who took me to the hospital. The police asked me a lot of questions. I gave no answers."

My body stiffened as I absorbed this unusual change in the conversation and waited for more.

"A week later, I bought more Ecstasy with the money James and I had saved up together. I brought James his share, twenty-five tablets. I wanted to talk. He was devastated by what he had done to me, as I was still healing from two black eyes and a broken right cheekbone. I was a swollen mess, unable to see out of my left eye for days. What James didn't realize was I had forgiven him before he ever threw the first punch."

Levi took a deep breath and continued. "That same night after I went home, James swallowed all twenty-five Ecstasy pills at once, causing malignant hyperthermia (super high, deadly fever) and dehydration, leading to kidney failure. I was too upset to attend the funeral."

"Three months later, Katie discovered she was pregnant. The next day, she was found dead in her bed, an empty bottle of Vicodin on the nightstand. After the suicides, I completely cut off from the world, having no interest in anything, hating myself and wanting to die, too. One afternoon I leaned over the side of my mother's bed and put a gun to my head. When I pulled the trigger, my hand that was so shaky that I missed, and the bullet shot past my forehead into the wall."

"Please tell me you're not going to try that again," I said, as a wave of concern passed through me. I was deeply taken by Levi. Feeling strange inside, I was shocked by the intensity. "I've been happily married for twenty years!" I thought, "but I wouldn't like Jack to walk in here right now."

"I won't ever kill myself," Levi said. "I have gained a new perspective."

"And what's that?"

"A person is like a glass of water, with the water representing the level of depression that person holds, an energy that can never be destroyed. If he commits suicide, his energy ends up spilling over to parents, relatives and friends, who fill their glasses with sadness, grief and anger. Suicide is selfish."

"What happened after you shot the wall instead of your head?" I asked.

"Doctors diagnosed me as bipolar and gave me Wellbutrin, an antidepressant, and mood stabilizers, Lithium and Depakote, which turned me into a lobotomized zombie. I stopped taking them."

"I totally get that!" I said. "When I was pregnant, I was terrified of giving birth in a hospital and being coerced into having an epidural shot just so other patients wouldn't hear me scream. I opted for natural childbirth on a farm, with a midwife and no drugs."

"Well, the thing is," Levi said, "I still self-medicated, and I partied hard for years afterward. I took Ecstasy and cocaine to bring myself up and Vicodin to get stoned and feel better. Finally, afraid I was going to die, I stopped it all and went cold turkey."

"So how did you handle the mood swings?"

"I tried some hippie nonsense," Levi said, "and it seemed to work."

"Like what?"

"I ate a healthy diet, got a lot of rest, exercised and meditated. I had a bit more control during the manic and depressive episodes, and the moments between episodes became clear, rather than cloudy from the medications."

"Will it ever go away," I asked, "the manic depression, I mean?"

"I can't say that I won't be bipolar anymore. I can tell when each phase is starting, but I still have no control over the symptoms, such as the racing thoughts and irritability. I do have control over my actions within the phases so that I don't endanger myself or cause trouble. I meditate as a sleep-aid, and I have support from my friends, sometimes asking them to hold my wallet so I don't overspend when I'm manic. When I'm depressed, I watch good movies and comedies, exercise more, meditate and do activities I enjoy."

"I feel so sorry for you," I said. My eyes watered, and I felt a genuine pull toward him.

"Best of luck," I said, as he stood up.

Just then I thought since I was working so hard on the book, I might be attracting people like Levi whose stories also need to be told, the universe fully supporting my path. Smiling to myself, I thought of the full glass of water Levi talks about, the water now representing the lessons that will spill over to help so many others.

The next morning, deep, penetrating pain drained me to the point of nausea. I had the sensation of a ball of energy growing in my lower abdomen. As I shifted my body, the pain radiated into my joints, like sharp knives slicing into my flesh. The pain in my thighs and muscles continued throughout the day as I considered my pain the enemy. The same afternoon I joined a class at Sweat Yoga, with the temperature 103 degrees in a room that lacked ventilation. I tried to connect on an emotional level to my pain place, making it my friend and calling it "Fred." Every time I got near Fred in a pose or a stretch, I wanted to puke. Holding myself back, I maintained my balance.

"Stop thinking so much," the yoga instructor advised. "It would be much better if you could just stay out of your head."

I moved into the camel pose bending my body as far back as I could while on my knees. Reaching Fred with this movement, intense pain shooting from all directions, I cried, unnoticed, my tears and sweat dripping to the floor. I looked at myself and forty other people on the mirrored wall and became dizzy. I gripped my towel and sat down, hoping the spinning would stop. Overheated, I began to crawl toward the exit door.

"Wait!" the instructor yelled. "Keep with it. You are not supposed to leave the work. You need discipline."

"Look, I have a very old pain," I said. "It hurts a lot. I thought I was going to throw up on your carpet."

"Why didn't you say so," she said. "I am honored that you chose to clear that old block here with us."

Thrilled as though she had won first prize at the state fair, she was flattered that my Fred had come to her studio.

"You just do what you need to do," she said, "but next time, stay in the room."

11
Cold Turkey

Fred was in my nightmare. He hurt like hell and woke me up.

"Eventually, I will turn you into love, Fred. Someday I will find the memories embedded in your rock-hard existence. There was a time when I thought I needed your friendship, as a last resort, to silence the horrors; that if we spoke to each other the pain might disappear. I don't need you anymore. Since my first job after university, you were the lower back pain that I experienced almost every day. Lessening your pain with massage, I learned to swim in your world. Computer-generated muscle scans taken by Dr. Marie and Dr. Grace say you don't exist, that I am fine now. But we know better, don't we Fred, my dark, parasitic energy?

Bouncing around my lower back, pelvis and abdomen, stabbing recklessly like the sharp point of a butcher's knife, you have made me your slave. If you would please just let me go Fred, I promise that I will become your admirer. Remember, if I wanted to, I could shoot you up with cortisone like I did twice before.

When I stretch, you feel better. Breathwork meditation relaxes you, Somato Respiratory Integration connects you, and Pilates loosens your grip. Healers have tried to send you out to space by having me imagine you in colors and shapes. An Emotional Freedom Technique therapist had me think of you while tapping on acupressure points. Sometimes for a few minutes, you disappear for no apparent reason, going underground, and ecstasy emerges, a tease of normalcy. You are a quagmire, Fred!

When I take Vicodin for my neck, I don't feel you at all, but taking pills to make it through the day is not how I want to live! Numbing what you want me to someday discover is not my long-term goal. Intuition is telling me the closer I move toward the suffering, to you, the closer I will be to freedom. Experiencing your pain without pills, getting to the other side of it, is the answer. Don't you see that I am ready now to accept the stories you hold?

Glory be the day when you will reveal all so I can throw myself into making us one. How much deeper do we go together? Let's party, Fred, because I am ready to make you my friend in order to let you go."

The next morning as a thick, murky sensation of pain began to grow, I thought, "Things have to change now." I called my neighbor.

"Hi Mel," I said. "I'm really sick. Would you be able to take my kids to and from school today?"

"Of course," she said.

When the kids left and the house was empty, I perspired a thick, gooey sweat, changing from hot to cold to freezing before I wrapped myself in three blankets and sat down on the carpeted living room floor. I listened to my inner guidance, deciding not to swallow the Vicodin. I was fearful of the risk that the sharp pain could overpower me; yet, I was strong enough to handle what would come.

"Take another pill," a sly voice whispered in my head.

Refusing to succumb, I sat still and experienced each subtle wave of pain, staying in a cocoon-like position on the carpet all day without food or water and vowing never to take another Vicodin. Each moment of agony, exhaustion and delirium was scary as I sweated out the toxins, my body sore and my mind fearful; yet, my intuition told me it was the only solution. The gooey sweat on my body froze as I clenched my knees in a fetal position, praying to God for help. Stiff and still, I never relaxed, even though I was depleted. I subsisted on will and strength that came from somewhere. I was going to get to the other side of what seemed to be a vise grip, an energy holding me where I was.

I thought, "If I could survive this morning without Vicodin, I can survive anything."

I sat under my blanket for six hours, hunched over, sweaty and freezing, the pain permeating. A surge of what felt like flames travelled from my head to my toes before I made it through the darkness into the light. I rose as though I had been resurrected and took a warm shower. Afterward, I was able to raise my left arm higher to spread on body lotion. Just then I thought of the orthopedic surgeon who had warned me I would lose all receptivity in my left arm if he didn't operate. I was ecstatic I had instead listened to my inner voice telling me I could heal myself. I threw out all the pain pills in my medicine cabinet.

The next morning, I called the Audi dealership, discovering it would cost $3,000 more to exchange the gold Audi for a different color. Next, I searched for convertibles on the Internet, crying off and on for two days as if I were mourning the loss of a loved one.

"This isn't you," Jack said. "Do you know what kind of deal we got?"

"I know. I don't know how lucky I am. I don't know what's wrong with me."

"You must have had some sort of trauma."

"No, there's no trauma."

Surprised by the words spewing out of my mouth that day, I was depressed, scared, and acting out of character. Shaky and ungrounded as if a separate energy was manipulating me, I slid into bed that night desperate to rid myself of what seemed like evil. I shifted gears and focused on the positive by making a long list of appreciation and changing my energy. "I appreciate my family and friends, I appreciate the birds and bees in the yard, I appreciate my house, I appreciate my mother, I appreciate my dog, and I appreciate the beach, the wind and the trees."

Instead of the strange energy disappearing, as my appreciation list got larger, that energy got stronger, not letting me forget how much I hated that Dakar Beige Audi. No matter how hard I tried, the tension persisted. Crying, I buried my face in the pillow until I fell asleep. I woke up in the middle of the night. I nudged Jack, kicking his leg with my foot, a movement he hates.

"How could I have been so stupid? How could I have let this car thing happen?"

"Well, you did," he replied. "Go back to sleep."

"I can't." I got up and went into the den to do breathwork. Unable to take in much air, I was stuck, pain piercing through my chest like a log lodged straight through to my back.

After dropping the kids off at school in the morning, I drove toward the market for groceries. All of a sudden I saw black, the camera shutter closing. Fear set in for a second before my vision lit up again, the shutter opening.

I was a small child about six years old sitting in the back of the gold Bonneville, which my mother was driving. She pulled into Bishop's Market in Beverly Hills, and parking on a slope, she said, "Vait here, I neet to tek somtink from da butcher."

Alone in the car, playing around, I hit the long, skinny stick-like thing on the steering wheel shaft, and the car began to roll backwards. I had released the brake by accident! On my knees on the passenger seat, I stared out the back window watching the scenery move. Too scared to jump out, I froze. Heading toward a busy two-way street, I wondered if I would hit the Bishop's Market wall or if I would roll straight into the traffic.

Two men jumped behind the car, trying to hold it steady. Pressing against

the back bumper with all their might, their faces bright red, they looked as
though they might roll right underneath the car.

Just then, my mother came out of the market with her packages.

"Hit the brake lady!" one man screamed.

She opened the car door, grabbed the brake and pulled up on the stick,
stopping the car.

Hearing this story, Jack and the kids understood what I had been going through the past week. They forgave me for the way I had behaved, understanding that childhood trauma can cause weird behavior and anxiety.

"I knew your mother had something to do with this!" Jack muttered under his breath.

After I recovered from the car ordeal, I focused on my writing again and spent a good amount of time perfecting the story I had written about Levi, the young man I met at Starbucks.

Walking into Lola's room, I was holding the latest version of the Levi story. Lola was straightening her bangs with a flat iron getting ready for the Freshman formal.

"Hey, I just wrote a new story. Can I read it to you while you're doing your hair?"

"Okay, Mom."

Reading the story, I noticed that at the same moments I felt emotion, Lola turned away from the mirror and stared at me, engaged in the story.

"Mom, there are so many kids at my school like that. They are depressed, cutting or have eating disorders. It's pretty awful."

"Why are they so depressed?"

"Different reasons. I know one boy who cuts his wrists with a pencil sharpener during math class because his parents fight all the time. This other girl says she has depression because her mother did. Then there are the girls who just don't eat."

12
Bathing Bagels

On our way to New York for a family get-away, Jack, the kids and I left the house in the early morning. We stepped into a cab heading for the airport, looking forward to liberating ourselves from the mundane responsibilities that kept our hamster wheels spinning. The middle-aged East Indian cab driver eyed me in his rear view mirror. Uncomfortable with his interest in me, I made light conversation with the kids.

"Aidan, are you excited to go to New York?"

"Yes, I can't wait." He snuggled closer to me and then closed his eyes, with his head on my lap. "Wake me up when we get there," he said.

As Aidan slept and Lola stared out the cab window, I wondered what I was doing when I was their age. Unable to remember much, I was envious of Jack, who remembered every date and detail. However, I was certain that as a child, I had never taken a plane to New York while coloring images of Sponge Bob using clear-ink, rainbow-colored markers.

Overpriced and small, our hotel room in New York was nonetheless a welcome sight after the long flight. I filled the bathtub with bubbles, slid in, leaned back with a satisfying sigh, and began to daydream.

Back home in the bathroom of the house I grew up in when I was nine years old, I heard my mother yelling from the kitchen.

"Tek a bat!" (Take a bath.) This was an unusual request; she didn't often think I needed to wash up. Her view was that Americans take too many baths.

"Tek a bat!" she yelled again.

Getting undressed, I turned on the bath water and stepped into the lavender-hued tub, which was surrounded by beige and green tiles.

"Do you hef zop?" (Do you have soap?) my mother yelled.

"Yes," I answered, assuming there was soap. Closing my eyes, I relaxed into the warm water.

My mother entered the bathroom. "Ver iz da zop?"

"Oh, I thought there was soap."

"Liar!" she yelled. She reached down and pulled me out of the tub by my hair, pushing me through the door.

"Go avay," she yelled.

I stepped out of the bath and wrapped myself in a white plush bath sheet as I walked toward the hotel room window and looked out at the New York City view. After I dressed, we took a taxi to the Carnegie, a deli famous for extra-large sandwiches—one was more than enough to feed a family of four. I decided on the oatmeal and fruit combo, while my kids and Jack ordered a fish platter with lox, white fish, sturgeon and bagels. Our waitress was a sweet woman who had run many times back and forth to the kitchen because she kept forgetting parts of our order. She wore red rouge, bright red lipstick and royal blue eye shadow. Her eyebrows were drawn on with a dark brown pencil as if a toddler had done it.

"Where ya' from?" she asked.

"LA."

"I worked as a deli waitress out there for twenty years. Do ya' know Nate n' Al's in Beverly Hills and Junior's in Westwood? That was a lifetime ago.

The two brothers at Junior's were the greatest guys to work for; dreamy eyes, down to earth, unaffected by the money, you know. They were menches, good people. Now let me tell you, Mel from Nate n Al's was a different story, always giving me a real hard time about everything. He was a tough one."

Every Sunday morning I had brunch with my friends at Nate n Al's when I was in high school, and always wondered why all the other kids had charge accounts except me; they never had to come in with any money. An account would have made sense for my family since it was the only restaurant my mother frequented. An expert at deli, the food she grew up with in Poland, she often purchased packages of salted meats and fish. In fact, the man behind the deli counter asked her to marry him. She said no. She never did the right thing.

After our deli breakfast, we visited the Metropolitan Museum, the Guggenheim, Toys R Us, FAO Schwartz and Times Square.

Somewhere between Saturday night and early Sunday morning in the hotel room, while I was sleeping next to Jack, I dreamed.

Lying naked in a white bathtub, with the warm water soothing my skin, I saw candles around the tub. The room was dimly lit, with shadows of the candles dancing on the grey and brown stonewalls and stone floors, built hundreds of years ago.

Luxuriating in the steaming water, I was at one with myself, and at peace. My body was beautiful, round and sensuous in the play of shadows and candlelight. I had a wonderful connection, as if in that place in meditation when spirit enters, with pure love, and the satisfaction you are right where you are supposed to be on the path of life.

"This is it," I thought, in the quietness of the room. "Nothing could be better than this."

All of a sudden, a loud male voice entered my consciousness. "Thanks for the porcelain," he said.

My eyes widened with shock as I recognized the voice.

What was this voice doing in my private bathing space? How did he manage to slice open my thoughts?"

Scared and humiliated, I awoke in the hotel room, startled and disturbed, riddled with guilt. I considered it my fault he saw me naked; my thoughts attracting him into my space. Blaming myself for somehow bringing him in, I couldn't understand what was happening. Enjoying what I thought was my alone time; he took away my innocence, clarity and purity. The tone of his voice, dominating, powerful and condescending, it was as though he was saying, "I am here because I can be, and there is nothing that you can do about it."

His voice seemed from a past life that saw me as the butt of a joke, a powerless plaything whose life didn't matter.

I sucked in my discomfort while managing to enjoy the rest of our trip. We went to Central Park, ate hot dogs on the street corner, and dined on Northern Italian cuisine. When we returned home, I was satisfied I had made the most of my vacation and I began to plan the next trip.

I looked forward to returning to my healing rituals. After everyone had gone to sleep, I put on the breathwork disc. After a few minutes, I was on a country road.

Seeing myself as a wounded animal, I was limping by the side of the road, a large camel-colored, spotted deer hobbling around in search of a solution for the hole in my abdomen where I had been shot, a painful place that clenched my lower back. Searching for answers in the darkness, I continued walking along the road, eager to find what I was seeking. I fell asleep.

Waking up on the couch the next morning, I repeated the breathwork, taking air into my lower belly and upper chest, and releasing. On that day, I saw what seemed to be souls or spirits. Now, I see them often when I am awake and in dreams. They come to me in amazing detail as faces of all sizes, groups, couples, energy and colors.

For example, at a retreat in Sedona, while I was doing breathwork, I saw two Native Americans with strong, proud faces in my mind's eye. They had colorful and ornate feathered headdresses. These images, souls or guides show up at random and most often after a lot of energy has moved during breathwork. If I see souls, I am happy and connected to the universe; if I don't, I feel stuck, as though there is more that I need to work on before moving on to the next best part of me. I am at the growing edge of something wonderful as I watch my own process unfold.

Still focusing inside myself on this early morning, I saw the beautiful camel-colored deer again. She was not a deer in the headlights, but still an injured deer, walking alone in darkness by the side of the road. Searching for help, she struggled with a painful limp, while still appearing strong. On one level I was the injured deer, trying to figure out how to heal myself. On another level, my mother was the injured deer, stepping out of the concentration camp gate, injured, looking for help; her vibration passing through to me.

Coming out of the meditation, I thought of a recent news story about a lone driver on the 405 freeway. He was on his way home at 2:00 a.m. in Los Angeles in 2010. A bullet hit him just like it had the deer. The shooter was an anonymous villain who did not know the person at whom he aimed, never considering the ripple effect on the victim's family and future generations, as if throwing a stone into a lake.

In another similar incident in April of 2012, I was late picking my kids up from school. When we headed onto the Harbor Freeway, I saw a black Honda Accord whose window had just been shot out by a bullet, the sick game of a sniper. A young man was injured and lying on the ground. Had I been on time to pick up my kids that day, might it have been me?

13
Jewish Guilt

Lying in her bunk next to five other women, she shivered in a thin dress that served both as uniform and nightgown. She couldn't wear the too-large clogs in the snow, as they made her feet bleed. A small blanket shared between the women did not cover them all, leaving some to freeze. Physically, emotionally, and spiritually frozen, having been left for dead, with shaved heads and malnourished, the women were skin and bones, with their eyes bulging out.

When I saw those emaciated images from the Holocaust on TV, I cringed, because my mother had looked like that—walking death, until the gates of hell opened, the war was over and she was free.

Dazed, she walked out of the concentration camp and along the street looking for anyone. A German woman noticed her and invited her in for a hot bowl of soup. She led my mother in, fed her, bathed her and dressed her—strange and luxurious comforts.

"I want to adopt you," the woman said. "I have no children of my own, you see."

"You can't," my mother said. "I have a family."

"I am so sorry," the woman whispered. "They are dead. Everyone is dead."

Having waited for so many years to see her family again, it was unimaginable no one was waiting for her. Gathering her strength, my mother said goodbye to the woman and set out to continue her search. Discovering the woman was telling the truth, my mother met only a sprinkling of Jewish people. They stuck together because all they had were each other.

Filled with insatiable guilt about what happened to my mother in WWII, I told myself that holding onto what haunted me, a gnawing in my gut, would not help my mother heal. I was only hurting myself with these thoughts, taking on energies that didn't belong to me.

Celebrating Lola's brown belt in karate, she and I went to a café near the studio. Just twelve years old, Lola had decided to stop karate before she earned a black belt. She felt she could protect herself, which was the point of all her lessons. Over lunch, I thought about how a university friend, Liz Beth Wasserman, had made the decision to end her life. Her father was a college counselor and her mother was a high school teacher.

Her father was a college counselor and her mother was a high school math teacher. While we were at university, Liz killed herself by ingesting rat poison in a locked bathroom. Her psychiatrist had decided she no longer needed the antidepressants and cut her off cold turkey, a fatal mistake. The withdrawal from anti-depressants, if not done gradually, can lead to suicide.

Liz was in love with her father and jealous of her mother, an Electra complex also known as "Daddy's little girl." Although I doubt she slept with her father, the thought had crossed my mind.

I asked Lola, "Isn't it strange on the one hand you have grandma, who struggled to hold onto life during the war and on the other hand, you have Liz Beth who threw her life away?"

"Look, Mom, Grandma was only eleven when the war started. She wanted to know about life because she hadn't experienced it yet. That's why she tried to stay alive."

"You're saying that Liz Beth had lived enough life?"

"You lived in Beverly Hills. You had money. Didn't you ever want to kill yourself?" Lola asked.

"Yeah, I wondered if I were better off dead. Then I thought, why should I die? So I thought about killing my brother instead. I plotted about poisoning his cigarettes, but I didn't have it in me."

"No one saw what was going on inside your house, mom. Maybe no one saw what was going on inside her house either," Lola said.

"Good point. In fact, I had always wondered about that. Did anyone know what was happening and just look the other way? In the beginning, the rest of the world said they didn't believe what was happening in the concentration camps. If you ask grandma if people on the outside knew what was happening to the prisoners, she would say, "Yes dey knew.""

I told Lola, "I was watching a YouTube video of a German woman who had been part of the Nazi youth. She was asked by a reporter if she and her friends knew the Jews were being systematically killed in the camps."

"Of course we knew," the woman said. "The gossip around the neighborhood was that the lampshades were made of Jewish skin."

"Oh God!" Lola said.

I said, "This morning I wrote in my journal about how guilty I feel about what happened to grandma, even though I had nothing to do with it."

"Me, too. I always feel guilty about it, too."

I said, "Guilt is common among children of Holocaust survivors because we can never make up for what happened to our parents or grandparents. We can't make it better no matter how hard we try, forever chasing the unachievable goal of making them happy."

"You make me happy, mommy!"

"Thanks, Lola!"

After the long drive home, I was weak, face swollen, equilibrium off, and the lower back pain worse. The swirling circle of soreness grew wider and more aggressive, making my back so stiff I wanted to cry. "Is that you Fred? You snuck up from behind like Clint Eastwood!"

Touching my face, I cringed from the soreness of my cheeks and gums. Just then, I made the connection that my back pain was directly related to my chronic sinus infections. I imagined my body was a noisy lit up pinball machine, the pinball was hit hard by flippers, rolling from my lower back to my sinuses and back, a continuous bumpy rhythm, affirming that Fred was a relentless parasite, sticking like glue.

On a mission to fight the impending sinus infection, I went to Dr. Marie's office for an NSA entrainment and to Dr. Grace's office for a chiropractic adjustment, before purchasing a bottle of garlic tablets, a natural antibiotic. Emotions coming up, my face burning, I was like a balloon pumped up with too much air, about to burst.

At home doing bills and paperwork while the kids and Jack were out, I couldn't think straight. I spritzed myself with healing sprays and rubbed on essential healing oils designed to support the body and chakras. The sprays transform the energy in a positive way. I put on the meditation disc, and lying on my couch with a pillow under my knees and an eye pillow on my face, I covered myself with a blanket while holding the ocean stones David Elliott had specially selected to help me ground and focus. Sending air to Fred, my breath became automatic. It took control of me as though I were on a fast ride at the amusement park. An image soon emerged.

A little girl, I peeked into the den where my mother watched television from the rust-colored couch. The bookshelves in the wood-paneled room were filled with books that Allan had read, including collections of Shakespeare and Edgar Allan Poe. The floor was a cool Italian terrazzo marble.

Every day, mother watched "Worlds at War," which featured the horrors of the Nazis and WWII. Engrossed in the program on this afternoon, she motioned me to join her on the couch. Sitting down, I saw planes flying over Europe, bombs dropping over towns and villages, and dead bodies piled high in rows and being bulldozed into gigantic, horrible mass graves.

"What is this?" I asked.

"History," she replied, without explaining her connection to it. "Worlds at War" was a normal part of my everyday life. Like that demonic guy in "Clockwork Orange" whose eyes were clipped open while he watched violent images as part of a fictional aversion therapy, I was, in a sense, forced to do the same, viewing the horrific aftermath of evil.

"Why do we have to watch this again when Scooby Doo is on the other channel?"

"Not now!" my mother answered.

Scrutinizing the screen as if she were looking for an ally among the naked refuse, she would not look away. I saw bodies in ditches or lying in organized rows. I viewed piles of eyeglasses, shoes and clothes.

It was as though my subconscious was ready and forcing me to remember what my life was like as a young girl. When I had looked at those gruesome scenes, my mind detached, locking the energy in my body, compartmentalizing it, so I could, back then, focus on my homework.

Emotions rose to my throat as I continued the breathwork. Needing to scream in order to release it, I grabbed a pillow and covered my mouth, making a long guttural whine, like a mouse being swallowed by a snake, not giving a damn if the construction workers remodeling the house next door could hear. In tears, I felt a great relief, even though Fred still lingered.

For the next few days, images of dead, naked bodies were on my mind. I faced them head-on, trying to understand why I might be remembering them now.

During my next session with Dr. Marie, the same dead-body images appeared, clear and disturbing, just as they had in the "Worlds at War" episodes. I cried as my body shook in terror. Moments later, the horrific images clouding my mind were replaced by a glowing red light, easing the tension before a clear white light emerged connecting me to spirit and love. I was part of something much bigger than myself—a universal energy. I found that I could create these images in the presence of a good healer.

"We're done," Dr. Marie said. "Whenever you're ready, you can sit up."

Later at home, I made dinner while the kids took baths. Wearing her fuchsia American Girl pajamas, Lola came out carrying a pink comb.

"Oh God!" she whined. "I have to comb my hair tonight. Will you do it for me, Mommy?"

"Okay," I said. "You don't know how lucky you are, Lola. Grandma used to plow through my hair as if she were raking leaves."

Our back door was always open on sunny days when I was six years old. I sat in the warm spot on the step, my head in my hands, watching the garage, waiting for my daddy to come home. He would be smiling and glad to see me.

Banks of blooming flowers grew along the sidewalk and against the pink wall, while the green lawn spread out to my favorite tall tree in front of my mother's bedroom. I climbed the tree and found a thick branch to sit on. Daydreaming, I stared across the yard at the clotheslines, where bed sheets blew in the breeze.

After I had my bath that night, I sat on the step by the back door waiting for my mother to comb my tangled, wet hair, my face flooding with tears as she ripped through my thick mane with a small cheap comb. Crying and screaming, I begged her to stop. She repeated this scenario every few days, as my hair regimen became my nightmare. When my mother reached her limit, she would open the breakfast room junk drawer and fish for the dull scissors. She cut my hair unevenly to just above the shoulder.

"Why can't she just take me to Tipperary on Dayton Way where all the other kids get their hair cut?" I wondered. "You get to sit in a sports car with a lollipop

in your mouth."

One evening after dinner while we were watching "All in the Family," a tall, gorgeous brunette with long flowing hair appeared on the screen at the commercial break. She washed her hair while sporting a wide smile, rinsing with clean water before putting lotion on her hair. Seconds later, she combed through her hair easily, swinging her locks from side to side.

"Wow! She's so lucky her hair doesn't hurt," I thought.

A few weeks later I was using Billy's bathroom when I noticed two bottles sitting on the edge of the tub that looked like the ones in the hair commercial. Reading the bottles, I sounded out the letters as I was just learning to read. One bottle said Flex shampoo, and the other was Flex conditioner.

"Wait a minute," I said to myself. "This is the lotion that makes your hair easy to comb." The words "tangle free" were right on the bottle in iridescent green.

"We have this in the house! Why didn't mom show me how to use it on my hair so it wouldn't hurt?"

Allan and Billy had never said anything about conditioner, yet they watched me crying on the porch. "I don't belong here with these people!" I thought. "They don't love me. And where is my daddy?"

Even after I explained the purpose of the conditioner, my mother still refused to listen. So, wise to the ways of my family, I snuck into Billy's bathroom, turned on the shower and used the Flex products just like the girl in the commercial, smiling, applying, smoothing and rinsing. I exited the shower just like she did having no more tangles, no more pain, just manageable, beautiful hair.

By the time I was eight I had long, healthy hair. I wanted a stylish haircut and longed for the "gypsy" shag. I begged my mother to take me to a hair salon for my birthday. When she finally agreed, instead of taking me to Tipperary salon in our Beverly Hills neighborhood, she took me to a seedy salon on Hollywood Boulevard, at a time when that area was still pretty rough, with prostitutes walking around, cigarette butts on the ground, and heroin addicts sleeping at bus stops.

I sat in the salon chair and told the hairdresser what I wanted. "A gypsy shag with long layers," I said.

He began cutting my hair when my mother whispered something in his ear. He nodded and was cutting off large chunks before I realized what was happening.

Staring at myself in shock, I was still as a stone. "It's shorter than a man's haircut!" I thought.

I looked like a cross between an androgynous French model and a concentration camp victim. I was so torn up inside, my eyes watered.

"Your mother told me to give you a pixie cut," he said.

"She lied to me again! And on my birthday! What is wrong with her?" I thought.

I sucked in the emotion, compartmentalizing it deep in my body, remaining silent. I hated the stylist for listening to my mother and, of course, I hated my mother for making me look like a boy. I stared at myself in the mirror, holding back the tears.

Once outside the salon, tears streaming down my face, I cried. "Why did you ruin my birthday? Why do you always ruin every thing? I hate you!"

"Iz very niz de her," my mother said. (Your hair is very nice.)

The Nazis shaved my mother's head for many reasons. They wanted to avoid vermin infestation in the barracks, and also used the human hair to make materials for the soldiers. The hair was pressed to make boot liners, seat cushions and upholstery. It was also much easier to spot bald escapees. Maybe most importantly, hair was cut off to humiliate.

Until my hair grew out, I was still flat-chested and mistaken for a boy. Girls in the restrooms gave me dirty looks, especially when I wore my burgundy baseball shirt with "Alix" plastered on the front.

"Are you a boy or a girl?" someone always asked.

Jack, Lola, Aidan and I drove up the coast toward Venice Beach to get our hair cut. Graffiti covered the walls at Paper Clip, an all-purpose salon where people from all walks of life straggled in off the street, often without an appointment. The salon was in an edgy neighborhood filled with interesting restaurants and shops.

Our hairdresser, Taylor, was oblivious to her own authentic beauty. Her long, wavy blonde hair, intoxicating blue eyes and sexy figure were striking. Conversations with Taylor were never boring, as she always found new ways to screw up her life. She was a wild, gorgeous mess you had to love.
"Yeah, I met him at this bar and he had some weed and ya' know . . . . I thought we had something," she said. "He hasn't called me in a week. I'm not getting any younger, I want a kid, and my rent is too high. I'm all stressed. See these hives all over my body? I'm telling you, I just don't know how I survive."

That night I applied oils and grabbed my ocean stones to ground myself before I began the breathwork—breathing into my belly, upper chest and letting it out. "God, tonight, please give me what I need." An image materialized in my mind's eye.

In my mother's white-and-crystal powder room off her bedroom, I picked up a fancy silver hand mirror and brush. Applying her dark red lipstick to my nine year-old lips, I admired myself while I brushed my hair, pretending to be Snow White, with the dwarfs and forest animals scampering around me. Wandering up the hallway, I stood before the mirrored coat closet near the den, confused as I saw partial images of Billy pushing me into the closet. I heard the door lock, and I wondered how long and how many times he had locked me in.

Billy moved out of the house that year to live with his girlfriend Jenny, in the valley. They invited my mother and me over for lunch. Jenny was tall and slender with light brown hair reaching below her shoulder blades. She parted her hair on the side with a simple white barrette. She was genuine, sweet and smart, a girl-next-door type wearing jeans and a blue T-shirt, trying to make a good impression on my mother and me.

On the drive home, my mother said, "She's not Jewish." My mother thought only Jews should be with Jews. Her friends would never approve of Billy dating Jenny in any serious way.

Fortunately, this new relationship gave me an opportunity in which I could move into Billy's old room, large with blue walls, a walk-in closet and adjacent green- and cream-colored tile bathroom. Two large windows overlooked the flower garden and the clotheslines in the distance where my mother hung laundry.

"Mom, why can't you buy a dryer? Everyone else has one."

"Who nids a dryer," she said. "Da tinks smell goot from di flowers outzide."

Allan came home from university in the middle of the school year and settled into his room down the hall.

"Why is Allan home?" I asked.

"Vay all d qvestionz?"

"Because he sleeps all day!"

"Vat iz it your biznis? Gey avek." (Go away.)

Rummaging through the breakfast room junk drawer, I found a silver key underneath the papers, pens and odds and ends. The key locked all of the doors in the house so I kept it in the nightstand next to my bed.

A few nights later as I was sleeping, I awoke, hearing loud screams. Allan was yelling at the top of his lungs in German. I understood every word, as German was similar to Yiddish, the first language I ever heard.

"Ve gayts du michigana hunt? Ve gayts due Yid?" he yelled. (Where are you going crazy dog! Where are you going Jew?)

He sounded like a prison guard rounding up Jews in the ghetto, his voice monstrous and unreal. I feared him as though I were a prisoner and slid into the farthest corner of my mattress, pressing myself against the wall and covering my head with the blanket to muffle the sounds. "Please God, make him stop."

Every night afterward I thanked God for showing me the key so that I could lock my bedroom door. Never relaxed, I curled up in my blankets, hoping that Allan would not rise up in the night like Frankenstein.

One afternoon when my mother and I were home, Allan screamed, "I am going to kill you! You dirty Jew!"

My mother pointed to my bedroom and said to me, "Cloz d door, don vatch."

These words reminded me of what had happened to my mother. "Da Nazis made a ghetto in Ozerkov. Dey came und dey med us stay in von room," she explained.

(The Nazis herded all of us into one room in the Ozerkov Ghetto.)

From my room I peeped through the keyhole to see Allan slam his fist through the den door, and then he backed away in a domineering stance. He wore only his light green boxers, and his legs seemed too thin to support his hanging gut.

He ripped down the five-foot-long bronze doorbell chime and watched it hit the marble floor with a whack. Picking it up, he walked through the living room smashing everything in his way. Glass shattered on the marble floor. A blue vase and a gold statue hit and dented the wall. My world was falling apart as though a bomb had been dropped on our house. Staring in disbelief, my mother simply said to him, "Vat are you doink?"

Allan went into his room and closed the door as though he was Norman Bates running the Bates Motel in "Psycho" and it was just another normal day.

Later that night as I was getting ready for bed, I used my key thinking I would be safe as long as Allan didn't smash in the door. As I closed my eyes, in a "fight or flight" state of mind, I hoped I wouldn't wake up to the sounds of his expert rendition of a Nazi soldier.

"This is Beverly Hills!" I thought. "Why does everyone think this is such a great place to live?"

Frustrated when I awoke the next morning, I said, "Don't you see that Allan is sick, Mom? There is something wrong with him."

"No! Der is somtink rong vit you," she said.

I was the culprit, the crazy one. I had better be quiet and not cause trouble.

While my 5th grade friends were on trips to Europe, Tahiti, Mexico or other exotic places with their families over the holidays, I was home with Allan— loud, mean, violent, crazy, monstrous, selfish Allan. Sometimes he was so out of control that neighbors called the police, then he was sent to the hospital to have his medications adjusted. Hospitalization for Allan meant a short vacation for me where I could feel free.

Billy came home one weekend, went into the kitchen and opened the refrigerator. He pulled out the fixings to make himself a snack of broiled, bubbly American cheese on toast. Watching him eat the crunchy warm meal, I wished he had offered me some. He came by the house often as if it were a 7-11. His presence had an aura of importance, delighting the rest of the family while it lasted. He was always too "busy" doing whatever it was that he did to stop by more often, though never accomplishing much. Always negative and struggling, a fish in a glass bowl despite the ocean of opportunity in front of him. We needed him to be the sparkle in our dreary lives leading the way, holding up his staff, as if he were Moses leading us to the Promised Land.

Billy left an old record player and some albums in his room, paving the way for me to make up a dance to "Crocodile Rock" by Elton John. On the rare afternoons when Allan wasn't home, I danced to the music. Had he been home and I disturbed him, he probably would have smashed the record player to bits.

"Allan scares me," I said to Billy. "He's going to hurt me."

"What do you want me to do about it?"

"Help me. Make him stop."

"Calm down. Don't make such a big deal out of nothing."

One day after school I walked in through the back door, the quiet indicating my mother was not there. Tiptoeing into the house, I put my backpack on the laundry room floor, snuck into the kitchen for a snack, and did homework in my bedroom. An hour later, I returned to the kitchen for a glass of juice when I heard his heavy footsteps.

Startled, I ran through the laundry room and into my bedroom. Grabbing the key from my nightstand, I locked the door.

I watched the crystal doorknob turn back and forth. "You bitch!" he screamed. "I am going to rip you apart with my bare hands! You are scum. You think you are so smart, but you are nothing. NOTHING! NOTHING! You will always be nothing!"

Whimpering, I was afraid of what Allan might do to me while my mother wasn't home. I imagined my escape, jumping out the bedroom window like 007, the house on fire, bullets flying.

After a while, it was quiet. Silently, I snuck into the hallway and called my mother's friend Danya.

"Please, come and pick me up before he hurts me," I begged.

"Okay," she said. "I comink now," Danya was, also a Holocaust survivor who lived in the richest part of Beverly Hills with her husband Carl and her two children, Mark and Rachel. Danya had a turkey neck that hung low and loose skin under her arms. She was an amazing cook who served the best chicken soup while often telling me I was going to inherit all her gaudy jewelry.

I went back into my room, locked the door and waited for her.

An hour had gone by when I heard Allan ranting from the other side of the house, "I was the star quarterback at Beverly Hills High School," he yelled. "I was King Lear, you know, in the play. King Lear, the quarterback, Berkeley, I could have been a great actor. I could have been like Richard Dreyfuss."

"Where is Danya? She should have been here by now." I thought.

Scared, I unlocked the door and ran to the phone. This time I called the police.

"Beverly Hills Police Department. May I help you?"

"He's going to hurt me," I said.

"What's your address?"

"227 Maple Leaf Drive."

I hung up the phone and ran back to my room, locking myself in. Minutes later, the doorbell rang. Allan answered the door still in his boxer shorts, his potbelly hanging out. Through the keyhole, I could see even from that distance his surprise. A great actor, he changed his expression from angry to calm as he spoke to the two police officers.

"Yes?" he said.

"We had a call about a disturbance here, sir. Is everything all right?"

"Fine," Allan said.

"Is there anyone else in the home?"

"My sister."

"May we see her?"

The pivotal moment in my life had arrived.

I walked down the hallway proud as I passed Allan. Having the upper hand, I was taking control. Once outside, I faced two officers, one of which was an African American female. She had her hair pulled back into a tight ponytail.

"We know about him," she said. "And I understand. Look, as long as you are under eighteen and he hasn't hurt you physically, we can't do anything." She cleared her throat. "As soon as you turn eighteen, you need to get out of here."

This angel, a stranger, offered me a life-changing epiphany, an out that I had never before considered. As though I were a mountain climber, each perilous step taking me closer to the summit of Mount Everest. From then on, I thought of every day as being one day closer to freedom.

After the police left, Allan stayed in his room. An hour later, my mother came home.

"Vay you call de poliz?" she asked. "You don do dat! Dis iz our bizness!"

"Danya was supposed to come and get me," I said.

"Eich gaveist. (I know.) I spoke to hair. I tell hair not to come."

With my stomach in knots, and proof that Danya didn't care either, I disappeared into my room. Face down on the pillow, I asked God, "Why doesn't anyone love me?"

"Eir vill git besser," (He will get better) my mother said from the other side of my door, lying to herself, trying to drag me into her denial fantasy.

An hour later she returned, knocking at the bedroom door. "Na, coom eppis essen." (Come and have something to eat.)

There was always a meal after the storm, such as hot stew, chicken soup with matzo balls and apple strudel. Filling my belly, I felt better; food giving me the strength to survive another day of absurdity, the extra pounds proving my confusion to food being friend or foe. The food in this circumstance was soothing and helped me forget the horrible dramas of the day. Other times, the food was offensive because the love I received was conditional upon how much I ate.

The next afternoon after school, I went into the kitchen and saw my mother sitting at the breakfast table reading the newspaper. She never looked up as I grabbed a cold, hard red apple.

Allan entered and asked, "Why do you always buy rotten fruit, mom?"

My mother was silent.

Taking a satisfying, crunchy bite, I headed to my bedroom to spread my homework out on the carpet. Allan suddenly appeared like a forbidding apparition, all 250 pounds of him standing six feet tall, calm and out of character, hovering over me. The chewed apple bits made their way down my throat in a gulp as I scanned the room looking for an escape route.

"Hi!" Allan said, as jolly as a Jewish Santa Claus. Although I didn't buy his friendly persona, I still wanted to believe he could change like my mother said he would.

"What are you doing?" he asked.

"Homework."

He approached and sat cross-legged in front of me in jeans and a white T-shirt sporting a warm smile. Hoping he was trying to connect, I was scared and delighted, like I was playing tag on the freeway during rush hour. Reveling in the possibility that this time would be different, I relaxed. Then he yelled, "Stop bothering me!"

"What?" I asked startled.

"You are a horrible sister!"

"What do you mean?"

"Stop it!" he yelled. "I can't take it anymore."

Frightened, I burst into tears and screamed, "Get out of my room!"

He rose like a lumbering giant mammoth and headed for the door, turning to me with a weird, sinister half-smile, his hidden agenda revealed.

A minute later, my mother ran in, red faced. "Vat you did?"

"Me? How could I possibly do anything to him? Have you seen how big he is?"

She threw me a dirty look as she twisted her blue dishrag, trying to strangle the life out of it.

I heard them talking in the hallway. "She bothers me all day! I don't want to see her anymore! I want my own apartment!" Allan yelled.

"Okay," my mother said. "Hack me nish in cop. You vill git." (Stop hitting me over the head with this. You will get it.)

This cunning ploy, a theatrical skit intended to get my mother to rent Allan an apartment, was at my expense. My only wish was that my mother would send either Allan or me away. Like an infected, pus-filled pimple, I absorbed their neuroticisms, keeping everything inside me, without breaking.

14
Lego My Heart

Aidan walked over to the stove while I was stirring mac and cheese. His eyes were big, sweet and innocent, his light brown hair a wild, cute mess.

"Mom, I want a Lego Death Star. It's really cool. It's a round floating base for space with lots of pieces—3,880 of them."

"How much?"

"Uh, it's like, well it costs $400."

"You're kidding, right?" I asked. "For a bunch of plastic?"

Upset, Aidan stared at his feet. He seldom asked for much, except for a good steak once in a while and saurkraut on his hot dog. Wanting to nurture his desire to build and create, I offered him a quick solution.

"Grandma gave me $100 for your birthday. I'll give that money to you now and you come up with the rest."

Aidan smiled. After a few seconds, he frowned. "How am I supposed to get $300? I'm only a kid."

"By doing extra chores. I'll give you a dollar for every five discs you upload into Daddy's iTunes."

"Boring!"

"You could make $800," I said. "And Daddy will be happy. It's a win-win situation."

"Okay, I'll do it!"

Aidan grabbed a pile of discs from the shelf. He worked on the computer inputting discs in the morning before school, in the evening after he finished his homework and on the weekend. He stayed up so late he often fell asleep in the office chair.

Watching Aidan work, I noticed he looked a lot like Billy. He was tall, with curly, dirty-blonde hair and a quiet demeanor. Billy, unlike Aidan, had never finished anything he started, having so many projects lying around, halfway done, with parts strewn around my mother's house.

Billy moved into my mother's garage when I was 18 years old, just before I moved up north to attend university. Turning the garage into a bedroom and work area, he painted and made sculptures. Quiet and nice one moment, angry and mean the next, he could not control his emotions. As careful around him as I was with Allan, I walked on eggshells for fear one of them would snap.

One day, after I had packed my suitcase and put it in the car, I walked down the hall when suddenly a pair of cold, rough hands wrapped themselves around my neck and squeezed hard. As though in a Hitchcock movie, Billy came at me from behind.

"Stop, you're choking me," I whimpered, struggling to breathe.
I was dizzy and unable to escape. My body went limp, allowing him to push me down to the ground, ready to die like a mouse between a cat's jaws. Fear and adrenaline rushed, shocking and confusing me. Footsteps pounded on the floor as Allan came out of his bedroom.

"Get off her, you asshole," he yelled as he grabbed Billy's hands and pried them off me.

"This is none of your business," Billy said, with eyes glazed over and face frozen. Like two crazed Jewish cowboys, the two of them were hunched forward,

ready to fight.

Fortunately, that day Allan hated me less than he hated Billy. Maybe the doctors had changed his meds that week. My mother was resting on her bed with her eyes closed, even though she heard the commotion in the hallway.

Billy worked in the family business and helped my mother collect rents. One day, I noticed that instead of depositing the rent, usually in the form of bank checks, he had collected it all in cash and had the wrinkled bills piled up high on his bed.

"Mom, look at this," I said.

"Oy," she responded.

We knew something was wrong when he, just then, walked into his room, a man of thirty, tall, bloated, depressed and medicated, his glassy, watery eyes surrounded by dark circles and embedded deep into his face. He looked like he was on drugs.

Wanting to "fix" him, I tried to play parent.

"Maybe if you got a job, everything would fall into place."

"F*** you," spewed out of his mouth.

That next weekend, I went to Colorado and attended my second Gate (a community educational experiential weekend open to members of NSA practices), wanting to go deeper into my healing and hopefully relieve more pain and stress. I was face down on a portable table when NSA founder Dr. Donny Epstein touched the painful place in my back. He evaluated the shape, position, and tone of my spine in relationship to my life, the mysteries soon to be revealed. As I arched up instinctively into the "forward facing dog" yoga position, he touched a spot on the back of my neck.

"Who told you that you had to be responsible for everyone?" he asked.

"My mother, I guess."

Donny Epstein pulled his hand away from my neck. When I lay back down on the table, a sudden surge of energy travelled through and out my body, creating a wave. It was as though I had been liberated. With an exquisite gentle touch, he changed my life that day; a tension forever released making me feel lighter and more flexible. Only then did I fully realize the depth of what I had just let go of. I was not responsible for everyone's tsuris (Yiddish for problems). Relaxing afterwards in the lobby outside, I realized that I, alone, was responsible for focusing on the tsuris. "Letting go" was a misnomer. "Letting go" really means grabbing onto something better. NSA made more energy available in my system leading me to better thoughts. Attention to the Tzouris hindered me from helping myself and others find solutions and love. When I made this connection, I was eager to make use of this new energy coupled with the guidance I had gained to claim a better life for myself and others. Absorbing this new understanding, my mind began to wander.

My mother met her friend Eugenia at a Holocaust remembrance ceremony in Los Angeles where they became fast friends, both being from Europe and living in the same neighborhood. Emilia was Eugenia's daughter, a successful talent agent. They came to our house often to eat lunch. Adorned in colorful silk scarves, they enjoyed my mother's tuna salad sandwiches on challah bread.

Emilia delighted in the layer of turmoil underneath those satisfying lunches. She took pleasure in our family's plight, aggrandizing her status because she had a relative who was a Holocaust survivor. Staying within the confines of Beverly Hills, she was rarely seen in Culver City or downtown, those places rough, scary and foreign to her upper-class European sensibilities.

I listened to her ramblings over lunch, about what a respected talent agent she was as she name-dropped Natalie Wood, Anthony Hopkins and Peter O'Toole, calling them by their first names. "And when I was casting for that film with Tony, we talked about politics and danced together. We had so much in common, what a wonderful man."

"Who are you talking about?" my mother asked.

"Hopkins of course," she said. "Anthony Hopkins!" She said his name in a

snobby sort of way as though she had just puffed on a long cigarette holder during the golden age of Hollywood while lounging on her velvet couch in silk pajamas.

Emilia and my mother came from different backgrounds. The only things they both had in common were they lived in Beverly Hills and were Jewish.

Oblivious to the drug culture, they didn't notice when my brothers and many of their classmates were high. First generation immigrants as Emilia and my mother were, had to focus on survival—learning a new language, finding work and raising a family. Drugs never came into their consciousness; they had no experience of them.

The next generation, on the other hand, had an easier life and could afford more. The drug scene was rampant and kids could buy almost anything. Some of my friends' parents kept cocaine in their medicine cabinets and marijuana in the linen closets. One friend knew where her father kept his roll of hundred dollar bills. She and her siblings would grab a bill to buy a gram of coke or some Quaaludes. Sometimes she shared with friends, her parents never noticing when we were all high, lying under the palm trees around the swimming pool. I was fortunate not to have as much money as they did, a fact which forced me to apply myself at work and school.

I returned home from the Gate a new woman, eager to start shopping and preparing for Thanksgiving.

I was driving to Los Angeles to pick my mother up and bring her over for the traditional family meal when my cell phone rang.

"This is Cedars-Sinai hospital. Your mother has just been brought to the emergency room. She had a sudden heart attack and stroke," an administrator told me.

The stress on me was unbearable as I sat in the waiting room wondering if she was going to live or die. Jack and the kids were an hour away when Tola, an old friend of the family from Poland, had heard the news. She called me on my cellphone.

"Iz all on you, izn it?" (It's all on you.) Tola commented.

Thank God my mother would be okay and was resting comfortably. She was a survivor in every sense of the word, a trait she passed on to me within my genes. When I finally got home, I was stiff as a board so I put on a breathwork CD, reclined on the couch and began the pranayama breathing. My brain and body were appreciative of the rest. Billy appeared in my mind's eye.

"Me, Allan and mom don't need you here," he said, as if he were the spokesperson for the family—the mob boss deciding who was going to get whacked. During those rare times when he helped my mother with groceries and dishes, it was usually in the presence of friends and neighbors.

Pinkis Yaroslavsky and his wife came over for lunch. They joined me at the dining room table as we watched Billy bring in dishes of hot food from the kitchen. Billy displayed his other side, hoping to give a good impression. He appeared helpful, a confusing sight for me when I was most accustomed to seeing him high on crack, plotting to steal the silverware.

Mr. Yaroslavsky said, "Billy das iz a gootin kind. (Billy is a good boy.) Takin care off da mitter." (Taking care of his mother.)

Billy's sudden helpfulness was a con he brought out for older Jews in the inner circle who still considered him a boy.

Little by little, my mother stopped asking for Billy's help, his importance dwindling as she gave me more responsibility. Like a ghostwriter, I was invisible and taking care of the family business from behind the scenes. My mother was too embarrassed to admit to her friends I was taking care of two grown men and their mother. It was bad enough I was the youngest, and I was also a girl. Billy threw out my tennis trophies and spoke badly about me for attending university instead of staying home, always making me the scapegoat. My mother's friends didn't notice what was happening in our house. It was as if I were just another Jewish lampshade.

15

A Kosher Christmas

Sometimes it was hard to believe that I could just live a normal, happy life, like when we drove to Lake Arrowhead to meet another couple and their two children for a restful weekend. One night we all went out to dinner at an elegant, dark and noisy restaurant with fireplaces and cozy brown leather couches. It happened to be Christmas Eve.

Jack and I, Maya and her husband Joshua, sat at one end of a long wooden table with the four kids at the other end. A compact young man with a well-groomed beard and long side burns appeared at the head of the table, gripping a large stack of leather-bound menus.

"May I recite the dinner specials for you?" he said.

"Please," I answered.

"We have a duck breast in an orange muscat reduction served with a wild rice pilaf and vegetable medley; a grilled veal chop with mashed potatoes; and a succulent roasted lamb shank served with a rustic port wine sauce."

"No pork!" Maya demanded, lifting her right hand in a STOP sign. "I want absolutely no pork in my order!"

Guests at nearby tables turned their heads, her Israeli/American accent echoing throughout the large room.

"Very good," the waiter said, taken aback. "I will let you know if there is any pork in your order. What would you like to have for your entree this evening?"

"I will take the salmon please," Maya said.

The waiter looked at Maya and said, "I hope this isn't too personal a question, but are you an Orthodox Jew? By that I mean, are you kosher?"

"Yes, I am."

"Well then, I should let you know that there is Parmesan cheese in the puff pastry that surrounds the salmon."

"That's okay," she said. "Bring the cheese."

Jack felt the confused waiter needed some understanding of the rules of kosher law so he chimed in with an explanation. "Fish isn't considered a meat like beef, lamb or chicken, so dairy is allowed with fish as long as it isn't shellfish. Isn't that right Maya?"

Maya nodded in agreement. "Yes," she said. "Kosher people don't eat pork and don't eat dairy with meat."

Jack flashed his Cheshire-cat grin at the waiter and said, "But if you should have a craving for a hamburger topped with Swiss cheese, just throw on some bacon strips. It's a double negative. The cheese and the bacon cancel each other out. Your burger, like magic, becomes kosher again."

All of us laughed except Maya, who was extremely annoyed at the fact she was the butt of Jack's joke.

I ordered the duck and Joshua ordered the lamb shank with the port wine sauce.

After everyone had ordered, the waiter informed us he was also the sommelier.

"I won't be ordering any wine tonight," Joshua said. He was saving himself for the single-malt, twelve-year-old Islay whiskey he had brought with him.

I said, "I'd really like a nice glass of wine to go with my duck."

The waiter asked, "A pinot?"

"Yes! Perfect. Join me Maya?"

"Cain, betach." (Yes, absolutely.)

As I sipped my wine, I enjoyed the pleasant environment, the wood paneling, the dim lighting, and the view of the lake. Halfway into my mouth-watering meal, I finished my wine. Maya had saved her entire glass for her salmon, yet she still hadn't taken her first sip.

Joshua was eating his lamb shank with a hearty appetite when he looked over at his wife's full glass of wine. He reached over, picked up her glass and took a substantial and loud gulp.

"Good!" he announced.

Maya's face shifted from calm enjoyment to fury. Pissed off, she said something under her breath in Hebrew. "You ate pork!" she screamed. "Then you drank from my glass!" She gave him a long cold stare. "Now I can't drink my wine."

"It's not pork," Jack insisted. "It's port, a sweet wine from Portugal made from the skin of the grape."

"Yes, yes, it's port," I said, trying to be convincing. "It's a port wine reduction sauce that comes with the lamb. Try it! I'm sure it's wonderful."

"Maya, its port! Port, not pork," Joshua said.

She wasn't buying it. Her kosher radar in high gear, she refused to drink the wine. "I am not going to kiss you tonight!" she said to Joshua.

"Oh really, so how is that different from last night?"

"Well, I mean it tonight!"

Maya let her wine glass sit in all its reddish-purple glory like forbidden fruit. The dishes were cleared around the glass, and the dessert and tea were served. By not touching the wine, she let her husband know he had ruined her meal, one strike against him, so far, this evening.

I considered drinking her wine myself, but the negative energies surrounding the glass went back to biblical times. The glass remained full throughout the entire meal as if we were waiting for Elijah the prophet to come and drink it down. But just like at the Passover Seder, no Messiah appeared at our dinner table, and the glass remained full.

A little buzzed from my wine, I thought about how some people today are still run by practices that began 2,000 years ago when impurities were an issue in food. Being kosher means not eating pork, shellfish or animals with double clove hooves that don't chew their cud, a practice that bonds Jews together as a group. Although I am a Jew, I am not against pork. In fact, I love eating bacon for breakfast.

16

It Takes a Village

The rabbi was a sweet, fat man with broken-out, pasty white skin. He wore a suit and a yarmulke and kissed the mezuzah every time he walked in and out of a room. The Hebrew Academy stood majestic on Olympic Boulevard, an off-white façade flanked by gigantic silver lettering. Whoever talked my mother into sending me to Talmud Torah, an Orthodox religious after-school program two days a week when we were not the least bit religious, was an idiot.

I felt like an alien. Modest dress and keeping kosher were the customs followed there, but not in our home. My mother fried up bacon for breakfast, for God's sake. She didn't even believe in God! And why should she? God had betrayed her. So she turns around and sticks me in this school where I am supposed to honor God in the strictest of terms.

My teacher was a woman who was colorfully dressed and wore make-up to match. She wore her hair as if a large, brownish-purple eggplant had been placed on her head. She taught me the Hebrew alphabet, the only thing I learned.

One of my classmates, Rebecca, was cute, religious and connected to the congregation—her parents were very involved. Popular, she always wore heels with fashionable jeans and corduroys that had the perfect flair over the tips of her platform shoes. She had beautiful jewelry her parents gifted her just because.

Envious, I shrunk into the background of the class wearing the same pair of 501 Levis every day with a T-shirt my mother brought home after she happened upon a three-for-one sale. One t-shirt read "Do It!" in big, black bold lettering across the chest at a time when my boobs had reached maximum capacity. Men would whistle from cars as I walked down the street. Uncomfortable and not yet accepting of my new voluptuous body or the attention it attracted, I was angry at my mother for buying me clothes that made me look like a slut even though, in her defense, she didn't know what the words meant.

During dinner when my brothers were both home, I explained my predicament. "I need more clothes," I said. "I only have one pair of pants. Everyone makes fun of me at school."

No one said a word in my favor as though I were not even there, leaving me crushed. If my brothers had only helped me persuade my mother, she would have listened to them, only the males getting respect.

"Eat d'eggs!" my mother said. "I already peelt dem."

"Can I have a drink, please?"

"No, if you trink, dere vill be no room for d'food."

While I chewed, I was glad my mother had recently bought me a bra even though it had an industrial quality. It was such a sensitive issue, my boobs, the boys staring and the girls so jealous. Now my hormones were raging as my body became shapely.

I was going through developmental changes and would have had no understanding of what was happening to me if it were not for a sixth grade mandatory sex education film where I learned crucial details about menstruation and pregnancy. When my period came, I went to the drugstore myself to buy maxi pads like the ones I had seen on TV. It was lonely and scary to go through this important stage of womanhood on my own, but I had no choice. This wasn't the kind of thing about which my mother spoke.

Every move I made at that time was a mistake, each an embarrassing moment that could have been avoided if someone had clued me in. I had let one boy in my eighth grade class who lived nearby touch me down there, having had no idea what I was doing. He stopped suddenly to grab his Calico cat and toss her out the door like a piece of trash.

"What are you doing to the cat?"

"She jumps on my back when I screw," he said.

As I was a virgin, the fact he was already having sex scared me so much I ran all the way home.

My mother reminded me it was time for Hebrew school as I was finishing a bologna sandwich. She dropped me off at the side entrance and watched me go inside the building where I waited behind the doorway until I heard her drive away. Slipping out seconds later, I walked ten blocks west and three blocks south to my friend Jennifer's apartment. A year older than me, Jennifer went to the same elementary school as I did. Her mom had marijuana, loose leaves that were stored in a Smucker's jam jar hidden in the back of her pantry, but we never smoked, at least not then.

We hung out while her mother was at work, talked for a couple hours and grabbed a bite before I headed back to Hebrew school in time for my mother to pick me up.

"How vas d school?" my mother asked.

"The same." I kept ditching Hebrew school until the end of the year.

When I graduated with no repercussions, she and her Jewish friends were satisfied, and that was all my mother cared about.

"Oh, you vill hev a Bat Mitzvah anda Sveet Sixteen!" my mother said.

She would ignite my hopes for these opportunities for me to be recognized, soon brushing her promises off as though I had imagined them. I was drawn into believing her then let down, not knowing any better, until I did.

Jewish holidays were strange at our house because even the ones that were supposed to be uplifting and fun were times to mourn the dead. These holidays were solemn, focusing on the past, on the sweet memories of my mother's home before the war and on relatives lost. The Jewish day of mourning and atoning for sins was the high holiday of Yom Kippur.

Jack, Lola, Aidan and I went to the synagogue to pray and read from the bible on Yom Kippur.

"What's this holiday about again?" Aidan asked.

"We think about our sins this year, and we fast," Jack said.

"You know the time when I was watching *Family Guy* on TV and I didn't finish my homework? I really did forget I had any homework that night," Aidan confessed.

"You don't need to confess," Jack responded. "It's not like going to Catholic confession and spilling your guts to the priest. You're supposed to silently consider your sins."

"I can't think of a major sin I did this year," I said.

"Come on, Mom, we all sinned," Aidan responded.

"Yeah, I know. I'm trying to think of a good, solid sin, though."

We listened to the cantor sing the Kol Nidre, a prayer asking God to forgive our sins. As I listened to the cantor's beautiful voice something resonated within me. "Wasting time when I should have been writing, I let resistance get the better of me," I thought to myself.

Suddenly, I felt an energy surround me. Aware of its heavy presence, as though air had been syphoned from the room, it told me I would never finish the book. Sensing and resisting it at the same time I had no choice but to deal with this dark energy. While sitting in synagogue, I thought back to other times during my healing process when I experienced an obvious duality—my energy and another energy that wasn't mine. As I sensed both these energies within me, I thought about my mother's life.

Polish Jews made up my mother's inner circle. When she wasn't visiting with them, she often made new acquaintances more important and interesting than her own children. The Nazis had destroyed that worthy, self-loving part of her when they ripped her out of a normal loving environment. She categorized her friends in two ways. First, she based them on where they and their parents were from, and second if they had shared experiences, the right background allowing entrance into the dark places of her mind, a select few who could remember, commiserate, console, and keep each other company. They discussed this place where "monsters" had lived, confirming a comforting bond from having suffered.

When my father was alive, my parents were active members of the 1939 Club, one of the largest and most active Holocaust organizations in the world, taking its name from the year when Hitler invaded Poland. After my father had died, my mother attended few events there. Mostly, her close friends came to the house to visit.

Pinkus Yaroslavsky and his wife Anna sat and talked to my mother in the breakfast room, speaking in a low whisper as though talking about cancer. When I entered the room, they changed the subject by taking a bite of whatever was on their plate. After they chewed and swallowed, the conversation shifted to how was I liking school and would I like something to eat. Their innermost thoughts were secret, their silence impressing upon me how horrible the camps must have been, the Holocaust always being at the forefront even if it wasn't the subject of conversation.

Helen, my mother's best friend, came over often bringing home-made fresh-baked European cookies filled with raspberry jam and sprinkled with powdered sugar. One day, she came dressed elegantly as usual in beige-colored pants and a matching turtleneck, with a fashionable gold chain belt around her slim waist. Offering a sincere concern I hadn't experienced with anyone else, she warned me not to pick at all the food my mother left out. She said, "Mek sure to be a goot girl und tek care of your moder." (Make sure to be a good girl and always take care of your mother.) It was as if she were saying good-bye, tying up loose ends. She died a week later.

Around this time I was seventeen and driving a beat-up red Toyota. I was delighted when Tola, one of my mother's friends from Poland, convinced my mother I needed a BMW; Tola's family had some sort of car dealer connection. A month later I was driving a white BMW stick shift with tan interior and a sunroof. An ironic situation since BMW had produced the ovens used to burn the Jews in the concentration camps.

The BMW was another deflection from the dysfunction in my home, and made life somehow easier in the sense that I could better pretend everything was fine. Since I was in this place in life, I attracted similar friends who also had things to hide. Relating well to dysfunctional people in my age group just like my mother did in hers, I found friends with family problems or screwed up relatives more interesting than the boring rich kids with perfect families. The more complicated their families were, the more interested I became.

When I no longer wore bifocals in the ninth grade, I was attractive and had a slim figure from running laps on the track at school. I thought I was fat, a mind game that plagues young girls.

A cute group of high school boys who lived in the wealthier part of Beverly Hills, where the big mansions were, liked me a lot. Being Jewish and having gone to the same school, I was part of the group. We shared good times and laughs, the escape I craved. As a result, my life became a succession of highs and lows, as if I were bipolar, although I wasn't. Moments of grief and loneliness at home contrasted with momentous highs, great sex and wild escapades. Keeping my home life a dark secret, I lived on the periphery, my friends unaware of what I was going through. If they suspected the truth, I would be left friendless, or so I thought.

I admit I looked svelt in my string bikini as we lounged in the lit-up Jacuzzi in the dark, while the boys smoked pot and sniffed a few lines to enhance the high. After we had all taken a Jacuzzi at Eric's house, Daniel, my best male friend from high school, passed out cookies.

"Don't eat them now," he warned. "Save them for later."

"Why? What's so special about these cookies?" I asked.

"My sister boiled the THC out of a whole bunch of marijuana and made bright green butter," he said. "She used that butter in the cookie batter."

I carefully placed the cookie in a yellow dinner napkin. I took it home and kept it hidden in my underwear drawer—little did I know.

17

Battling a Devil in Drag

A perfect day unfolded in spite of the fact that I was balancing dueling energies. We took the red-eye from Los Angeles to New York during the winter school break. Lola was a budding actress wanting to see some theater, having already been in a few productions and commercials. Aidan was excited about the big Toys R Us, while Jack and I were interested in the museums, jazz clubs and new restaurants.

We bought tickets to "Mama Mia" on Broadway, and after a brisk, cool walk to the theater, we made it just in time to enjoy the musical. Uplifted and charmed by Abba's lyrics and music, we watched the performers dance and sing dressed in funky '70s costumes. After the show, we followed hungry theatergoers to John's Pizzeria, set in a building converted from an old cathedral with stained glass windows. We entered from beneath the lights of the bustling street. Ravenous, we wolfed down a messy, thin-crust, hot and gooey cheese pizza with extra sauce.

Loving the adventure and diversity of the city, and an escape from the normal pressures, I appreciated we had so many choices in life. When I was very young, my mother chose for me.

I asked, "Why do I have to live with Allan?"

"Vat ken you do? Dis is da laben." (What can you do? This is the life.)

Life just happened to my mother. She was unable to make her own choices about many things, due to learned helplessness brought on by her past. In general, she focused on being frugal. Food was the exception to the rule. Never had I gone without a meal nor had I ever seen anyone leave our house hungry, even though we lived most of our life as though we were dirt poor.

"Don't you have any other pants?" Julia asked me as we walked toward our next class in ninth grade. Julia was dark skinned and exotic looking, as if she had come from a long line of plump, Tunisian belly dancers. She wore luxurious designer clothing, and rarely wore an outfit twice. Feeling awkward in comparison, I glared back, wearing one of the two worn-out shirts I owned. Bullied on occasion, I was punched by boys and teased by girls, with the exception of one skinny blonde girl who hit me in the forehead with her fist. Unable to find common ground with girlfriends who were proudest of the contents of their walk-in closets, I was frustrated and prayed before bed.

"Please, God, give me some clothes. Take me out of this house away from Allan so I don't have to be scared."

I remember my mother sharing "Ve vent to verk in da textile factory. Ve vore clothes from dem in Aushwitz mit da bloot." (We went to work in the textile factory and wore the same bloodstained clothes from those murdered in Auschwitz.) The Nazis didn't want to waste material so they recycled the uniforms of the dead prisoners.

The next year, during one of the Beverly Hills High School assemblies, a teacher mentioned the school job board was a great way for seniors to find summer employment. "If I got a job, I could make money to buy clothes," I thought. "And, I wouldn't have to go home right after school!"

Although, I wasn't a senior yet, I relished the idea of having un-terrorized hours within my day and was eager to check out the job board. As soon as the last bell rang, I found where white index cards were tacked up. Scanning them all, I honed in on a part-time position at Cora's Clothing Store in Century City. While I filled out the employment application, I discovered I had to be sixteen years old to work; still fifteen, I lied about my age. Hired that week, I walked ten minutes to the store after school and worked until 6:00 p.m. every day, shelving and hanging clothes, keeping the store tidy and helping customers find outfits. After work, I went to the gym and worked out for an hour before I came home.

"Vay you bin comink home zo late?" my mother asked.

"After school activities."

Cashing my first paycheck was surreal. Money meant freedom. Now I could buy clothes! I designed my wardrobe, becoming my own person and loving the independence of shopping. Not having to beg and cry for what I needed, this was another step in loosening myself from my mother's grip.

One day, Sheryl, the store manager, called me over. With whitish skin and black curls holding tight to her head like an Afro, she wore thin, gold-framed glasses and looked a lot like Billy Jean King, the tennis player.

"I am suing this store," she said. "I have a lawyer."

"Why?"

"Sexual harassment. Tom has been inappropriate."

Tom was her supervisor. He didn't pay much attention to me.

"Will you be a witness?" she asked.

"Witness? I didn't see anything."

The atmosphere in the store changed as the lawsuit loomed. Supervisors from the store's main office checked in on us periodically. Not enjoying my time there anymore, I gave notice.

I returned to the job board at school with work experience now under my belt and having learned speed typing in an elective class. I applied for a receptionist/ secretary position in a real estate office in Beverly Hills. A silver-haired Hungarian Holocaust survivor interviewed me. Mr. Peter Frankel was a warm and likable man dressed in an Italian three-piece white suit and colorful silk tie.

His matching wide-brimmed hat hung on a coat rack in the corner of his office. On the wall was a framed photo of him wearing the same hat with his arm around Sammy Davis, Jr. He looked like Marcello Mastroianni in that hat.

Hired the same day, I made $100 a week working after school while maintaining excellent grades. The only person who read my report card was me. Three months later, my mother confronted me.

"Vay you nit to verk?" (Why do you need to work?)

"I like it and I need money."

As I was getting ready for bed later on, my mother came into my room and gave me forty dollars.

"Na, tek it," she said. "I vill give you evry week lik dis."

This money was her way of reining me in from becoming too independent. She wanted me home. Allan pestered her like Chinese water torture when I wasn't there. He used me as a target for his rage. Billy didn't want me to work either, seeing my efforts as showing him up. My mother did her best to keep me home, by instilling the fear of going outside.

"Do you rilly nit to go to Daniel's houz now?" (Do you really need to go to Daniel's house now?) she said in a worried tone. "You juz came from da verk."

"Yes, I do."

"Do you hev to go to da bich today?" She said on the weekend. "Iz a long bus ride und da vater iz a ganza calt." (The water is freezing.)

"No, I don't have to go the beach, I want to go to the beach."

From my mother's perspective, it was safer to stay in. If she hadn't stayed where she was supposed to be in the Polish ghettos or in Auschwitz, she would have been shot.

Having my own money was the beginning of my independence and I could not be stopped. My weekly income was $140, my allowance plus my salary, which was a fortune back then, though it was still not enough though to keep up with the lifestyles of my peers, who flaunted their designer clothes, expensive sports cars, exotic vacations and even investments. Often I overheard kids at *school discussing early morning stock trades they had made with their dads.*

Chloe, a girl in ninth grade, was tall, flat-chested and stick thin. She wore a hot pink Chanel suit to school, the skirt falling just above the knee and the fitted jacket just above the waist. She wore matching heels, and walked through the cafeteria as though on a Paris runway. Watching her swagger by, I chewed my greasy buttered bagel trying not to drip on the new jeans I had purchased at Cora's with an employee discount. Never would I have known her suit was Chanel were it not for the gossip. I felt as if I were from another planet.

Even though my life improved as I earned money, that policewoman's sage advice haunted me. I still dreamed about getting away from my family. Like the little girl in "Poltergeist" who was trapped inside the television, I rose toward the light, a voice somehow leading me.

Emilia, my mother's friend whom I hadn't heard from in years, phoned when she couldn't find my mother.

"She's at the dentist," I said.

"Oh, well. I'll call her tomorrow. How is the family?"

"Wonderful!"

"Really?" she said, surprised.

"Yes! They are great. Jack is doing well and the kids are happy at school."

"Oh, you're talking about *that* family," she said, remembering I was now married with two kids.

Empowered as I spoke to Emilia, gloating in my strength, showing her I had escaped the dysfunction and the "tsuris" (problems), I suddenly felt weak and unsure of myself. "Why is it if I stand up for myself, I feel bad? Maybe I am not supposed to be happy? Am I bad if I'm happy?"

Stuck in this limbo for weeks, unable to differentiate right from wrong and love from evil, I was confused as I struggled to gain control of negative thoughts, not wanting to get out of bed or answer the phone. Every morning, I had to convince myself I deserved my life. My happiness was always going to require shoveling away the dirt piled high on the dump truck of life. Moments when I had tried to prove myself worthy as a child haunt me still, an unbearable sadness.

After school, work and the gym one night, I came home with a smile on my face and sat down in the breakfast room. Billy and my mother were having a meal.

"Guess what?"

"Vat?" my mother asked.

"I got a raise today!"

"Oh." Her tone was disappointed, as though I had done something wrong. She cleared dishes from the breakfast table, avoiding the subject.

"Who do you think you are?" Billy laughed. "You're not special, you are nothing."

As if I were Wile E. Coyote, a gigantic boulder having fallen on my head after the dynamite blast, I went to my room. Staring at the ceiling, I had no hope, no will and no energy, wondering why I was even born. Now I'm even castigated for earning more money, which society deems as success. My friend's parents would have been proud. I was devastated, and yet, believing deep in my soul there was something wrong with them and not with me, I pressed on.

Often, my friend's parents regarded me as an example for their children.

"Alix, could you please hold Susie's money? She always loses it."

"Maybe you should study with Alix so she can help you with your homework, honey."

When I was in ninth grade, there were times when I was sick, unable to get out of bed in the morning and not having pleasure in anything. I asked my mother to please take me to the doctor because I was sure I had the flu. After examining me, the doctor said I was suffering from depression and wrote a referral. Annoyed, my mother ignored his diagnosis like she did everything else that had to do with me.

"Dere is notik wrong mit you."

I dealt with my depression and masked the sadness by smoking pot, snorting cocaine, exercising, working more hours, having drinks and dinner with friends, and having sex whenever I could. I did anything not to feel bad, to not notice that place where I felt unloved and had no self-love. It was as though I was desperate to make that last pull-up over the bar as I tried to achieve something significant before the negative voices pushed me down. Like John Belushi in "Animal House," with an angel on one shoulder and a devil on the other, I had to decide if I was going to join my mother and brothers in their suffering—a world of craziness, depression and dysfunction, or if I was going to allow myself joy.

Love and purpose replaced drugs and bad habits when I married and had children. Still, depression hit hard and heavy from time to time, to the extent I couldn't function. When this happened, Dr. Hyla Cass prescribed St. John's Wort, a natural remedy derived from an African plant, which kept me from feeling too low. I also made daily rampages of appreciation as per the Abraham teachings, and lists of what I love about myself and what others appreciate about me, as per David Elliott's book *Healing*. "I am worth it!" I told myself, and over time, I believed it.

Around this time I took the risk of letting myself really feel into the sadness of depression. Instead of repressing the negative energy and thoughts, I dove right into it, bathed in it, and to my surprise, it spiraled out of me within a few days, another huge release. I no longer needed St. John's Wort as I became accustomed to switching my thoughts to positive ones and gaining self-love. Other positive side effects were that it meant I was happy most of the time while attracting wonderful and creative new people into my life.

One afternoon I watched Oprah interview a family with a seven-year-old schizophrenic girl, out of control and dangerous, who had only short bouts of normalcy. Both parents were at their wit's end.

"We are afraid she might hurt her younger brother," the mom radiated concern.

"Yes, and she may take her own life," said the dad. "Keeping both children safe is our biggest concern."

The parents had spoken to multiple experts. "Our solution was to separate the kids by renting two apartments next to each other, one for each child," said the mom. The parents traded off each night, giving one parent a stressful night and the other, a restful one. They kept the little boy safe while keeping the schizophrenic girl engaged. She needed to be busy all the time, otherwise she connected with the demons in her head.

"You look very relaxed," Oprah said.

"We take antidepressants to get through this," the mom said.

My upbringing was just as bad—a little girl living in a big house with a mentally ill man, sixteen years older, whose diagnosis had changed depending on the doctor of the day. No one considered keeping him separate from me.

"Why wasn't I on a talk show?"

"You are d helty one," my mother said.

"So?"

"Zo, vay you fight wit him?"

"Oh, so the healthy one has to let the crazy one be right even if he is wrong?"

Damned if I did, damned if I didn't. Whatever decision I made, I was wrong. Blamed for being healthy, I couldn't win. The more ill my brother became, the more love he received from my mother. Never did I see an emotional incentive for him to get better. And consequently, I saw my mother enjoy those times when I had a cold or flu so that she could dote on me, the only time I felt love. If one wanted to be loved in my family, one had to be sick.

"I herd you sniz," my mother said. "Und caffink laz night." (And coughing.)

"I'm fine."

While on Dr. Marie's massage table one morning, the shutter in my mind's eye closed. An image emerged.

Walking from our house on Maple Leaf Drive to Vista Elementary School, my mother wore her snug-fitting chocolate brown pants and matching shirt. Her outfit always stood out in front of the white colonial office building.

"Von culor lookz azoy rich," (One color looks so rich,) she said. Caring about how she looked, she ate a bran muffin every morning before school and drank eight glasses of water during the day.

On our way to school, we passed the savings and loan where she had her savings account, and stopped to admire the bronze statue of a mother with her three children, standing tall in front of the white and red brick building.

The image changed suddenly and I saw myself at 14 years old, a high school student in the 9th grade. My mother was parking in the lot behind the same savings and loan to make a deposit. Once inside, I saw my mother had a tear in her eye. She showed me her savings passbook. The balance was huge.

"Wow, where did all that money come from?"

"I zold da bildng." (I sold the building.)

"What? To whom?"

"Da uncle. I nided money."

"But isn't that building worth a lot more? You didn't tell anyone?"

"No. Vat could I do?"

As though my heart had been torn out, I couldn't believe my mother created another mess, letting her wealthy brother-in-law shortchange her. Showing me her bank balance, her youngest child in high school as opposed to someone from her inner circle, she might have been looking to me as the parent now.

"Why do you always do the wrong thing?! Did you talk to Billy?"

"He'z in da hospital too."

"So you sold our share of a building?"

We both cried.

Staying healthy and strong for my present day family was foremost on my mind. Pilates helped me stay supple and flexible. Gina, my Pilates instructor, always offered the right exercise when I had a back or neck issue. Half Japanese and half Italian, she was the perfect combination of both nationalities. Laughing to myself, I wondered if her parents, like Jack and me, had arguments over whether to go out for sushi or Italian.

I was lying on the Pilates reformer machine, a wooden bed with weighted resistance straps.

Gina ordered, "Get on your hands and knees. Grab the wood on the sides. Keep your arms straight and your core tight. Now, pretend you are holding a newspaper under each armpit. Pull yourself forward without dropping the newspapers."

Just then, I remembered my father had always held a newspaper under his arm, an image long forgotten until I met the medium that talked to dead people.

My massage therapist, Becca, told me about Mr. Angelo, a medium. One of her clients went to see him after her father passed away. She had such profound experiences visiting with her father through the medium she made an appointment every Monday at 1:00 pm. If she was early, she would wait until her father arrived and lecture him on his tardiness. Envious of her success connecting to her father, I wondered if I could connect with mine. I made an appointment.

"To prepare for our meeting, I want you to think about your father. Talk to him when you are driving down the street or taking a shower. It will help the communication."

In the days leading up to our meeting, I pretended to speak to my father about my fears and aspirations. When I arrived at the office, I sat in the waiting room, where on a wall plaque were the words, "I speak to dead people."

In his office, Mr. Angelo sat opposite me as I sat on his couch. Recording our session, he said, "I can see people standing on either side of you. If you see my eyes staring in either direction, don't be alarmed."

After a few moments, he stared at me and looked to my left. "Your father is here with us now," he said. "He loves you so much. He says he has always loved you. Your father is tall and strong, standing in a gray suit and striped tie, with a newspaper under his arm."

"Yes, that would be him."

"He has a wonderful smile. I can see it, and bright green eyes. He took you on a family vacation when you were three, with your mother and brothers, right?"

"Yes. It's the only time we ever took a vacation together."

Waking us up in the early morning darkness, my father drove us to Murrieta Hot Springs in the gold Pontiac Bonneville. The motel had a pool in front of our rooms. My brothers were in one room, my parents and I in the other.

As he carried me in the pool the next morning, I felt safe in my father's arms. Smiling in the sun, my mother waited for him to return me to her as she sat at the pool's edge, dipping in her toes. Never having learned to swim, she was afraid of the water.

"There is a man, an old friend of your father's, standing on the left side of you now telling me about a party at his house in the mountains. You were there with your parents."

"Who is the friend?"

"His name is something like Danko."

"It's Drezenko, I remember!" Wealthy and important in the Jewish community, Drezenko was a close family friend of whom my mother had spoken highly. "Dey froz hiz body ven he diet, like Valt Dizney," she said.

"He always played with me," I said.

"He loved you."

"He did. I remember what that felt like."

"He tossed you up in the air and tickled you, too."

"Oh my God! I remember laughing so hard I couldn't breathe." My memory banks were reignited as though a magic wand had tapped me on the head.

"You smoked pot with your mother-in law," he said. "She wasn't feeling well."

"How did you know?"

"She loves you very much."

"You have a disappointing relationship with you own mother. She was never there for you."

"Yes."

"Your father is telling me he was watching over you when your brother was taking care of you. You were small."

"I don't remember my brother taking care of me. I do, however, remember him helping me pick out my first car, a pleasant surprise."

Billy taught me how to drive a stick shift. Driving to the beach and back was an exciting day. He put his hand over my mine while helping me switch gears on that sunny day. I wondered why he was being so nice. He didn't do much without getting something in return.

Elated by the medium's consultation, I couldn't wait to tell Jack what had happened, the events he reminded me of, and that my father was there.

"He has some kind of gift, obviously," Jack said. "But you don't know your father was really there."

"There you go again, being your skeptical self, always having to have some kind of proof for everything," I yelled. "If I say it was my daddy, you should believe it!"

"How can you prove it? Maybe he was reading your thoughts."

Jack may have been right about how the medium absorbed information, although I couldn't admit it. My biggest quandary was what I was going to do with the rest of my life. The idea of channeled fatherly advice calmed and enticed me so much I made an appointment to see Mr. Angelo a second time.

He was quiet that day.

"I want to talk to my father," I said. "I need advice."

"No, I can't do that."

"Why not?"

"I just can't."

Mr. Angelo stopped our session, refusing to tell me any more. I was shattered, and vowed never to return. I left feeling betrayed; he had cut me off cold.

On my way home, I thought about the holes in my memories of childhood. I couldn't remember much about growing up and had few stories to tell.

Jack remembered every detail and date, so why couldn't I? As my mind wandered, I recalled an old photograph of me sitting on Louise's couch.

Louise was a tenant who occupied a patio apartment in the building my mother managed in 1975. Sitting with Sparky, Louise's black and white dog, I was smiling brightly all of seven years old. Cute and pretty and already beginning to develop, my body was bursting in the tight clothing my mother made me wear. My long bangs were pulled back to one side with a brown barrette.

Louise was a bone-skinny redhead with thin lips in her mid-forties. Like Sissy Spacek in "Fried Green Tomatoes," she wore a big white floppy hat and a flowery dress as she got out of her white Studebaker that Sunday after church.

Eager to see her dog Sparky, she unlocked the front door. Greeted by her faithful companion, she pulled open her drapes, taking in the view. She saw me outside, jumping over the cracks in the sidewalk. I was standing by for my mother, who was inside waiting for a repairman.

Grabbing a small glass bottle out of her purse, Louise came outside.

"Hello," she said.

"Hi!"

Twisting open the bottle, she sprinkled me with liquid.

"What are you doing?"

"It's holy water. It will save you." She danced and dripped water on me, her body moving jagged and quick as though possessed. "Jesus will save you. I'll pray for your salvation."

I was more curious than alarmed, having never seen holy water, and not believing in Jesus in that way. Jews don't believe that Jesus rose up from the dead or that he was the Messiah.

"Would you like to come inside for a soda?" Louise asked.

"Sure. Okay."

Visiting with Louise, loving her dog more than anything, I stayed in her apartment while my mother was upstairs. It was time for lunch and I was hungry.

"Bye, Louise. I'm going to find my mom."

Giving Sparky a big hug, I kissed him on his forehead.

"Bye, honey. God bless. Praise Jesus!"

I entered the vacant apartment where my mother was standing in the kitchen. I said, "Please, can I get a slice of pizza, mom? I'm so starving!"

"You cin vait. Ve vill eet at de home." (You can wait. We will eat at home.)

"I'm hungry now!"

Not wanting to miss the repairman after having waited for hours, she wouldn't budge.

"Call him! Why don't you ever call anyone to check if they are coming? Please give me some money to buy a slice. I know how to walk there. I'll come back fast, I promise."

"Okay," she said.

She reached into her purse and pulled out a few dollars. I grabbed the money and headed down the street toward the "Piece o' Pizza" stand, aware my shorts were too tight, making me look too voluptuous for my age. I had no sexual desires, even though my body was beginning to develop.

Thinking about the cheese pizza I would be devouring, I kept my mind off my pants. While I was ordering, a man in dark sunglasses walked up behind me. Slim and wiry, older than Allan, he was wearing faded blue jeans and a white T-shirt. He smiled, "Beautiful day."

I nodded.

"Are you here alone?"

"Uh, well, my mom is waiting for me."

He looked around and saw no one. Moving in closer, he smelled like musk and stinky hair gel.

"I'm Jeff. Wouldn't you like to go for a ride with me?" he asked, pointing to a white, dented Pinto in the parking lot.

"No, my mom is waiting for me."

I picked up my food and turned to leave.

"Come and check out my car," he said. "It's so nice inside."

My intuition was heightened, a warning to get the hell out of there. I gripped the hot pizza slice on a paper plate in one hand and a bottle of Coke in the other. I ran, never looking back. Later that year, a sexual predator with a similar description to the man at the pizza place was arrested in Maryland, after molesting young girls all across the country.

18
Testing the Waters

J aime, our neighbor from down the street, was pushing a stroller past our house. She caught my glance as I stuck my head out the open front door. "Hey!" I yelled.

Jaime's blonde, blue-eyed daughter, Samantha, jumped out of the stroller and ran toward the rope swing hanging from the flowering Jacaranda tree on my front lawn. Lavender flowers falling from the tree painted the street like a Monet. Samantha sat on the swing with a gigantic smile showing off the wide gap between her two front teeth.

Pregnant, Jaime wore skin-tight, faded jeans, a cherry-colored tank top that hugged her expanding breasts, a straw hat and matching red flip-flops. Gorgeous and magazine-cover worthy, she wore lots of make-up. If a photographer showed up out of the blue, she was ready.

"She's a hot mom!" my friend Oscar once commented as he watched her dance at a bar one night.

Forty pounds overweight, I felt eons away from being even close to a hot mom. I was bummed, because for the first time I had to buy size fourteen pants.

"Are you losing weight?" Jaime asked, as she parked the stroller.

"No, I'm just buying big!" I stretched the waistband out as far as it could go. "This way I can breathe!"

We both laughed.

"I am trying to lose weight, but it's hard," I said.

"Don't use the word hard," Jaime insisted. "You are putting negative energy out there, making it even harder on yourself. Say to yourself, 'I am in the process of losing weight.' Put a positive spin on it!"

Samantha jumped back in the stroller, and Jaime walked away. Looking down at my cellphone, I saw a message from Lola. "Mom, is it okay for me to shoot a BB gun with Kelan? Her dad will be supervising."

Shooting had never entered my parental domain beyond an occasional arcade game. "What is she, Rambo? What are they doing over there, training her to hunt?" If only she had stuck with the piano lessons, none of this would be happening. The incident reminded me of Reuben.

Reuben lived down the street from us. We were in the fourth grade and hung out together most days after school. One day, he took me behind his garage where he had lined snails up on the concrete wall. He pulled out a BB gun and shot snails off the wall one by one, like a cowboy in a showdown.

"Where did you a get the gun?"

"My dad keeps it in a locked cabinet. I know where he hides the key."

Reuben then poured rubbing alcohol on the cement below us and lit the ground on fire.

Reuben always had the latest books, toys and games. He had a Ping Pong table and all the Barbie and Ken dolls. Every board game I had ever seen on TV was stacked neatly in his playroom beneath the TV set. I wondered why I didn't have any of the things that Reuben had and figured something must be wrong at my house.

"Mom, why can't I have toys like Reuben?"

"You don neet dem. Iz stupid doze tings."

Could Reuben's family really be stupid? His mom was a pediatrician and his dad owned a men's clothing store.

We played outside almost every day. Our neighborhood was made up of an eclectic group of kids. Three Spanish-speaking boys lived across the street in an off-white house with brick trim. They wore white button-down shirts, ties and gray or black slacks to their private Catholic school. They were always afraid to make a mistake. One day the oldest brother, Jeffrey, showed me how to singe a corn tortilla on the stovetop flame. We spread on mayonnaise and rolled it up. For years, I thought mayonnaise on a tortilla was a Latin delicacy.

Next door to them was a modern-style house that was inhabited by dark, exotic-looking Turkish sisters—I never figured out how many. Older boys often rang their doorbell late at night, and Abe, their younger brother, was short, mean and ugly. He used to punch me in the stomach just because he could. Being a tomboy made me an easy target, until my mother found out.

Fuming with anger, she walked across the street, pounded on the door and yelled at his mother. I was surprised she stood up for me. I felt a new family loyalty. In that moment, I understood that within my family I had no power, but if anyone came up against me from the outside, they'd better watch out! It was our family against theirs. Even in a family as weird as ours, we watched out for each other.

19
The Piano

S omeone from my mother's inner circle of Holocaust survivors from the 1939 Club must have talked her into buying that Story and Clark upright piano that stood in our living room.

I stared in awe at the piano when I was nine years old. Futzing with the keys, I fantasized about how my piano playing might sound if only I knew how to play. An extra-large window framed the piano and me. As I sat on the bench I could have been the subject of a Marie Cassatt painting. Opening the window wide on sunny days, I pretended to play music, hitting any keys. "What's the point of the piano without lessons?" I asked my mother. "Why is it even here?" I cried and pleaded in frustration for months, as many of my friends had been taking lessons for years. When I reached an emotional tipping point of exhaustion and was too upset to eat, my mother finally took a serious look at my self-inflicted, gut-wrenching pain. A few days later, she had some news.

"I finded a piano titcher," she said. (I found a piano teacher.)

My mother's method of doing research was unorthodox. God forbid she should ask a parent at school or friend for a referral. Word of mouth from a stranger on the street or in Bene's bakery was where she got most of her information, as though still in the shtetl in the Warsaw ghetto, isolated from telephone books, *libraries or schools.*

The first time we drove to Miss Schwab's, the new piano teacher's home, we drove out of Beverly Hills toward La Brea, passing a private Christian high school with a gigantic cross in front, a lifelike Jesus hanging down. On the right side of the street were Spanish-style duplexes where weeds popped up through cracks in the sidewalks. Stepping over them, we arrived at number 666 ½ and walked into a dim, narrow corridor and up worn steps in stale, stagnant air, the sound of our shoes on each step like a guillotine coming down. My mother rang the doorbell. Hearing no footsteps, I hoped she wasn't home.

"Come in," yelled Miss Schwab from a distant room.

Hearing her nasty, raspy voice, like the wicked witch in "The Wizard of Oz," I knew everything I had dreamed had turned upside down and would never be right—another fine mess my mother had gotten me into. In a living room desperate for light, we stood between old antiques and dusty, musty junk. Oval picture frames with black and white photos of unsmiling people took up the walls.

"In here," Miss Schwab cackled.

In another room, as cluttered as the first, was a black baby grand piano near the window. An enormous woman was sitting in a wheelchair.

"I am Miss Schwab."

"Hi," I said.

"Halo," my mother said.

She wore a white, see-though, mu mu-type housedress and had gold-rimmed glasses stuck to her swollen face. Her short, thin, greasy gray hair covered her shiny forehead. A curious thick residue masked her large facial features. Her hands were not the curved and well-maintained hands one would associate with a pianist; instead, sprouting from her wrists were five fingers reminiscent of oversized baguettes sporting three-inch long fingernails. A gold wedding band on her right hand was so tight it looked like her finger would pop off.

I was overcome by her scent while having to sit on the piano bench and listen to her talk. Fortunately, she asked me to open the window behind her, a short reprieve.

My mother sat in a large, tufted red leather armchair and watched as Miss Schwab fixated on my every move. Grasping a long bamboo stick while I played, she sat at attention. If I made a mistake in tempo or reading a note, she raised her sagging, flabby arm up high and slammed the stick down on my fingers. Pain shot up my arms as her fingernails hit the keys like tacks dropping to the floor. She also pounded her fists on the keys, making my spine shiver. My passion for the piano dwindled, and was replaced by fear.

"Mom, why does she have to hit me?"

"You vanted piano lessons."

In school only until the fourth grade before being forced into the Polish ghetto, my mother remembered it was common in old Europe to discipline kids by hitting them on the hands with a stick. Comfortable with those teaching methods, my mother often went to the market during my lesson. When she left, Miss Schwab confided in me. She told me her secrets and dreams, a welcome distraction.

"I dreamed last night I was a cherub rising up to the heavens with the angels. They were taking me with them."

I visualized Miss Schwab surrounded by Michelangelo-type cherubs with golden, curly hair, bright red cheeks and round little bellies. Heading toward a blue sky dotted with puffy white clouds, the angels rose. I could see Miss Schwab rise up in her wobbly wheelchair and struggle to lift her wings, all 300 pounds of her, with a bamboo stick forever stuck to her chubby fingers. Thereafter, when the stick came down, I imagined her being hoisted up to heaven with a forklift and then dropped down below, where she belonged.

More interested in appearances than what was really going on in our house, my mother summoned me to play the piano any time a friend came to visit. Sitting in the living room sipping coffee, eating Pepperidge Farm cookies, her guests sat and listened.

"Play it again, play it again," she demanded, as though I was a paid performer. My piano playing made us seem "normal" and presenting me as a talented girl took the attention off my brothers.

Today, thirty years later, that same piano stands in my living room. My children play it. When I hear Aidan play "21 Guns" by Green Day, I am proud he was taught with positive reinforcement and love.

20

Healing Tree

Over time, I heard about many healers through word-of-mouth at school, Pilates and through friends scheduling regular sessions for the healing modalities that were tried and true for me along with new ones. The more healing I did on myself, the more traumatic memories were released from my body and there was no turning back. I had an intuition that holding onto trauma might lead to disease. As a result, I was diligent. On a typical week, my schedule included a variety of treatments: corrective chiropractic, medical massage, Pilates and NSA, for example. Afternoons, I went grocery shopping, cooked and ran errands before picking the kids up from school.

Determined to be normal like everyone else, I wanted a chance for happiness, a body without pain, a mind without fear, and a life of total choice and freedom. Somehow in the back of my mind I grasped all of this was achievable—an inner voice telling me I had a bigger purpose in this world. I plugged ahead, wishing, dreaming and fantasizing about being happier and more self-confident.

While the kids enjoyed an afternoon grilled cheese sandwich with a cup of tomato soup, I was dealing with pain again, though this time able to handle it without Vicodin. All the healing experts from the day were unable to heal the sore spot in my lower abdomen. Throbbing pain traveled from there into my coccyx, wrapping around my lower back. "What secret is stored in there, Fred?" I asked.

Aware of a powerful clenching accompanied by finger-like jabs into my lower abdomen, I wanted to understand what was inside this pain. "Please show me what I need to know; I am ready to deal with this!" I begged. Hoping to resonate with my subconscious, I was determined to bring messages from my pain to my brain.

After everyone was asleep that night, I walked into the bathroom, closed the door and turned on the light. I stared at myself in the mirror, not recognizing my reflection. I saw a clone of myself that looked old, tired and worn out. I've always been told that I look ten years younger, but today I looked ten years older. I had a puffy face and circles under my eyes. In the den, I started the two-stage breathwork, putting forth the intention to like myself, feel great and look as good on the outside as I did on the inside. I thought back to my youth.

Today, I turned thirteen. It's 1977. I stared at my reflection in the mirrored closet; I liked my long, thick brown hair, my slender yet curvy body and my new womanhood. The bronze doorbell chimes hung to the left and a vivid painting of a peacock to the right. In the living room, two blue velvet couches and two golden velvet armchairs surrounded a lacquered wood coffee table. An ornate stained glass window took up most of the back wall.

I admired my new outfit, a cream-colored, tie-front blouse and a flowing printed skirt covered in tiny lavender, black and brown flowers.

"Will Billy or Allan be here for my birthday?" I asked my mother.

"No."

Unsure if their absence was a curse or a blessing, I was sad my brothers didn't make an effort to come to my party, and yet I was happy I wouldn't have to worry about Allan embarrassing me in front of my friends. The happy and the sad cancelled each other out, leaving me numb and in birthday party limbo, a place where I could never truly enjoy it.

A few weeks earlier, I had handed invitations out to fifteen school friends— everyone was coming. My mother decided card tables should be set up in the front patio near the marble stairs. The tables would rest on slate stones surrounded by blooming May flowers, dark green bushes and large abalone shells that sparkled in the sun.

"Where will we get tables?" I asked.

"Danya haz dem tables," (Danya has the tables,) she said. "Ven da Tata vas alive, ve had dem tables. All da frenz vood come to play cards." (When your father was alive we had the tables. All our friends would come and play cards.)

I remembered those card parties. I had peeked into the smoky dining room when I was four, watching couples laughing and enjoying themselves, the men smoking thick cigars and drinking scotch. My mother refreshed their drinks, put out ashtrays and served hot hors d'oeuvres, ensuring all her friends from the 1939 Club were well fed and comfortable.

"Mom, did you play cards back then, too?"

"No, I don like dem cards."

"Did you like having the parties?"

"No, I hat-id-it. Vas shtupid. Un d smoke, terrible."

Many things my mother didn't know how to do, like playing cards, she would look down upon, making her seem discriminating as opposed to being unable to understand how to play.

"Did you think about a birthday cake?" I asked.

"Yez, I ordert from Bene's."

My mother came through with bakery goods, as she came from a long line of women bakers. My great-grandmother owned the only bakery in Ozerkov, Poland. In the center of town, the bakery was where all the hungry children came after school for a snack. They stared through the window at all the fresh-baked fare, one of my mother's happiest memories.

The day before my party, I walked into the kitchen where my mother stood, dressed in her favorite chocolate brown outfit. She stared straight ahead.

"What is it?" I asked.

"Iz da kek." (It's the cake.)

Towering on the table was a magnificent, three-tiered cake creation. My mother had missed out on most of her birthday celebrations, a fact making me feel like a second-class citizen undeserving of this spectacular cake, my existence unjustifiable. I admired the ballerina figurines placed on three levels of pink and white buttercream frosting and wondered what it would taste like.

"Chocolate and vanilla inside?" I asked.

"I tink zo. I don no."

"Why ballerinas?"

"Oh, d balerinas , der azoy butiful," (The ballerinas, they are so beautiful,) she answered. "I never zaw zuch a tink in my life."

"Mom, can we please have pizza delivery on my birthday?"

"Yez."

"Promise?"

"I promiz."

"Lunsh iz redy!" my mother announced at my birthday party.

I was excited to have Jacopo's pizza. I went out into the patio with my friends. My mother came down the marble stairs carrying something large while holding her blue dishrag. She set it on the table and lifted the lid off an old turkey-roaster. She had filled it with home-cooked spaghetti. As she spooned the spaghetti onto plates, my heart sank. I understood the pizza was a lie, another promise broken. My insides twisted themselves like her blue dishrag.

I was awakened early by a dull pain on the right side of my pelvis, so unexpected that I was eager to explore what was behind it. Just like the Whac-a-Mole arcade game, the energy in my body would pop up, demanding I pay attention. At this point in my healing I had no choice but to deal with whatever was happening in my body, usually through breathwork and meditation. I worked through one uncomfortable place after the next, staying with it until it released.

In the den I put on a breathwork disc, closed my eyes and focused on the pain in my pelvis. "It's not you, this time Fred. It's different." The size of a quarter, the pain was sharp in the center of my pelvis like the point of a pen. Fear kept me from going too deep into the small space; my breath slid over the pain instead of into it. After a while I connected, having developed a skill, an inner practice, in which I could see the pain and blocks in my body as they arose. When I felt the sensations brewing inside, I sent my breath to those areas, pushing through, getting to the other side, vibrating with intensity. It felt as good as it did bad, like ice on a sunburn. Through the darkness, an image emerged.

Chills ran through me as I was seeing the coat closet in our house. Was I being pushed into the closet? I thought so, but couldn't be certain. I walked away from the closet and saw a man put on a white doctor's coat. Smoothing down the sides of his coat, he looked satisfied with whatever it was he had been doing. It was as though it were all in a good day's work. The man was Billy.
"Was Billy playing doctor?" I asked myself.

Quivering, I didn't want to stop the breathwork when the disc was over. I wanted to go deeper. I jumped up and pushed the start button on my DVD player again and continued. As I stared into the darkness, two straight white lines shot out in front of me like lightning bolts stretching out into the distance. The white lines became the borders of a residential street. Flowers sprouted up, trees and bushes rose on the same lovely street that was on my route home from elementary school.

I walked home alone, eleven years old, enjoying every house in my neighborhood. Each was different with outdoor decorations worn like women's accessories, from porcelain gnomes to flowing angels, metal sunflowers, wooden farm animals, birdhouses, wreaths and even mezuzahs. The smell of cut grass filled the air. I skipped along the sidewalk trying not to step on any cracks. I was free in the warm sun, with no one else around. Walking home was the hour of the day I could imagine, fantasize and just be.

As I turned the corner, I saw our house. Billy came into focus standing outside the back gate. His face was swollen and bruised, his jaw was bleeding and his eyes glazed over. Beads of sweat popped through the razor stubble on his face.

"Billy?" I asked.

"Go home."

I didn't argue. I walked into the kitchen through the back door. I smelled something appetizing cooking on the stove.

"Dinner is going to be good tonight," I thought.

I put my books down and looked for my mother. I found her resting in her bedroom. "How vas de school?" she asked.

"Fine. Did you see Billy outside?"

"Vat you vud like to eat?"

"Anything."

Obviously, there was a lot to block out this afternoon about Billy. My eating her food would enable us both to do just that. As though she were a waitress at a local diner, my mother entered the breakfast room carrying plates, plopping down the green salad, the tuna salad, the egg salad, the cold cuts, the cheeses, the fruit salad and a gigantic plate of sliced challah and rye bread purchased fresh that morning. Enough food to feed eight, it was all for me. There was nothing more important to her at that moment than my eating her food.

Overwhelmed by this feast, I didn't know where to start. My mother grabbed my empty plate and loaded it up with a heaping spoonful of everything. Satisfied with her creation, she set the plate in front of me.

"Eat!"

She sat across the table from me and watched as I ate, listening to me chew and swallow.

"Is this tuna?" I asked.

"Yez itz a tuna."

"Really?"

"Uf curse it's a tuna—vat are you talking?"

I accepted the fact that the mysterious flavored stuff that looked like tuna was indeed tuna. Later I found out the truth.

Finishing my plate, I watched my mother dip the serving spoon into the fruit salad.

"No! I can't eat anymore."

"How about jus dis little bit. It's fruit. You ken eat fruit. It's dietetic."

"I'm full."

Later that same afternoon, I roller skated along the sidewalk wearing knee-high tube socks with two blue stripes at the top and yellow "Ditto" short-shorts when my mother had come outside to water the lawn.

"Look at me," I said.

"Oh, very niz skatink," my mother said.

"Watch, I can do a trick, a turn."

As I gained momentum for the turn, the metal wheel of my skate caught on a tree root. I flew into the air and had to choose between landing on the cement, head-on, or on the grass. Like an aerial acrobat, I angled toward the grass, feet first, then knees, and chest. The needles of the grass pierced my skin just before I felt the thick padding of earth beneath me, my chin landed last, smashing down on the edge of the cement with a cracking sound. Lying there motionless, I felt warm blood ooze.

"Oy," said my mother.

Getting up, I felt like a loser. Worse than that, my chin was stinging.

"How is my chin?"

"Oh, iz notink." (Oh, its nothing.)

In the house, I went into my bathroom and looked in the mirror. A bloody scrape had loosened the skin and a two-inch flap was hanging down. Washing the blood off my hands, I thought I could see my throat through the deep opening in my flesh.

"Mom, I can see my neck!"

"Iz notink. Don tink zo much."

Even I, at eleven years old and in the sixth grade, recognized that this was something!

"You need to help me mom. I need stitches."

"Vat you van me to do? You are makink sometink out of notink."

"Take me to an emergency room please!"

We drove for an hour across town from Beverly Hills to an emergency room on Temple Street somewhere between Chinatown and Skid Row, even though there were hospitals nearby. We waited for two hours in the emergency room because my injury was not considered as important as the gun shot wounds or stabbings. I looked up through the thin blue sheet covering my face and I watched the shadow of the doctor stitch up my chin as though he were creating Frankenstein. I was numb, thankful for the anesthetic.

When my mother was in Auschwitz, she developed a boil larger than a baseball on her leg, She had to have it cut open and the infection squeezed out, with no antiseptic or pain killers. She told herself her injuries and everything short of death was nothing.

The morning after my breathwork session in the den, Jack, Lola, Aidan and I went for a walk with Bone, who had a white, heart-shaped birthmark on the top of her light brown head. I listened to the crunching sounds of our sneakers breaking the dried leaves as Bone scurried after a tennis ball. The tall eucalyptus trees that lined the trail had a relaxing scent so hypnotic that I began to daydream and see the tree in front of our house in Beverly Hills in my mind's eye.

The massive, leafy tree on our front lawn stood between the stained glass window and the ivy hedge separating our house from the Plotnick's. If I climbed into the branches, I could sit in a little space that was the perfect size for my rear-end, enabling me to peek over the hedge. I thought not everyone was as fortunate as me to have her own tree, which had been here since before my father died. I loved sitting in it and beneath it, and leaning against just like the little boy in the Shel Silverstein book The Giving Tree. *My tree was like a friend who understood me, who wouldn't leave me. The tree gave me a sense of support and a solid foundation when I was thirteen.*

One late afternoon I stood under the tree, contemplating whether I should climb higher than ever before. The more I thought about it, the more I was ready for the challenge. Watering her plants out front, my mother must have seen my gaze upward, and the wondrous look on my face.

"Donchu climb dat tree! Iz dangrous!" she warned. "Don do it."

Dangerous? Any danger that I had ever known came from inside the house. Waiting patiently for her to turn off the hose, I listened as her footsteps sounded on the marble walkway. I heard the gate squeak closed, and more footsteps until the screen door slammed shut.

It was dusk and the neighborhood kids were heading home for dinner. Soon it would be dark, a good time to make my climb. I gathered all my strength and pulled my strong body upward, moving from branch to branch. I became one with the tree, intertwining myself with the spreading branches, transported to another time and place. Climbing higher and higher, the soft breeze blowing my hair into my eyes, I looked up at the stars shining against the new night sky—it was getting dark.

And then, my foot slipped. I plunged down, tumbling through the branches, hitting the ground with a loud thump and a crack as my butt hit first. My head flew backward, smashing against the tree trunk. A loud, resonating thud zipped from ear to ear, echoing through my brain. A few seconds later there was a rippling pain in my head, and I was dizzy.

"Oh my God. I fell. But I'm alive." I was frightened, shaky and aching, unsure I could move. My head felt strange as I raised my hand and touched the sore spot. A warm, oozing liquid covered my fingers. Even in the darkness, I could see the thick dark blood. I had cracked my head open!

Delirious, I was afraid of what my mother would do if she found out. I sat there, blood trickling down my head, too proud to admit she may have been right. Leaning against the tree, I pulled myself up with what little strength I had left. My vision was blurred as though I was standing in front of a different house in a different world. Careful and slow, I dragged myself up the marble steps and through the gate. I quietly slipped through the front door and down the long hallway until I reached my room. I closed my door and grabbed the key locking the door. In my bathroom, I put a wet washcloth on my head. The bright red blood soaked into it faster than I could rinse it out. "Oh my God, there's so much blood."

"Mom, I'm going to sleep. I'm really tired," I yelled.

"Gootennight."

Putting a towel on my pillow to soak up the blood, I turned off the light and put my head down. "Please God, let me wake up in the morning."

Drifting off to sleep, the only thing I could do was to have faith.

The next morning I awoke, depressed, with a sore head. Unable to wash my hair over the gash, I moved the long hair covering the spot on the back of my head so no one would notice. Drained, I used every ounce of strength I had to appear normal. I walked into the breakfast room dressed for school and sat down to eat. My mother noticed nothing different. The next few weeks I was depressed with a headache, and went on with my life, ignoring the pain.

Many years later as I was doing breathwork, I relived and then released the concussion I received from falling out of that tree. It's amazing how our bodies can hold on to trauma unless we do something to release the blocks.

It wasn't long after, that Aidan was on the Cubs little league baseball team. He was ten years old and in the fifth grade. Hit in the head with a baseball while at bat, he fell over, a piece of his helmet pressing deep into his temple. Jack rushed him to the emergency room to check his vital signs and make sure there was no bleeding in the brain. He had a concussion, which resulted in depression and temporary loss of vision. When he felt a little better, he did breathwork with me every night before he went to bed. He enjoyed the meditation, slept better and woke up happy.

One night after breathwork he came into my bedroom to say good night. His eyes looked different. He told me he was seeing the numbers on the baseball scoreboard in his head blur just like he did when he was hit with the baseball. He had relived the traumatic experience and released it from his body. In the days that followed, he was less afraid to play baseball and was looking forward to our family ski trip.

We finished our last ski run of the morning on a sunny winter day at Big Bear. Placing our skis in a rack, we headed to the lodge where we peeled off our jackets and thermals down to our T-shirts and sat outside soaking up the sun. We ordered lunch while watching skiers pour down the mountain. Enticed by the sweet smell of barbecue, we ate our grilled burgers. Jack and I shared an ice-cold beer that we had buried in the snow earlier. We were acting a little silly, mixing alcohol with altitude.

"Everyone gets a bear name today!" I announced.

"Why?" Lola asked.

"Because we are in Big Bear!"

"Aidan, you're cozy-bear. Lola, you're teensy-bear."

"What about me?" Jack asked.

"Hmm, how about Jack-in-the-bear-stock?"

I laughed hard at how silly I was. My eyes watered and my vision blurred as I remembered I had once been called "Pooh Bear."

"Pooh Bear!" Allan yelled. With his waist-length hair hanging loose around

his shoulders, he came through the gate with a huge smile on his face, wearing a beaded necklace over his white T-shirt. He was on summer break from university.

At first, I loved hearing the sound of "Pooh Bear." Those endearing words made me feel special. As I grew older, I heard the words more often, many times a day.

"Pooh Bear! Pooh Bear! Ha ha ha!" Allan said. "Remember when I used to call you Pooh Bear? You were so cute when you were little!"

"Who who who who," he continued, as if he were Tigger and I was Eeyore, the donkey. He had a laugh like Sam Kinison and he kept repeating himself, like Bill Murray in "Ground Hog Day."

The clown act that had been funny when I was six, stopped being entertaining when I was 14. I had endured years of listening to the same old script. One afternoon, I was spreading my notes and books on the dining room table.

"Vat you doink?" my mother asked.

"I have to write a report."

"Okay, I don boder you. I bring a sanwheech."

Allan walked into the room. "Pooh Bear! Pooh Bear! Ha ha ha!" he yelled.

"Remember when I used to call you Pooh Bear? You were so cute and little! Who who who who!"

"Stop, please," I begged. "I have to write a paper."

"I don't give a shit about your paper."

Hearing the yelling, my mother entered the room.

"Not now," my mother said to Allan.

"But...."

"Not now."

He turned around and walked out.

Proud of Allan, my mother saw him as a genius, discussing politics, religion and world history. He was a great debater. Relatives and friends came over to hear what he had to say about what was going on in the world, while my mother cooked a hot meal. And yet, something made him stop working. Something messed him up. My guess was that he had a genetic predisposition to mental illness triggered by my mother's experience that may or might not have emerged from doing hard drugs while at university in the 1960s.

Allan would often run into kids from Beverly Hills High at Nate n' Al's or the Century City Mall. "Do you know my little sister, Alix?" he would say. "I used to call her Pooh Bear when she was little."

I fell into an abyss of wishing I had normal brothers, a father that was alive, and a mother who could guide me. I was sad that I had ever been called Pooh Bear. "Change your thoughts," I said to myself. Within seconds, I blocked out the past and focused on the present moment, not giving the negative a chance to linger. This was a skill I'd developed from listening to the Abraham discs I purchased once a month. Putting the Abraham words into action and watching my life change, I was hooked on always searching for the next best-feeling thought. "I am enjoying life with my family on this beautiful ski slope," I thought, looking out at the mountain. Closing my eyes, I felt joy and love, and on that mental plane, I drove home from Big Bear calm, satisfied and complete.

The next morning I longed to do breathwork. I walked into the den in my blue and white flannel teddy bear pajamas and began the meditation.

Through the darkness, a whitish circle emerged, floating above me in my mind's eye. It was the same size as my face. An outline of facial features became clear within the circle as someone familiar, but whom I couldn't quite place. Frightened at first, I soon became comfortable as I watched the materializing face with its tired eyes and sad expression.

After the disc was over I stared up at the face for a long while, until I was interrupted by a knock at the door. I saw my mother's outline through the clouded glass. Opening the door, I was struck by her facial features pulled tight by a pink scarf that was tied in a knot under her chin. Her face resembled what was floating above mine minutes earlier. She looked like a Russian babushka (grandmother). Having a hard time sleeping the night before led her to take two buses to our house without letting us know she was coming.

Remembering when I was 15 years old, our house smelled like chicken soup, garlic and roasted meat. Danya's son Mark was visiting. Danya was one of my mother's closest friends, a member of the '39 Club. Mark and Allan were both twenty-nine. I was sitting on my bed, lying back on Billy's old blue comforter, writing in my diary. Without knocking, Allan and Mark came in.

"Is that a diary? What's in it? Secrets?" Allan asked.

Mark swiped the diary out of my hands, holding the book high while I jumped up on my tippy toes trying to grab it.

"Mom, help! They stole my diary. That's mine! Give it back!"

Mark started to read it aloud. "I have a crush on the cute guy across the street, one of the Catholic boys."

"Stop!" I cried.

"He's so tan and cute and I love the way he looks at me. His eyes are green."

Hurt and embarrassed by this invasion just as if an ax had just sliced my head open, I wanted to die.

When I told Loretta, my EFT practitioner, I asked her, "How can two university-educated men do something so cruel and uncaring?"

"Education in the 'school of life' has a lot to do with it. How someone was raised as well as their inherited nature come together and form the personality that interacts with the world. If a youngster was bullied as a child, they learn two things: What it feels like to be victimized and how to bully. They learn bullying by experiencing being bullied. Our behavioral choices are often limited to the behavior we have been exposed to, particularly in childhood."

"What if they were just assholes?"

"There is a growing study called epigenetics that holds that we are psychologically and physically shaped by the experience of past generations. So much more is passed on to us from past generations such as lifestyle, life experience and current affairs, through to the most mundane of experiences. Epigenetics shows us that the world we live in can impact the world we pass on to our children. One can only wonder about the epigenetic impact of the Holocaust on your brothers and their behavior. That said, it is not an excuse for what was done to you. What they did was inexcusable."

"Between the way I was raised and the epigenetic impact on me, no wonder I am spending countless dollars trying to heal. I'm healing generations, not just me."

21
Let Them Eat Rum Cake!

Minnie Langkston came to Beverly Hills High in the middle of the school year. We were 14 years old and in the 9th grade. From Australia, her family was in the wholesale jewelry business, importing from around the world. She had blue-green eyes, short, layered blonde hair and a great accent. She invited me over to her house and we became fast friends.

Minnie's mom picked us up after school. Arriving at their house, I was in awe of the Romeo and Juliet balcony on the second story. The house felt good. Minnie was excited to show me her room, which was filled with albums, a stereo, books, memorabilia, games, magazines, oil paints and water colors, an easel, sports equipment, family photographs and assorted other things piled high in a corner. I would have cherished any one of her things.

A few people outside my family had given me nice things on occasion. Emilia, my mother's friend, gave me a necklace with a delicate green emerald pendant when I was twelve, a time when I should have had a Bat Mitzvah. I understood no matter how much we had in our family, I wasn't supposed to get anything. I had no idea of the value of the necklace and felt undeserving of it. Someone better than me should have been wearing it.

One day the necklace disappeared. I never figured out who lifted it. Allan,

Billy and Danya's son Mark had often rummaged through my room. Emilia asked me about the necklace years later. Not knowing where her gift was, I saw in her dark eyes how much it hurt her and learned in that moment how much thought, love and care she had put into that gift.

The abundance at Minnie's house reminded me of a time before my father died when there was music, color and life in our house. After his death, like a snowball melting into nothing, my mother sat by, watching our home and our lives deteriorate. Living in the barren barracks of Beverly Hills, I lived a life in black and white while I imagined everyone else lived in Technicolor.

Minnie and her siblings, two brothers and a sister, got along well even when they teased each other. I was confused and envious as I watched them interact, not understanding why my family was so different and why no one treated me nicely, the way Minnie was, at my home. My body tightened and tensed as I tried to comprehend if I was loved or unloved, if I was good or bad, and if I was supposed to be living in that house in which God had decided to drop me. I felt awkward, uncomfortable and wanted to run away from there, tortured by their connection contrasting with all I had ever understood.

A handsome, slender silver-haired man in a grey suit and tie, Minnie's father, greeted me with a smile when he came home from work. "Nice to meet you, Alix! Great name you have there!

"Dinner's ready!" yelled Minnie's mom. "You sit here, Alix, between Minnie and Lizzy."

Mrs. Langkston served pot roast, mashed potatoes and asparagus spears with fine silverware. Despite living in California, I had never seen asparagus before and was unsure how to eat it. I watched how everyone cut into their food trying to copy them with little success, especially with the asparagus spears that popped up like Mexican jumping beans simultaneous with the sound of my knife hitting the plate.

"Let me help you, Alix," offered Mrs. Langkston. She cut my asparagus in half-inch pieces, enabling me to pierce them with my fork. Embarrassed by my

lack of etiquette, I was quiet the rest of the evening.

The next day at school, Minnie ignored me. "What's wrong? Why aren't you talking to me?" I asked.

"You're not my friend," she said. "You're just the first girl I met."

Like spilled milk, our relationship was spoiled and could not be salvaged. Quiet, shy, awkward and distant, I was confused and unable to navigate the language of Minnie's life. Like a tourist having stepped out of a time capsule buried since the '30s, I walked into a normal home as if it were a foreign country, a recurring pattern in my life time and again. No one wanted to be my friend because I wasn't like everyone else, which was no surprise, considering my mother thought Beverly Hills was a small village in Poland. She walked around our neighborhood daily for exercise, to clear her head and to get away from Allan's screaming. She would drop in on people without calling first, a practice considered rude and improper. Whatever had been accepted in her village in Poland during the 1930s was her rule of thumb. She never made a doctor's appointment or a restaurant reservation either. She was surprised when the doctor wasn't expecting her and somehow she always managed to get squeezed into his schedule. She did this with the honesty and innocence of a child.

Besides homework, I never did much of the things other kids were doing like listening to music, going to concerts, going out to dinner and interacting in a healthy way. I just tried to study hard, work a lot, stay alive and get jeans that fit.

That summer, I went to Israel with my mother, where we stayed with her distant cousin Malgosha. Appalled that I didn't know how to eat in the European style, she taught me table manners when I was fourteen, putting the fork in my left hand and the knife in the right. I appreciated being taught how to eat.

A headache stretched from the base of my neck to the top of my head, while I felt a sharp stab in my lower back. According to the latest chiropractic scan, I shouldn't have these symptoms.

"All white bars! Wonderful!" said Dr. Grace.

The proof that my muscles were communicating with my brain was in the colored bars on the computer screen, white being best, meaning my nervous system was working at its best. But I was still in pain. Dr. Grace was so happy with the results I didn't have the heart to tell her the truth, since she had done all she could thus far.

Fred was relentless a week before my menstrual period. He was unreliable and would pop up randomly, even disappearing for days at a time. When I tried focusing on Fred while doing Hot Yoga in 103-degree heat for ninety minutes, my emotions came up in a fountain of tears, which no one noticed. Red as a beet after class, I drank a bottle of water before wobbling in to take a cold shower before going home. Drained, I crashed on my bed, each individual pore open as my body detoxed. Falling into a deep sleep, I dreamed.

Danya's son Mark drove up to our house in his orange Lamborghini. "Wow! Cool car!" Cindy said. She was my best girlfriend in tenth grade. I had started to fit in a little more at Beverly Hills High, and was using my peers and their families as role models for how to act in society. Little did I know Cindy's friendship wouldn't last long, as another girl pulled her away, probably claiming I was too weird.

Mark had wavy blonde hair and wore fashionable sunglasses with his three-piece designer suit as he sat tall, with the engine revving. He flashed a grandiose smile that reminded me of the pervert at the "Piece o' Pizza" place who had tried to get me into his Pinto when I was seven.
"Want to go for a ride in the Countach, girls?"

As the scissor car doors lifted and we squished into the passenger seat, Mark gave Cindy an invasive look as if he had X-ray vision that saw through her clothes. She had wavy dark blonde hair and bright blue eyes, plump lips and a voluptuous figure in tight blue jeans and a long sleeve turtleneck. She and I shared the passenger seat. We sped away on the tan leather seats, hardtop off, wind blowing through our hair.

Returning home, Mark followed us into the house and the kitchen. My mother was stirring something in a saucepan with a spoon. She was barefoot, wearing a clingy flowered dress.

"I didn know you ver comk today," my mother said to Mark.

"I had to visit my favorite person," he said, smiling and giving her a kiss on the forehead. "And besides, Cindy's here today!"

Cindy and I turned red. Mark's flirting with her made us both uncomfortable, although my mother noticed nothing.

"Na, you stayink for dinner. I mekking stuffed pepperz!"

"Great!" he said.

Mark grabbed a glass and filled it with water. As my mother turned back toward the stove, he pulled out two blue-green pills and popped them into his mouth, washing them down in one gulp.

Wanting to finish our homework before dinner, Cindy and I sat on the living room floor, our backs against the blue velvet couch and our books spread out on the coffee table. Mark breezed in, plopped down on a chair and pulled off his loafers. He loosened his tie and ran his fingers through his hair. He reclined until he was almost flat, and his breathing became faint.

"What were those pills you took in the kitchen?" I asked.

"Quaaludes. You guys want some?"

"No thanks."

Children of Holocaust survivors, Mark and his sister Rachel lived a lavish lifestyle in an exclusive part of Beverly Hills with Mitzi, their black Doberman, and their parents—Danya and Carl. Their neighbors were Vidal Sassoon, and some famous movie moguls and sports team owners. Often I would see Vidal walking his Yorkie terrier through the hilly streets. One day while I was visiting, Danya was standing in the kitchen snacking on Mitzi's dog biscuits.

"You're eating dog biscuits?" I asked.

"Yez, dey are goot! Tasty!" she said. "Dey mek goot tinks for dogs. Van a pice

a kek?"

She pointed to a fresh rum cake sitting on the kitchen counter. Rum cake was her specialty. Aromatic and fluffy, the frosting was a light mocha-rum with finely chopped nuts over the top. Her love for the past held in each slice a memory of a time she and her mother made those cakes together, serving them on blue and white china plates. Yet, hidden somewhere beneath the creamy goodness was Danya's remorse, her contradictions and her confusion. Her giving me cake was a mixed message; every scrumptious bite I took turned into a mouthful of guilt.

While she watched me as I chewed, I read her mind. "You are not good enough to eat this cake. You are alive and they are not." Danya had guilt about being a Jewish survivor. Even though she and her husband remade their lives and became wealthy once again, she cried inside for all the lives lost. She looked at me as though I were the culprit, eating her rum cake when the rest of her family, many of whom looked like me, had been thrown naked in a ditch. I was damned because I would never be guilty enough and I would never know how good I had it.

Danya served the rum cake drizzled with sweet wine on Shabbat and on all the Jewish holidays except Passover, when you are not supposed to have wheat flour, yeast or breads that rise. Brisket, roast turkey, chicken soup with matzo balls, salads and potatoes were plentiful. I enjoyed the taste of the food on the one hand and I suffered through the hopelessness and grief-stricken atmosphere on the other. Engulfed in the aura of a funeral, I felt alone during the holidays, savoring the mocha frosting, mixing the delightful with the grim, the only child in attendance.

Danya and Carl lived on the highest street in the neighborhood, Robin's Ridge. Their house was bare, like it was about to go on the market ready for sale, even though they had lived in it for the past thirty years. The floors of the long, curved hallways and the bathrooms were of Italian marble. The view of the city from the swimming pool was breathtaking.

Every evening at 6 p.m. sharp, Carl watched the evening news, sitting on a rickety foldout chair, leaning forward with his legs crossed. Everyone else sat on a worn brown couch. In the far corner of the room, a black, upright piano no one played sat beneath gold-framed graduation pictures of Mark and Rachel. The bedrooms were minimal, each with a bed and a little nightstand. Multi-millionaires living for years in an almost unfurnished house, they ate meals off a small, white Formica table in the kitchen.

The fancy dining room was never used. As if in a store window, it had gold and red linens on the table; black dishes and glassware were stored in a black Formica armoire. Carl was an investor who enjoyed nurturing his hefty bank accounts. Guilty about surviving the war and damaged from the trauma, he gave everything to his children. He gifted Mark the orange Lamborghini after Mark was accepted to medical school. Like a mediocre wine turning bad with age, Mark was now a worse person than he was when he stole my diary. Fed up with his negligence, his patients switched to more competent doctors, and the American Medical Association tracked him down for malpractice.

His parents and my mother taught their sons to become the center of their own lives, the only people who mattered. I didn't much matter, a fact that may have saved me.

One Shabbat at Danya's and Carl's house, the table conversation was about Caroline Kennedy, the daughter of JFK.

"She is azoy notink," (she is so much nothing,) Danya said. "Plain, no mek up."

"Von day, she vill do da pitzin, (one day she will take care of herself)," my mother said.

"What does 'pitzin' mean?" I asked.

"Pampering doink tinks to look besser (doing things to look better)," said Danya.

Jealous of their interest in Caroline Kennedy, I wanted them to notice me. Sitting right in front of them at nine years old, I needed clothes and a new hairstyle. I needed to learn this 'pitzin' thing.

22
Blood Fred

I had a dream.

I wore a frilly white nightgown, the kind my mother always wore. I was running down the hallway toward the kitchen, happy and innocent. Then everything went black. In those moments, I had been taken, stolen in such a way that I couldn't feel my body. My perpetrator remained invisible. "Was I wearing a blindfold? Was a blanket over my head? Was I drugged?"

Remembering the times everything went black, I couldn't remember ever waking up. Desperate to see through the darkness in my dream, the shutter opened.

I remembered when Jack and I were in Ibiza, an island near Spain, when I was still single. I swam in the sea in front of a secluded beach where everything seemed perfect. All of a sudden, I froze. I was scared something awful was about to happen. Just then my leg fell as though it dropped from underneath me, like when you step down and nothing is there. Screaming from pain in my lower back when attempting to step, I struggled to stay afloat, dogpaddling until Jack pulled me out of the water. As if he were cradling a baby, he placed me on the sand.

The next evening, I participated in my second writers' group conference call. A thick energy surrounded me while my mind tried to convince me I was unworthy. "I am damaged, beyond repair! And who is going to want to read my book anyway?"

I stayed on the call even though I was in crisis, wanting to pop like a balloon as I sat in my bedroom. The drapes were closed and I couldn't see the yard. Hard to speak or move, I was like a fat woman forced to wear a burka, but wanting the world to embrace me stripped naked. Wanting to throw myself through the drapes and glass window, I imagined the glass cutting into my skin, blood releasing and me breaking away to the other side, a soothing respite.

In spite of the negative voices, I was determined to write, create and share my truth. Desperate and scared, I moved forward with each page. Thinking of the hummingbird in the road that flew above me before I joined the writers' group, I stuck to the goal of completing this book.

Journal Entry April 30, 2009
This has been the longest day ever, with a sinus infection and Fred pounding into my lower back, plus taking care of the kids and doing laundry. I love my babies. I love Jack. I want the suffering to end. Should I get a rescue dog or a new puppy? Point me toward the light, please. Where are my animal guides? It seems like the squirrels, crows and a cute white dog in my visions, are my spirit guides trying to tell me something. The hummingbird must be one of them!

"The pain in my sacrum is still there," I said, my tone still hopeful as I explained my frustration to Loretta at our next session.

"You have to stop being so angry," Loretta said. "The anger clenches inside you, causing pain! That's why you keep getting sick with sinus infections. Your resistance is way down."

Asking me to stop being angry was like asking an alcoholic not to crave a drink.

"You need to release your anger before you can forgive your mother so you can heal."

"I'm too angry to forgive."

"Why do you take such good care of her?" Loretta asked.

"Because she's my mother and I feel responsible. It's my duty as her daughter to take care of her."

Loretta stared at me.

"Oh, you want me to say that I take care of her because I love her, don't you?"

"If it's the truth."

"The truth is that I love her because she is my mother, my blood. And I hate her for what she inflicted on me. So, it's both."

As I left her office, I became aware of the connection between my anger, my blackouts and my pain. That night as I tried to sleep, I thought about how inadequate I was when I started high school, still dependent upon my mother to guide me when there was no guidance to be had. As a result, I ran my whole life by the seat of my pants, hoping to make the right decisions, and I am still doing just that.

Journal entry date May 15, 2009

I thought back today to when my mother sent me to the Beverly Hills Recreation Department Sleep-Away Cross Country Ski Trip when I was thirteen. While there, I let a cute older boy, Josh Goldstein, touch my boobs over my turtleneck more than once, in a dark corner at night—I liked the attention. The camp counselors weren't sure what to do. Keeping an eye on me, I heard them whispering. In trouble without really understanding what I had done wrong, I honestly didn't know how to behave with my pre-teen hormones getting the best of me.

That night after everyone went to bed, I lay down to do the breathwork.

After a few minutes, I saw myself as a 'tween.

I broke out of my tomboy cocoon. Tall, with long hair, a new me appeared in the mirror every morning, baby fat having stretched into leanness. Looking more like the girls in the teen magazines and less like a "porkster" wearing bifocals, my new inviting self was now somehow intriguing. I was considered cute, pretty and even beautiful in some circles, all a part of me I couldn't own in my insecurity about myself. Guilt about being alive was what I understood. As a result, my outsides were looking a lot better than my insides.

While hiding this sadness, I wanted to understand boys and was confused about when to say yes or no about anything. One day, two boys each wanted to meet me after school on the corner across the street from my house. I hoped they would miss each other. Mick showed up right on time, all too eager. Right away he was too young and boring for me even though we were the same age. He was asking me out, making plans, hoping for more—I saw his mouth move but I didn't hear his words, my brain shutting off. All I could think about was the other boy, Noah, who drove up while Mick was still standing next to me, an awkward moment.

When Mick left, Noah gave me a big hug. Noah was cultured, mature, handsome and a few years older. He stared into my eyes moving his face toward mine as though he was going to kiss me, then he moved his face to the right. Like a hungry cougar, he bit hard into my cheek, his mouth a suction cup on my face. Pushing him away as if he were a deadly green insect on the cover of National Geographic, I tried to pry him off. He let go a few seconds later, smiling with satisfaction.

"What are you doing? That hurt!" I screamed.

"I'll see you soon," he said, as he walked to his car and left.

As I washed up the next morning, I looked in the mirror and gasped at my reflection; a deep purple bruise on the right side of my face was the size of a big mouth! "It's a hicky! How am I going to explain this to my mother over hardboiled egg on buttered toast?"

Noah had put his mark on me. Not wanting anyone else to have me, he did a territorial sort of thing, like a dog peeing on a fire hydrant.

"Serves me right for making a date with two guys at once," I thought.

"Cum bekfas is ready!" my mother yelled from the kitchen.

I rummaged through my messy bathroom drawers and found a bottle of liquid make-up. I spread it on my face, but it didn't cover the bruise. Desperate, I grabbed a Band-Aid, stuck it on my face, and went into the breakfast room.

"Vat happen?" my mother asked.

"It's a gross horrible zit," I said. "It's bleeding! I had to cover it so it won't get infected."

I walked around school all week wearing a Band-Aid stuck to my left cheek.

"What happened to your face?" Reuben asked.

"I was bitten by a dangerous spider."

23
Self-help and the Shrink

J ack was supportive of my writing endeavor, making my dream much easier to chase. I had wanted to be a writer since I was in elementary school, first journaling on notebook paper before tearing it to shreds. I could trust no one.

While boarding the plane to New Mexico for my first writers' retreat, I saw Mara. She was heavy-set with shoulder-length red hair and wispy bangs offset by thick, Chartreuse glasses, the cat-like kind with pointy corners.

"I hear we are a small group," she said. "There's supposed to be an Italian guy. I think his name is Giuseppe."

As I walked to the back of the plane and settled into my seat, I thought of the Italians in my past and began to write, the material flowing into my brain as though I were a secretary taking dictation from the Universe. Valentino, the Italian waiter with whom I had once lived, showed up in my mind.

He was a monumental male specimen with all the stereotypic qualities you would expect from an Italian. Valentino loved good food and wine. He was gorgeous with black curly hair and deep brown eyes. His chiseled features turned heads. Unsure of what a guy like that was doing in love with me, I wasn't complaining.

In my early 20s and fresh out of university with a new public relations job, I thought of Valentino as the chocolate buttercream frosting, the best part of the cake. We lived together in a Spanish-styled duplex on 6th near Fairfax and adopted two black kittens we named Nails and Piccolino, Picco for short. I played house with Valentino even though I had no thoughts of marrying him. He was my escape, my excitement and a toy I could add to my collection of things helping me forget my family problems and the fact I didn't feel loved. There was no better way to forget my troubles than with great, mind-blowing sex where nothing else mattered.

Valentino had a twin brother, Enio. He was as dreamy-looking as Valentino, but unpredictable and aggressive. One time, in a jealous frenzy, he pulled hard on his girlfriend Ila's earring, ripping her earlobe. I was puzzled as to why she loved him even more afterward.

She and I became very close, as though we were sisters-in-law, closer than I had ever been with another woman. She had short brown hair, light hazel eyes, and supple olive skin. Seductive, elegant and sophisticated, she also had a dark side after a glass of wine and her usual line.

We hung out with fascinating people: models, photographers and artists, all looking for a good time. Everyone was using cocaine as just a part of the LA culture. Cocaine helped keep my secrets and pain repressed. Numb to my emotional self, I looked great, had fun with friends and stayed up until the wee hours of the night.

I pulled out the self-help book from the seat pocket in front of me and opened it to where I had left off. I read that children who had been sexually abused could grow up to be workaholics. In order not to remember, they cut themselves off from spirit. "That's a strange coincidence," I thought. "I'm a workaholic and I would do anything not to feel."

Ila introduced me to the I Ching, the Chinese book of hexagrams. We got together often to read each other's hexagrams, six coded lines divining the future based on a series of coin tosses. These intimate pow-wows fascinated me because the hexagrams were on target. As though I had an inside track on something I didn't understand, I was on a spiritual path.

One night at Ila's house, Enio brought over an Italian gypsy named Drina, whom he had met at a bar. In her late 40s with long, harsh wrinkles embedded in her face, she looked like Willie Nelson, wearing torn blue jeans, a white T-shirt and a headband which held the strings of dry hair away from her face.

Interested in the I Ching as well, Drina visited Ila and me often, usually bringing us a few lines to sniff.

One day at Ila's apartment, Drina brought out her Tarot cards.

"Want me to read cards?" she asked.

"Okay," I said.

"First you shuffle. Then cut the deck."

I did as she instructed.

She pulled out the first card and concentrated for a minute, and then said, "You don't have a father. He died when you were very young."

She was either psychic or highly intuitive. Her ability to know my history was scary. A nervousness came over me, a pressing on my heart and a gasp for air. "Stop. I don't want to know anymore."

Annoyed, she proceeded to smoke a crack pipe. After she inhaled the substance deep into her lungs, she gestured for me to take the pipe.

"I don't do that."

She was agitated that I would not partake and stared at me, her eyes intense. "You try!"

"It's time for me to go," I said. "I have a big day at work tomorrow."

The next evening when I had arrived home after work, Drina was standing at my doorway.

I said, "I didn't know you were coming over. Come in."

"I have something for you," she said.

She handed me a sandwich-sized Ziploc bag full of large rocks of cocaine. "For you. A present."

Even though I should have refused, I didn't. We had a cup of tea before she left.

Soon, I found myself scraping the rock into a powder every day after work, depending on it, keeping myself closed off. I looked beautiful, slim, sexy and fun on the outside, my inner-self holding in all the pain and trauma I was neglecting to the point I could no longer feel it.

Drina came by my apartment one afternoon about a month later. "I go back to Italy to visit family. I want to leave this suitcase here." She pushed past me toward my closet and slid open the mirrored doors. She found a space in the back. "Tank you. I see you soon."

After about a year, I came across her suitcase in the back of my closet. Something didn't feel quite right; I perceived an odd energy emanating from it as I wondered how I had ever attracted Drina into my life. Fearful of keeping anything of hers, I got rid of the suitcase without ever having opened it. Driving to a faraway place, I threw it in a trashcan.

The writers' retreat stimulated so many memories that it was imperative to have more creativity and breathwork in my life. These two modalities worked together well as I tapped into my own gifts such as intuition in helping others heal. As a result, I planned to attend a Healer Training workshop in Los Angeles. The morning before the workshop I basked in bed, memories of Valentino lingering as I stared out of the big glass window toward the yard. Warm and comfortable under my covers, I sipped hot coffee and made lists of things I appreciated such as the vibrant trees and jewel-toned flowers. A gigantic leafy tree loomed high above the yard. I imagined that I could see through the gaps within the branches into the next dimension, an extraordinary place where I could connect to Mother Nature and be free. I had a striking vision of a beautiful naked woman jumping through a tree. As she leaped forward, the negative and dark parts of her were falling away as she moved up into the light.

I took the freeway toward the workshop and answered a call by speakerphone.

"Hello."

"Hey Alix, it's Daniel. Remember when I got kicked out of Beverly High for rolling a joint?"

"Yes. Why, are you high now?" I asked.

"No, of course not! Remember the time you fell off your skis and I blocked you from hitting that tree?"

"Daniel," I interrupted, "I'm going into a healer training right now. Gotta go."

At the Healer Training workshop taught by David Elliott, I checked in and met my partner for the day. He held space for me (i.e. concentrating on me and the immediate space around me.) He then applied healing oils while I did the two-stage pranayama breathwork, an ancient technique. I relaxed as spirit came into my body. It was a sense of ease and calm similar to when a dentist lays a lead blanket over you before an x-ray, a slightly heavier and connected impression. The intensity of breathing in a group can sometimes be stronger than doing it alone. Before I discovered this meditation, I had had no idea how much I lived in my head, my awareness now moving through my whole body and beyond.

As I did the breathwork, my psychic self kicked in and a vision of me where I live now, near the beach, emerged.

Having just awoken from a recurring nightmare, I was forever stuck in a university building, lost in a maze, never able to graduate. I rubbed my eyes and walked into the den. Standing between the cherry wood shelves and the olive-colored chenille couch, I looked out the glass doors facing the garden. I wished I could slip in and out with ease, while a strange invisible force was keeping me inside.

It was the mid-morning break at the healer training when I was considering calling Daniel back. I thought, "Why do I put up with him?" When I was younger, I was attracted to unpredictable personalities and enjoyed the entertainment value and the escapism. Now, I can see I have slipped back into this erratic pattern like a person released from prison who, even though he is free, moves into a studio apartment with no windows. Leaving this prison was not as easy as I thought it would be; the psychological barriers were ingrained and very difficult to eradicate. The truth was that I now stood on a new platform with as much behind me as in front of me, having the choice of who I wanted to become, my inner guidance shining through.

The lights were low as I stretched out on the floor after the active breathwork. Inhaling through my nose, I rested, when in my mind's eye I became Raquel Welch in "One Million Years B.C," svelte in a shredded bikini. Staring at my hot, sexy new self, I transformed before my own eyes into a prehistoric drawing of a cave woman from a 1950s science textbook. I was her. I became muscular with protruding veins, hunched over with my long arms almost touching my feet. My breasts were exposed but camouflaged by my wild, tattered hair. Wearing only a loincloth, I took my axe and swung at a glass door, breaking it into a million pieces. Sharp edges pierced my skin, blood spurted and just as I lifted my foot to step through the door, the cave woman disappeared.

Perplexed by my vision, I wanted to do breathwork again as soon as I got home. After my family went to sleep, I burned sage to clear the energy in the den, laid blankets on the couch, and put in a breathing disc before turning off the lights. Wanting to see where my mind would take me, I changed consciousness fast and got out of my head when an image emerged.

A junior in high school, sixteen years old, I worked in the Beverly Hills law office of Beckman, Berman and Penske, along with five lawyers and two paralegals. "Ambulance chasers," they hired me to type and correct legal documents and answer phones. Fitting in with the office culture, typing 60-80 words a minute, I had long brown hair, blown straight and a cute figure. Fashionable clothes, concert tickets and dining out were now affordable. No one knew the other reason I was working in an office was to avoid being terrorized at home. I pretended to be just a regular kid.

Well-prepared each morning, I brought a snack to school so I wouldn't have to go home afterwards. Sitting on a bench in Beverly Hills, I took five minutes to eat and compose myself before going to work. Late in the evening, after a long day, I tiptoed into the house careful not to rile Allan. Sometimes my mother left a hot meal for me. If Allan ate it all, I broiled meat or fish and made a salad.

After dinner, I finished my homework and picked out clothes for the morning, wanting to get into bed and fall asleep before anything happened. I sometimes wondered how many nights my mother had gone to sleep at my age questioning if she might be alive in the morning, sad this was the connection I made between the two of us. Often, I prayed before I went to sleep.

"Please God, don't let him hurt me."

Sometimes on the weekend I went to Daniel's house on the top of Laurel Canyon. One day I met Kenny there. He was sixteen, an artsy kid who drove a light blue pick-up truck. His wild, thick blonde hair stood up in all directions as if he had planned it. The next Saturday Kenny came over to my house. We went in my room and I locked the door with the key. Without warning, Allan began pounding.

"Open this door, motherf****!" Allan yelled.

Backing away from the door, he turned around. I could hear his pounding footsteps as he ran down the hallway, through the kitchen and laundry room toward the bathroom connecting to my bedroom. I ran, seconds ahead, locking the door from the other side.

"I'm going to kill you both with my bare hands! Open this door, damn it, or

I'll break it down!"

Stunned, we pushed out the bedroom window screen, jumped out the window and landed on the grass. We ran as fast as we could until we reached Kenny's light blue truck. We drove away and I had nowhere safe to go.

"I want to kill him," I said.

"Me too. I'll help you," Kenny insisted.

"Maybe there's a way to poison his cigarettes." Murderous thoughts derived from my desperation.

I returned home late in the evening after Allan was asleep. Still shaken from the incident, I went on with life as usual.

The next day, I went to work at the law office dressed in crisp white shorts and a coral blouse. I was typing legal briefs when, all of a sudden, I felt a warm flow at the seat of my pants. "My period!"

My white shorts were covered in blood I had no way of concealing. I poked my head into the office of a paralegal, Christina.

"I have an emergency! My period, it's bad. Please just tell everyone I'll be in tomorrow." I ran home, sneaked into the house and locked my door. Sliding into bed exhausted, I fell asleep.

William Berman, Esq., the managing lawyer at work, stared at me the next afternoon for longer than he should have while sitting on the corner of my desk.

"I just love these rainy days," he said, looking out the window. "Great for business."

"The rain brings business?"

"The rain brings car accidents!"

The cutest of the lawyers, Nick Penske, had light blue eyes, wavy sand-colored hair, and had different women leaving messages for him every afternoon. He rang my extension.

"Hi Alix. Would you come into my office, please?"

I grabbed my paper and pen, walked into his office and sat down. He got up and closed the door behind me.

"Do you know what day it is today, Alix?"

"Tuesday?"

"It's National Secretaries Day."

"Really, I didn't know there was a National Secretaries Day."

"Yep. I wanted to give you something special today."

He showed me a small plastic container about the size and shape of my thumb.

"What's this?"

"A bullet. It's filled with cocaine. Let's celebrate! Just take a big sniff."

He put the bullet up to his nostril, his thumb covering a small air hole, and inhaled. He handed it to me next and watched with a smile. Nervous at first, not wanting to seem uncool, I inhaled a tiny dose of the white powder. A minute later, I returned to my desk revived and eager to update legal briefs and take phone messages. After a productive afternoon, I thought cocaine was magic. Everything bothering me disappeared and I felt increased energy.

The fact that cocaine was illegal made snorting it all the more fun. Even Mr. Johnson, my high school English teacher, wore a small coke spoon charm on a chain around his neck. Everyone wanted to be in his class. "If my boss and my teacher are doing cocaine, it must be okay."

Smiling, I headed home. When I arrived, my happiness dimmed as I saw the warped entry gates, a reflection of what was inside. My mother held on to the same worn-out stuff like the now-stained orange satin comforter she covered me with after I had climbed to the roof when I was four. Masking the nose-itching stench of Allan's cigarettes, she opened a window and placed soap bars between the linens.

Allan kept a blown-glass vase next to his bed with cigarette butts and ashes, a super-sized ashtray. When the vase filled up to overflowing with particles floating though the air, my mother would come in and clean it and the room. She cooked, cleaned and did laundry for us, never teaching us how to do anything for ourselves.

The couch in the den was a splash of lovely autumn colors. Pine bookshelves spanned the entire wall, housing Allan's books: Shakespeare, Edgar Allan Poe, Plato and textbooks on politics, psychology and law. Impressed by the books before I was able to read, I thought Allan was the smartest person in the world, and so did my mother. She looked adoringly at him when he spoke, catching his every loud word as he held forth about politics and history. To her, he was something special, and in retrospect he probably was. I listened to his speeches too, not so much because I was interested in what he had to say, but because I wanted to be included.

I came home from high school one day and found Billy waiting for me in the den, with the shades pulled down. The rays of the sun seeping in through the cracks highlighted the dust motes that looked like smoke swirling around his form. Motionless, he stood there. He had asked me to buy cocaine for him at school. He was waiting for the small paper envelope filled with powder I had purchased from Gary, one of the more entrepreneurial of my classmates. Wanting my brother to love me, I would have done anything to get closer to him. I pulled the gram out of my pocket. He grabbed it and said, "Thanks." Then he left me alone in the dark. I was nothing more than a means to an end.

The day after my breathwork in the den that had brought back so many high school memories, Jack, the kids and I were driving to Palm Desert with family friends for my forty-fourth birthday when I saw a bumper sticker on a red Corvette that read, "I Survived My Childhood." The bumper sticker sparked my thoughts. I felt appreciation for my life, my family and all I had been through, thanking my higher power, that which I think of as God or Source, for helping me through those tough years of my upbringing. I remembered how I had prayed every night to be set free.

I sat in a tangerine-colored armchair on this hot spring day in the desert, looking out over the golf course watching my kids and their friends run through the sprinklers, squealing in their soaked pajamas with smiles as big as crescent moons.

"Happy Birthday!" Jack said. "Any thoughts about the day?"

"Yes, as a matter of fact. I predict one year from now, I am going to feel and look better than I do today."

"Wow, positive! Looking forward to it!" Jack said with his signature Cheshire-cat grin. He had watched me first-hand jump in and out of pain with relentless courage, reliving childhood traumas and getting to the other side of it where my heart began to open as I claimed my power and tapped in to universal energy, the flow, and God in a new way.

"I am looking forward to becoming stronger, healthier and in shape, being a better mom and completing my first book! Happy Birthday ME!" I said.

I visited a nutritionist because I was fat and couldn't digest. She advised me against eating gluten, the protein in wheat, barley and rye. My sinuses and skin cleared, and the watery bloat and heaviness in my gut was gone, along with ten pounds of weight. Jack and the kids were also gluten intolerant so we changed our eating habits.

"Vat? Broit iz not helty?" (What, bread isn't healthy?) my mother asked.

The concept of bread not being healthy was like telling my mother people throw out chicken after having boiled it for hours to make chicken stock. My mother would cut up this "laundered" chicken, mixed it with mayonnaise and call it tuna.

During and after the war, my mother held tight to her happy memories, hopeful she would re-experience the sounds of children laughing and the smell of bread baking. Sometimes she would imagine herself back in Poland with the family she was born into instead of with us in Beverly Hills.

My mother and the mother of my childhood friend Rachel were both Holocaust survivors. They brought the two of us girls together to play when we were little. Now years later, Rachel and I met for a quick lunch at the Urth Café on Beverly Drive. I noticed how beautiful and slender she was after having four children. She had not changed much since high school. She had long blonde hair to her waist, hazel eyes and the perfect Jewish nose, unlike all those Jewish girls who had needed nose jobs.

We ordered a large salad to share and unsweetened iced teas. As we chatted, we watched four teenage boys follow Paris Hilton down the street, taking pictures of her as she window-shopped. Walking on as though she didn't notice them, she wore a flowing chartreuse skirt that hit just above her ankles, with silver sandals and an oversized, white cotton T-shirt.

"I always remember how your mom would spread loads of butter on toast for me when I came over."

Sipping my iced tea, I cringed at the fact that butter on toast was Rachel's fondest memory of my childhood home. She didn't see what was happening behind the façade of those hearty lunches, including a nudge from my mother to eat more, a constant push that still remains.

Food was sometimes like a drug for me, especially when I visited my mother. I took her to lunch at Fiddler's Bistro, an eatery with simple, great food in West Hollywood. She wore a pink shawl she knitted herself, a loose white sweater, matching pants and white lace-up shoes permanently tied so she could slip them on and off easily. Her face was make-up free with barely a wrinkle even though she was eighty-two years old.

The waitress, a tall exotic-looking woman with long black hair plopped down a bread basket with a bowl of roasted vegetable puree. My mother spread the puree on the flatbread with obvious pleasure. I pushed the basket away as I made myself a silent pledge I would not partake. I found each piece of bread tempted me as though it were a line of cocaine laid out on a mirror in the '80s.

"Oh, iz azoy git I ken stop," (Oh it's so good I can't stop,) she said.

"The bread is a drug for you, isn't it?" I commented.

My mother always ate her meals slowly, wanting me to finish mine before she finished hers, even pressuring me to eat the food left on her plate. Growing up, she stuffed me with a little extra, an expression of her love, and praised me for being such a good girl. My life became a battle of wills in which my mother wanted me to eat while I resisted. Even though she was coming from a place of love, I stopped her from pulling that stunt with my kids. "They have their own food," I said. "They don't need yours, too."

Thinking back to when I was in eighth grade, I remembered a Shabbat dinner where I wished I were dead.

"Dinner iz reti," my mother said.

My mother's friend Emilia and Allan were at the table when I arrived. Emilia was dressed in an elegant and colorful Hermes outfit while my brother was dressed in a T-shirt and jeans. When Allan didn't speak or move, he looked handsome, with his olive skin and blue-green eyes, eyes like my father's. It was his words and harsh body movements that made him ugly and intimidating, especially when he was angry; the possibility he was going to kill me was always in the back of my mind.

My mother was about to serve the first course of chicken soup. Carrying each soup bowl from the kitchen one at a time, filled to the brim, she was careful not to spill a precious drop. She once told me, "Jus to mek da chicken zoop for shabbis, my moder had to buy d chicken to kill and bless it, tek off all d feathers at home and den cut it up." (Just to make chicken soup in Poland when she was small, my mother had to buy a live chicken in the market, take it to the butcher to kill it in a kosher way, bless it, take all the feathers off and home and then cut it up.)

"Why do you have to fill the soup bowl to the very top?" I asked. "I never eat that much."

"Eat vat you can."

The four of us sipped the hot soup in silence.

"I had a good day at school today," I said.

"Don talk," my mother said. "Juz eat."

"God damn it, Alix!" Allan yelled. "You bitch! Who do you think you are?" With my face only a few inches away, he smashed his spoon down on the table with 250 pounds of weight behind it, his beastlike, bloodshot eyes blazing from

behind his messy brown hair, his chest hyperventilating. Scared, I ran out and into the bathroom. Locking both doors from inside, I fell onto the white bath rug and sobbed, my head against my knees, wondering why it had to be this way. Worse still, I knew I would be blamed.

"You are d helty (healthy) one," my mother insinuating I had to endure everyone's "mishigas" (craziness) as my punishment for being sane.

A quiet meal had once again turned into a torturous event in which I was the prisoner and Allan, large and scary, was my captor. I wanted to disappear wishing I were dead.

"Please, Alix, come out of the bathroom," Emilia, who wanted to finish her dinner, whined from outside the door. "It'll be okay now. He's calm. He's not mad at you anymore."

"Mad at me for what?" I asked.

Emilia didn't answer; her silence reinforcing there was no rationale to Allan's hurtful rages, no rhyme or reason to his craziness. Sometimes the outbursts were spontaneous and uncontrollable, other times they were premeditated bids for control and attention. He derived pleasure from bullying me and hurting others.

I opened the door ten minutes later and walked out with swollen eyes. Returning to the table like a puppy with my tail between my legs, I was scared I might be punished. Allan was satisfied for putting me through this drama as he sat staunch and stoic, his chest puffed out, the proud king of the house. By his side, my mother showed her allegiance with an angry expression. She came from a world where men could do no wrong.

Emilia pretended to be oblivious to the fact his behavior was allowed at my expense. My mother would never stop loving and supporting Allan no matter who he hurt. Her first-born son and favorite, he could do no wrong. I, on the other hand, was the family scapegoat, the focus of unmerited blame. Whenever something went wrong, the truth was twisted into something having to do with me. Blaming me made them feel better. Hating them, I often thought terrible things in Yiddish, a language rich with insults.

"Gey in drert arayn," I yelled in my head, meaning, "Drop dead" or literally, "go inside the ground."

"Sid dan an eat. Ve hev kek," (Sit down and eat. We have cake,) my mother insisted.

As I ate the chocolate mocha seven-layer cake, my favorite, I wasn't sure how to feel, having just been humiliated. The cake was the medicine I needed to get through the night. As I put the next forkful in my mouth, Allan changed his tone.

"I love Alix so much. She's my favorite sister," he proclaimed with a smile just before shoveling a mound of cake into his mouth, the cream sticking to his beard.

Wanting to get ready for bed after Emila had gone home, I was walking down the hallway when Allan approached, transforming once again.

"Vie giets du?" (Where are you going?) he screamed in German, like a Nazi prison guard. With clenched fists and a crazed look in his eyes, foaming at the mouth and ready to attack, he hunched over his bent knees. Scared, I froze. My mother came out of her bedroom and got between us, holding her hands out to separate us.

"Enuf for von night!" she said. "Iz time for da bed."

And that was the harmonious end to the Shabbat dinner from hell.

On Veterans Day, we planned to hike on a trail near our house and discuss the importance of this national holiday, but when I woke up that morning, my lower back hurt so much I couldn't change out of my pajamas.

"Guys, I'm really sorry, but I can't go with you today."

My eyes watering, I staggered to the couch. The pain had emerged after two weeks of flashbacks to the Shabbat dinner from hell. Overloaded with images of Allan's evil-eyed face and constant threats, I felt victimized and emotional, as if it were all happening to me again. Normally, I would block out my sadness by being busy with work, going out for a drink with friends or eating something fattening. This time I let myself get depressed and feel it all.

After a few days of this practice my sadness lifted, leaving me free and open. I had moved something within myself and I once again understood how important it was to feel in order to move forward.

Face down on Dr. Marie's table the next day I relaxed as she touched my neck. A gateway opened and released energy stored in my spine. As the energy moved, I saw myself locked in the bathroom during that nightmare dinner. Then I saw God's hand, just like the one reaching out to breathe life into Adam on the ceiling of the Sistine Chapel. The enormous spirit-like hand burst through the bathroom ceiling, spinning like a tornado before grabbing me and lifting me up and through the ceiling, freeing me.

This was a new vantage point of calmness, openness and clarity. I was able to intuit that most people become emotionally paralyzed when they attempt to face their fears. Hiding behind drugs, food or alcohol, they suppress those emotions too hard to handle. Out one night with friends at a local tapas restaurant, the subject of feelings came up with Leslie, my friend from high school who had brought me to my first breathwork event, having no clue as to the impact it would have on my life.

"I always have to be in control of everything," Leslie said.

"Why?" I asked her.

"Because when my twin sister died, I had to keep busy. I don't know what I would have done without that next appointment, event or lunch date."

"You would have had free time," I said.

"I am afraid of having nothing to do. I would be forced to think about my sister—too painful."

"She died over twenty years ago," I said. "Maybe it's time to think about her. Let yourself be free of appointments, distractions and substances for a while. Just let yourself be."

Leslie sighed as though I would never understand.

"Too scary..."

"That's the point! Facing fear and developing a new relationship with it."

"Maybe. It's an interesting concept, but not for me."

Most people have been hurt by loss. Seeing them in pain, I wish they could let themselves truly feel what is inside, getting to the other side of the pain and letting it all go.

Emilia's father had been a famous and respected newspaper and radio news reporter in Belgium before the war. Coming from such well-read stock, an intellectual snob with a sophisticated Belgian accent, Emilia pursed her lips together and nodded her head with interest when discussing the arts. With sharp facial features brought out by her violet lipstick and coarse black hair, she thought of herself as part of the Hollywood elite, a movie star-making talent agent. Dressed in solid color pantsuits adorned with Versace look-alike silk scarves, she enjoyed lunching with my mother at an Italian trattoria in Beverly Hills.

Her mother, Eugenia, was born in Poland and moved to Brussels after the war. I often listened to the three of them talk over tea and butter cookies when I was a child, as they reminisced about family life before the war. As they commiserated about the past, I was praised for my patience.

"Such a good and quiet little girl," Eugenia commented.

"Yes, what a sweetheart!" Emilia said.

Afraid to express myself, my fear translated into a repressed quietness, the result of Allan yelling at me, and Billy and my mother blaming me.

Emilia directed most conversations toward the entertainment business, name-dropping celebrities, discussing the Screen Actors Guild and criticizing new movies. "Catherine Deneuve . . . no American is like Catherine Deneuve," she said.

"Oy, zucha beuty," my mother added.

"You know, I met her while she was divorcing that British photographer."

"O, rily," my mother said. "You know a lot of dem very famous people."

"Now she is with Marcello Mastroianni."

"Oh, vat a couple. Dey are sometink!"

"Europe, there's nothing like Europe," said Emilia. "We had real theater, films and stars. Not like here."

She and her mother compared the entertainment business in Hollywood to that of Europe, shaking their heads in disgust. Emilia signed many actors who became movie stars in popular films until one day when there was a fatal accident on one of the sets. The cinematographer was killed in a gruesome crane accident, with blood everywhere. She happened to be on the set that day. Using that terrible experience as her excuse to stay stuck, she gave up her career and instead talked incessantly about the accident for the next thirty years.

After Eugenia passed away from natural causes, Emilia and my mother remained friends. They moved on with life as though nothing was happening to me. They denied the clear signs of abuse: a mentally ill, gigantic man running after and yelling at me in between his many days of sleeping. I never felt comfortable around Emilia or any of my mother's friends. I was constantly surprised no one ever came to my rescue.

As I grew older, I gained the confidence to try and change my life. "He really shouldn't be around me," I said to Emilia. "He scares me."

"Are you a psychiatrist?" Emilia asked.

"No."

Staying blind to the truth, Emilia was part of the problem, feeding into the dysfunctional system my mother had put in place. In return, Emilia had an audience, as though our house were a theater where she could act like a success and still think that she was impressive.

"Don't you see he's sick, Mom?" I asked.

She was silent, her small brown eyes blank. Her eyes seemed to say, "He's the normal one, my son, the genius. The rest of you are the ones who are nuts!"

Billy would live with us from time to time in the Spanish house. One of those times, when he was 28 years old, he thought he was in charge of the family. Standing out on the lawn looking over the property like a Texas billionaire surveying his oil wells, he spoke his mind, "This is all going to be mine."

"What about me?" I asked.

"You'll be all right."

Not taking care of me the way a big brother should, not protecting me from Allan, not standing up for me when I needed new jeans, Billy was not going to determine my future. I took matters into my own hands and confronted my mother when I was fifteen years old. I was going to take what's fair and everyone had better get out of my way. This girl was not going to get ripped off.

"Mom, do you have a will? Billy says he is going to get everything."

"I dunno vat vil happin. I don tink of dese tinks." Trying to escape my line of questioning, she moved to the kitchen, looking for dishes to wash. I followed her.

"You are the mother. Your will is not something I am supposed to think about."

"Zo don tink."

"You can't do nothing all the time! Sometimes you have to make a decision! Don't you have a lawyer?"

"Okay, let me tink," she said. "Da Tata (your father) had a lawyer before. Mr. Varren, he vas our lawyer, a nice man. His parenz ver from Vilna."

My father had written his will with Mr. Warren, leaving everything to my mother. I called his office.

"Do you remember my father?"

"Of course," he said. "He was a good man! How can I help you?"

"My mother has no will and my brothers are living with her. It's not a normal situation."

"Go on."

"Well, Allan is bipolar I think. Sometimes the doctors call him manic depressive, schizophrenic or something else. Billy works on projects when he feels like it, never finishing them. He used to help my mother, but not anymore."

"I'm sorry to hear that. Must be tough on you."

"Everything is falling apart. I feel overpowered. I'm worried about what will happen to me."

"Get your university degree," he insisted. "With a degree, you'll always be okay. Call Don Glass. He specializes in wills and trusts. My secretary will give you his number."

While Don Glass was working on a will with my mother, dividing her assets equally among her three children, Allan became worse, having many violent nervous breakdowns. He saw a psychiatrist, Dr. Mulligan, a few times a week.

"Why does the psychiatrist think Allan should live here?" I asked my mother.

"Vell, he iz da doctor," she said. "He knows vat to do."

"Really? What has he done? Allan's gotten worse!"

"Vat ken you do? Dis is da laben." (What can you do? This is the life.)

"Does this psychiatrist know that I live in this house too?"

"I dunno. I dunno vat he knows."

"Mom, you have to do something."

"He iz da sick von, not you," she said. "You hev to tek care of him."

"Screw that!" I yelled. "I am not babying that bastard like you do." Harsh words flew out of my mouth as I came into my own power. "I want Dr. Mulligan's number and I want it NOW!"

In my mother's room buried in a pile of bills and receipts, I found Dr. Mulligan's phone number. I called and said, "Hello Dr. Mulligan, this is Alix Resnick, Allan's sister. I need to talk to you. It's urgent. Can my mother and I come and see you? Okay, tomorrow at 4 p.m."

I confronted my mother. "We are going to Dr. Connor Mulligan's tomorrow. I just talked to him and made the appointment."

She was silent.

"Mom, say something!"

"Okay."

The next day after school, we drove to Dr. Mulligan's office in Culver City.

He was a short, stocky, dark-haired man with a big gut and wire-rimmed glasses. If I didn't know he was Irish, I would have thought he was a Hassid, an Orthodox Jew.

"Sit down, please," he said. "What can I do for you ladies?"

"I can't live with Allan," I explained. "He's ruining my life. I can't sleep and I'm afraid all the time."

He leaned back in his chair, breathing deep, his hands locked together as he took a few moments before leaning forward. He looked at my mother.

"Your daughter is right," he said. "She shouldn't be around him. It's not good for her. Allan should move out of the house."

"Oh, okay," she said.

Years of my begging and pleading to be free of Allan had never had an impact. After hearing one phrase from a large man behind a desk, with framed degrees on the wall behind him, my mother decided to listen.

My mother rented Allan a luxurious apartment in Beverly Hills, making the wrong decision. She never asked Dr. Mulligan for further advice nor did he offer a viable course of action. Never considering sending him to a place that might help him, a hospital or an institution where he could engage with people and receive therapy, my mother treated Allan as though he were not ill.

I thought, "Let's see how long Allan can live alone after his mother had taken care of him for his whole life." He didn't even know how to cook or do his own laundry.

Setting him loose when he needed medication, food and support, my mother did the worst for all of us. He lasted only a few months on his own before his neighbors called the police. He was arrested for being a public nuisance before returning to our house.

"Vat can you do?" my mother said.

"How about signing the will today?" I asked.

"Okay."

And she did.

24
Chocolate Sex

I opened the front door to get the newspaper on a beautiful Sunday morning, almost tripping on a large white paper bag on my doorstep. It contained a three-pound box of See's chocolates and a note signed by our neighbor Mr. Inaka, who we considered the meanest, craziest guy in the neighborhood. The note read "Thank you for cutting back the tree branches on the side of your house. I really appreciate it."

"Look what Mr. Inaka dropped off!" I said.

"What is it?" asked Jack.

"Chocolates."

"Is it factory-sealed?"

I placed the box on the kitchen counter, opened it and saw the loose chocolates in their individual papers.

"Nope, no seal. Do you think it's safe to eat?"

"I don't know. Maybe it's laced?" Jack's mischievous smile meant he remembered the bad blood between Mr. Inaka and me.

A week after we moved into our new house, we left Bone outside in the yard while we went to dinner. When we returned, she was sleepy, dragging herself to her comfy bed in the corner of the kitchen. The next morning, still sick, she didn't move a muscle. She just blinked.

Jack was on his way to a trade show and had left the house earlier that morning. Making a pot of tea while the kids were still asleep, I walked into the backyard and plucked a lemon from the tree. When I turned back toward the house and happened to look down, I saw pieces of hot dog on the grass.

"That's funny. I don't remember making any hot dogs." Picking up a piece, I noticed a chalky, bluish-white substance inside the meat.

"Oh, my God! It's a pill. These hot dog pieces are laced!"

Frozen, I stood there with two little kids and a dog, in a new house in a new neighborhood, staring down at poisoned dog treats. Adrenalin rushed through my body as I panicked, "How do I keep us safe?"

I called the police.

"I just moved into the neighborhood and found hot dog pieces filled with pills in my backyard. What do I do? I'm pretty sure my dog ate a lot of it."

"First, take the hot dogs to the nearest pharmacy. Find out the exact description of the foreign substance," the officer said.

With the kids still in their pajamas, we jumped in the car, dropped the dog off at the nearest kennel for her own protection, and headed to the local drug store. The pharmacist happened to be the mom of one of Lola's classmates. She took the pill out with tweezers and examined it.

"Extra Strength Tylenol PM," she divulged.

"Is it dangerous for my dog?"

"It's lethal to anyone, including dogs, in large doses."

Again, I felt an adrenalin rush, my heart beating faster. Hurrying home, I called the police again reporting what I had learned.

"We will send someone right over," a policeman confirmed.

As I waited for them, I couldn't believe the mess I was in. I wondered if my karma was acting up again, paying me back for something. This kind of situation would never have happened to Gary O'Leary, one of my old friends.

Like a color snapshot I hadn't seen in over thirty years, he appeared in my mind.

Taking a summer screenwriting course at a local university, I wanted to tell my story and express myself. I had drive, but no direction, no role models to emulate and no elders from whom to get advice, Overwhelmed by the size of the campus on my first morning, I felt like a flea on a dog, just trying to hold on.

During class break, I headed toward the campus café a few lawns away. Inside the beautiful old brick building, I grabbed a juice and Danish from the counter. I noticed a boy watching me as I sat down at a small round table. He was cute with black hair and green eyes.

He walked over with his coffee.

"I'm Gary. May I sit with you?" he asked.

"Sure. I'm Alix."

"What class are you taking?" I asked.

"Art and illustration."

Gary pulled out a pen and drew a caricature of me on a napkin while I finished my juice.

"Wow. You're good!"

"Jessica Lang thought so. My aunt got me a job working as an extra on a new movie. Most of the time we just sat around, so I was doodling." Jessica Lange comes over and gives me a $100 bill to buy my doodle. She told me, 'You are going to be famous one day!'"

I went home that Friday afternoon happy to have made a new and interesting friend who peaked my curiosity. At the same time, I was unaware of what the universe had in store for us.

I smiled to myself thinking back to my youth, this time with fondness, when my daydream was interrupted by a loud knock at the door. Two tall, muscular detectives stood there, both wearing dark gold-framed aviator sunglasses.

"Hello, we are from the animal control unit. I understand you have a problem here, ma'am."

"These are the hot dogs. You can see a pill inside each piece. My dog might have been spooked by something while we were out to dinner. This neighborhood has possums, raccoons and skunks. Maybe she was barking."

"This is very serious. You don't kill a dog because it barks," one officer said. "This isn't just a case of attempted dog poisoning. It's child endangerment."

They walked out into the yard.

"Who lives behind you?"

"A family with a dog, and a single mom with two little girls. She's really nice. There's no way it would be her."

"And who lives in the house to the right?"

"An Asian man who lives alone."

The officer measured the distance from where the hot dogs were found to Mr. Inaka's fence, figuring that the pieces had been tossed over the fence.

"I'm guessing he's the one who did it. What else can you tell me about him?"

"Well, there are always coolers sitting out in front of the trailer parked in his driveway," I said.

"Coolers? Filled with what?"

"I don't know."

The next day, a detective phoned. "Mr. Inaka does not live alone," he said. "He has a wife, according to the neighbors. Some know her from church."

"Strange, I never saw or heard a woman. He must keep her very well hidden."

Within the next few hours, undercover cops were parked outside, because a man capable of harming animals and children might be capable of worse. They watched his house for weeks. Everyone who lived on the street noticed the men outside in their nondescript cars.

The Sheriff phoned. "We asked Mr. Inaka about the hotdogs. He denied any knowledge and slammed the phone down."

"Well, that doesn't surprise me," I said.

"Well, hold on. Twenty minutes later, he called and confessed to the whole thing."

I wondered if it was Mr. Inaka's wife who had put the fear of God into him or if it was his lawyer. I couldn't believe he had confessed. The next morning, the doorbell rang.

"Who is it?"

"It's Mr. Inaka from next door."

I hesitantly let him in, leaving the door wide open, the undercover policemen right outside.

"I am very sorry for what happened," he said.

"You scared the hell out of me and my children!"

"Oh, God!" he said. He thrust his fist up in the air, as if it had a mind it its own and punched himself hard between his own hip and groin. Taken aback, I jumped. Memories of Allan slamming his fist through a door flooded my brain. Was Allan's Japanese clone living right next door?

Mr. Inaka calmed himself. "I am over-sensitive to barking," he said.

"You almost killed my dog."

"I'm sorry."

Mr. Inaka was now afraid of me, of what I might do next, as I had the power to put him in jail. The next day I found a typed apology in my mailbox along with a hundred-dollar bill to pay for the weekend kennel expense.

I took a copy of the letter and the $100 bill to animal control before agreeing to sign a report about what happened; in other words, I pressed charges, ensuring that Mr. Inaka would no longer feed Tylenol to his neighbors' pets. I received a call from the District Attorney's office and was asked about the case.

I said, "I want to be safe, but I don't want to ruin the man's life by putting him in jail. And I don't want to live in fear."

Undercover cops were parked outside for the next few weeks and then disappeared.

Just as I was thinking about Mr. Inaka and the hot dogs, Barry, our neighbor from around the corner, burst through the door without knocking. He had come over to watch a football game in his Sunday best—Old Navy shorts, a worn Tequila Bob T-shirt, blue baseball cap and flip-flops. He saw the box of See's chocolate on the counter and reached for it.

"Don't!" I yelled. "If something happens to you, your wife will kill me!"

He took a step back. His hands flew up in the air. "What are you talking about?"

"Those chocolates were sent from the man who poisoned our dog."

Barry and I examined the chocolates. We discovered a small hole in the dark soft chew and an unexplainable smudge on three of the solid milk chocolates. We didn't want to take a risk by eating it even though we had a relentless craving.

"I have an idea," I announced.

I called the See's candy store and spoke with the salesperson. "I think there might be a quality control issue with a gift I received. Might I exchange it for a fresh box?"

"Yes, of course! We guarantee all our chocolates. Please bring the box in and we will be happy to exchange it." I grabbed the chocolate and drove off to make the exchange.

Later, at home, I enjoyed the quiet. Listening to the sound of my own chewing, the soothing crunch of nuts in chocolate. I looked down at my dog, loving the fact that she was back to her old self, chewing on a rawhide bone.

As I languished, my thoughts again drifted back to the very attractive Gary O'Leary.

"I think I love you," he said one afternoon after class.
"What? No, no, no you don't," I replied.

"I do."

"You just think you do."

What I thought was a nice friendship, another stepping-stone in my life's adventures, was becoming complicated. Anything serious was too much for me to handle.

He pushed me against the wall. "I love you," he said.

He put his arms around me, holding me tight. He pressed his lips against mine, his tongue moving in deep. And in a moment I couldn't resist, a spark ignited through me. I wanted more.

He stopped and took a step back. "I am tortured," he said. "I want you more than anything."

"So why are you pushing me away?"

"Because this is a serious decision. I'm Catholic."

"So? I'm Jewish."

"I am waiting until I get married to have sex," he said. "That's my contract with God. I have to decide between you and God."

"Look, I don't have any religious experience except I was born Jewish. I don't really have a lot of rules."

I saw the struggle in his eyes and recognized the lust he thought was love. "Let's just be friends," I said. "Everyone including God should be okay with that." I had never planned on him liking me that much. It was incompatible with my life and I wasn't sure how to handle it.

After class, I saw him walking toward me, calm and confident. He had a fresh look on his face as though he had just walked out of a men's cologne ad, with his green eyes sparkling.

"Let's go somewhere," he said. We walked to the dorm room he had rented for the summer with his friend Stan. "You're the one," he blurted out. "I want you to be my first."

"What about God?"

"He'll understand."

He grabbed me and kissed me. He pulled off his clothes and mine and jumped on top of me, his warm skin tingling against mine. It was by no accident that he produced a condom. Not leaving much time for foreplay, he entered me before it was too late, the deed done within minutes.

Happy about his first time and having moved to the next level of manhood, he had made peace with his desires, a base from which his next relationship would blossom. For me it was another fine mess I had gotten myself into in high school. It was as complicated as the next Saturday night when Daniel called. I was home working on an English paper when my mother came out of her bedroom wearing a mocha-colored skirt and jacket with matching shoes.

"I be home from d veddink (wedding) at 11," she said.

"Okay."

Allan was in the hospital, thank God, and I was home alone. I had finished my English paper and put it in a red folder so it would be presentable. I had just turned on the television when the phone rang. It was Daniel. I told him my mom would be here until eleven. Little did I know what he was plotting.

An hour later that evening the doorbell rang. I looked through the peephole and saw a bunch of kids, some of them familiar. They piled in with bottles of booze, chips, dip and bags of who-knows-what-else.

"Daniel said we should come over. Is that cool?"

"Yeah, I guess."

The doorbell kept ringing. I was becoming a nervous wreck, seeing so many people in our house at once.

"Where are the tunes?" someone yelled.

"I got that," a voice shouted.

Finally, Daniel showed up.

"Why did you invite all these people over? I'm going to be in trouble."

"Don't worry," he said. "Everyone's going to clean up."

Kids were dancing drunk, yelling and mixing it up. My hellhole of a house had become Beverly Hills party central. Older than the rest of us, JJ wobbled over, drunk. Just making it to the bathroom, he closed the door. Daniel went in a few minutes later.

"Oh no, JJ," Daniel yelled. "He threw up on the rug. He's passed out."

"I'm going to be in the worst trouble, Daniel. There's barf all over my bathroom."

"We've got some time. Let's let him rest. You need to get out there and dance Alix! Everything will be fine, I promise. First, you need a drink," he insisted.

I followed him to the kitchen where Eric and his girlfriend Tami were making drinks.

"What do ya' got?" Daniel asked.

"Vodka grapefruit with a twist," Eric passed me a cup.

"It's good. It's sweet," I said after my first sip.

"There's a lot of sugar in it, that's the trick! The sweetness hides how much alcohol you're really drinking!"

All the kids, the music, the food and the doors slamming melded into a slow, zany spin as I danced to Led Zeppelin's "Stairway to Heaven."

"Shit, it's 10:30," Daniel said.

"Turn off the music! Everyone, Alix's mom will be home in a half hour. Clean this place up!"

Greg walked around with a trash bag while some girl he brought wiped up the tables with Pledge and a paper towel. Everything was back in its place except JJ, who was still passed out on the floor, hugging the rug. Eric and Daniel lifted him by his armpits, schlepped him outside and threw him into the back of Eric's car.

Back inside, Daniel put the soiled rug into the washing machine. He said, "Stick the rug in the dryer as soon as it's done so it's dry before your mom gets home."

The house emptied out. As I waited for the rug to dry, I watched a rerun of Starsky and Hutch. Five minutes before my mom walked through the door, the dry cycle finished. I put the rug back in the bathroom and put on my pajamas.

My mother was smiling, but within minutes, she noticed something was off.

"Vat iz da vashing machine doink zo far fin de vall she asked?" (Why is the washing machine so far from the wall?)

During the spin cycle, the thick rug had caused the machine to move a few feet across the laundry room floor.

"What do you mean?" I asked.

"Ah, notink. I am tiert." (Oh nothing, I'm tired.)

High school was the best time of my life and the worst. It was a reflection of heavy craziness and gloom counteracted by intense escapism. Puberty, sex and boys were never discussed and I received no encouragement or guidance at home.

Fortunately, I was attractive and "a nice young woman." Boys usually treated me with respect and gave me the gift of wild and fun times. I wasn't anywhere near popular in high school until my junior year. I moved from nerd to cool without much effort when Noah became my serious boyfriend. Even though he had begun our relationship by sucking my cheek, he later exposed me to the finer things, from exceptional wine, food and music to intellectual conversation.

Sometimes my escapes were extreme, like the time I was invited to Acapulco with Annie's family. She and I were close in tenth grade. Swimming in the ocean, parasailing for the first time, eating in a fancy restaurant complete with a Mariachi band, I felt like an important part of their lives. It gave me a taste of how normal people lived; I felt I had come from hell to heaven. I emulated what their family did and what other kids from good families did. I pretended I was normal.

Daniel often took my mind off family matters by taking me to a local sushi bar. He had been friends with the entire staff and was savvy about what to order. Afterwards, we might go to a movie in Westwood or to an impromptu party at someone's house. It was nice that things didn't always have to be bad.

One night, we piled into cars and drove up into the hills, parking just below the large blue tank of the Beverly Hills reservoir. I climbed up the tall metal ladder. Scared yet excited by the challenge, I walked on top of the tank and sat down in the middle. Looking up at the stars, I connected to something bigger than myself just like I did when I sat on my roof like a little Buddha when I was four.

The boys sometimes brought random girls along that I never saw again. They ran around the edge of the water tower after drinking vodka out of a big bottle, something I was afraid to do. No one cared where I was. As long as I ate something before I left, my mom believed anything.

"Mom, I'm going to Cindy's house."

"Okay. You vant a sandveech first?" she asked.

"Sure."

One time, instead of going to Cindy's, I went with Daniel to Palm Springs, where we were meeting our friends. Daniel "borrowed" his dad's dark maroon Datsun 280ZX and drove 120 miles an hour leading a ten-car caravan. He put both hands in his lap.

"Grab the wheel!"

"What?"

"I'm closing my eyes. Grab the wheel, Alix! If you don't want to crash, grab the wheel."

"Shit!"

I grabbed it and steered while he pressed the gas, heavy-footed.

"You are scaring me," I said.

"Woooo-hooooo!," he yelled, as if he were riding a bucking bronco, his arms raised high and his eyes shut tight, with a gigantic smile. A minute later, he took hold of the wheel as if nothing had happened.

The next Saturday night Daniel called. "My dad's letting me borrow the car again. I'm going to this party in the valley. Want to come?"

"No, I can't. I have to study for a history test."

I thought about how lucky Daniel was that his dad always lent him the sports car. "He's so lucky to even have a dad," I thought.

He called again. "It's Daniel. I'm grounded now because I called my dad to pick me up from the party. I was too messed up to drive. I took some speed. I called my dad, thinking he would understand. You'd think he'd appreciate me not wanting to crash his car in the way home. He's a psychiatrist. It's such crap the way he preaches about being my friend and caring. All he cares about is his car."

A prominent child psychiatrist with a thriving practice in Beverly Hills, his dad was often on CNN giving his opinion on the latest children's toy or trend.

Everyone was psychoanalyzed in their house, which gave Daniel the tools to psychoanalyze everyone else. He mixed this knowledge with a variety of recreational drugs, creating a fantasy of himself as a sort of superhero, a guy who looks at life from all angles while in a world of dreams and inventions.

I remembered the cappuccinos his dad, Dr. Karp, made us on the weekends. I enjoyed watching him steam the milk with the high-powered espresso machine as though it were a musical instrument. They lived in an upper middle-class community; his ex-wife purchased the house next door, just to piss off his new wife.

The next Monday, I entered my house through the back gate after a long school day. I walked quietly up the steps and perking up my ears like a guard dog I listened for Allan, my body tense. Tiptoeing through the house, I dropped my books in my room. Allan's room was empty.

"He must be in the hospital again. Thank God!"

My mother was lying on her bed with the shades drawn.

"How vas da school?"

"Fine. What are you doing?"

"Restink." (Resting.)

I finished up my homework when I remembered the chocolate chip cookie Daniel had given me. I opened my underwear drawer and dug out the cookie from underneath. My wild side wanted to eat it the entire cookie. My cautious side decided I should only take a small bite.

I sat down on my bed and my phone rang.

"Hey, it's Daniel."

"It is so weird you called."

"Why?"

"Because I just took a bite of that cookie you gave me last weekend."

"How much did you eat?"

"A bite."

There was a moment of silence.

"I need your help," Daniel said. "Greg is at my house now and he's really sick. Please, leave right now. Promise me you will get in your car right now, this second."

"Okay, I promise."

"Mom," I yelled. "I'm going to Daniel's."

In my little red Toyota, my first car, I drove north toward Sunset, turning right and then left onto Laurel Canyon, passing a little market on the left where Daniel told me Crosby, Stills, Nash and Young sometimes hung out. The road seemed to lean over to the right while my car leaned to left. The road seemed to be running away from me and not letting me catch up.

"Oh shit, it's the cookie! It's hitting me!"

As I tried to get to Daniel's safely, the white painted traffic lanes were slithering away like snakes chasing a rat.

"And I am here why?" I blanked out for a few seconds before remembered where I was headed. I focused as best I could on the road and moved with the traffic. Tree branches stretched out from their trunks like long arms coming toward me. The streetlights became rubbery, bending over with big eyeballs, staring down at me as if in a Tim Burton movie. Relieved, I turned into the cul-de-sac where Daniel lived, my hands and feet tingling as though I had just inhaled a tank of nitrous. I parked, staring out at the view, as a pinkish light flowed over the valley.

I teetered up the stone path through the entryway to the ornate front door, with it resembling a gigantic Hershey bar, the kind with no nuts. I crossed my arms and touched the soft, luscious skin of my biceps because my skin felt so good to me. I rang the doorbell. Dr. Karp answered the door with a smile, wearing a white button-down shirt and a burgundy cashmere sweater.

"Well, hello there, Alix!"

"Hi, Dr. Karp."

"How are you, my dear?"

"Fine, thanks. Is Daniel home?"

"Yes, go right up. I'm with a patient so you will have to excuse me." He turned and disappeared into his home office.

I stood alone in the corridor for a few seconds. I heard a scream, and then a series of small screams. "That must be the screamer Daniel told me about, one of Dr. Karp's patients," I thought.

I tried hard not to laugh as I walked into the living room, which was filled with artifacts Daniel's dad and his new wife had collected from their many trips to the Far East. I sat down on the white burlap couch between the large pillows and stared at the sculptures and tapestries. The many rows of Buddhas decorating the shelves were moving back and forth in a rhythmic dance. I got up off the couch and walked toward the carpeted staircase. As I stood at the base, I imagined my legs filled with blue, bubbly water and red gum balls. The escalator about to take me up to the next floor was broken.

"Shit, I can't move."

I heard my name, and looking up, I saw Daniel's face at the top of the staircase.

Daniel scrambled down the stairs and took my arm. "I'm going to carry you up the stairs now," he said. He lifted me in his arms and threw my arm over his shoulder, dragging me to his room where I sat down on the floor.

I heard a scream and more small screams.

"It's the screamer, isn't it?"

"SHH!" Daniel said, his index finger pressed against his lips.

"Your lips are getting thicker," I said.

"Shh! My dad is in with a patient. They might hear you! Don't mention the

screamer to anyone. Patient confidentiality."

I laughed so hard I howled, until my sides were getting sore. Quieting down, I became so cold I was shivering. Daniel threw a blue and orange Mexican blanket over me and put a pillow under my head. Lying back, I looked at the ceiling.

"It's so beautiful up there," I said. "It's like a kaleidoscope of blue and white tie-dye coming in and out in waves. Whoa, now I see the entire spectrum! What am I doing on the floor?"

I looked over at Daniel's bed and noticed Greg sleeping under some blankets. "What's Greg doing here?"

"He ate four cookies made with the THC butter. He's been freaking out for the last fourteen hours. That's why I asked you to come over. I didn't want you to go through this alone."

"I want to go home. I don't want to watch the ceiling anymore. Please make it stop."

I spent the next six hours watching spheres, rainbows, classmates, hair salons, earrings, green leaves, cream puffs, trees, silver and gold wedding rings, fish ponds and fat Buddhas. I had moments of fear turn to sadness, and moments of sadness turned to laughter all while Daniel talked Greg and me through it. When it was over, I had a new perspective on life, and a newly expanded mind. Drained, Greg and I looked at each other.

"I'm starving," I said.

"Me, too," Greg said.

Daniel disappeared into the kitchen and returned with two fresh, hot roast turkey sandwiches, a chocolate cake, milk and two pints of Haagen-Dazs.

Relieved the dog incident and Mr. Inaka had been handled, I was tired of all the drama. I dropped Bone off with close family friends the Shaffers before I drove to Palm Desert with the kids. We were ready to have fun and blow off some steam. I enjoyed listening to the hum of traffic mixed with the cacaphony of Aidan and Lola, each singing a different song out loud while playing computer games in the back seat. When they stopped singing, I turned on the radio.

National Public Radio was featuring a woman who had written a book about prom night. She discussed the styles and costs of tuxedos, evening gowns and limousines, and explained the psychology of how these crucial decisions are made. The prom theme reminded me that, in spite of everything, I did have special times. My prom was one of those times.

My boyfriend for three years in high school and the grand passion of my life, Noah invited me to the prom. Danya's daughter Rachel lent me her beautiful silver lamé dress and black sling-back heels.

A powder-blue limo arrived at my house and Noah gave me a corsage. With our friends in tow, we headed for the Beverly Hills High School prom at the Beverly Hilton Hotel.

The most incredible part was that while Noah wore a full leg cast under his tux, he wined and dined me all night and took me home afterwards. In severe pain, he still took me to my prom because he loved me. He looked so boyishly cute, with sweat beading down his forehead as he dealt with the intense pain of his crushed kneecap. He and his poet friend, Ursula, had been driving between Santa Monica and Malibu, heading south in a Chevrolet Cavalier, when they were struck by a stoned tennager who had crossed over the center line. I visited Noah in the hospital, bringing goodies and his favorite take-out.

Before I saw Noah, I saw his parents and two sisters, and the four of them hovered with worry. Holding back tears of relief as I saw Noah in the hospital bed, I camouflaged my concern with a smile.

"Where's Ursula?" I asked.

Noah's mom, Barbara, pulled me into the bathroom. She looked serious. "Ursula died in surgery," she said. "Please don't say anything to Noah yet."

Visibly shaken, I thought it could have been Noah who had died. Never before had I felt that kind of love and gratefulness for another human being. I cried in the bathroom at the prospect of almost having lost him. Pretending I was having an allergy attack, I used the bouquet of flowers as my excuse for sniffling. Thank God he would be okay.

Every now and again my persistent neck and back issues would bring things to a head. Here I was a married woman with two kids, five and seven years old, and desperate not to be a burden on my family. I feared Jack would have to take care of me for the rest of my life when I was the one who wanted to help everyone else. This need to heal forced me to connect with my higher self. I prayed a lot and asked the universe for answers, discovering I was on the path to integrating all the disconnected parts of me, with no turning back no matter how difficult the emotional, physical and spiritual work.

Part of my healing was letting go of Stella, Lucy and Daniel, whose friendships were once so fulfilling. As I did more healing and growing, I ended up with a whole new set of friends. Refocusing my energies, I was now drawn to people who wanted to teach, grow, experience and enjoy life, loving themselves without harming others and showing the world the real person within.

Lola wanted to show herself to the world, to be on stage, TV and in films. Called back after an initial audition, she jumped at the chance to have some fun. She pounced to the front of the audition room, an eager jackrabbit with a beautiful smile.

"Hi, I'm Lola and I'm ten years old."

"I love you!" the talent manager said. "Ya' got something for me, kid?"

Lola read her lines with another actor.

"She did very well," he said, "except her pitch. Be careful of her pitch. She's got a lot of voice. I want to work with her. Keep her in acting classes!"

Choked up, I loved the talent manager seeing her potential.

Journal entry (July 9, 2010)

As I thought about how I had been treated as a child, I became angrier!

"I am not worthless! Mom, you were never worthless either! You were just trained to feel that way by sick people who killed your family and stole your sanity!"

I am smoldering with self-doubt and the battle to get past it, feeling the spark of a deep chord, and my tears have flowed on and off for days. Having cried so much this week, I should pay myself $250 an hour for the healing.

I focused on what I wanted for myself, watching my relationships become stronger. Happy, content and enjoying my alone time, I was interrupted by an unexpected ache in my lower back—Fred begging for attention. Choosing to lie down and do the breathwork, I closed my eyes, directing my breath toward the discomfort. Massaging Fred from within with my breath, I sensed him turning away. "I'm too busy to deal with you today and play these games, Fred. Leave me alone! I have guests tonight." Many times I could pick and choose when to process Fred. Other times he gave me no choice. Tonight when Fred demanded my attention, I had to say no.

Sitting in an antique café chair at the mosaic-tiled table the next afternoon, I drank a cup of tea while taking a ten-minute break to enjoy the garden. Listening to the symphony of birds, I admired the surrounding colors— green, purple, orange and white—and the leaves and petals swaying in breeze. Jack joined me as he enjoyed being outside in the evenings, watering the plants with Bone by his side. He connected to and appreciated the nuances of nature, back to a time when there was no cellphone, television or computer. Breathing in the fresh air, listening to the subtle sounds of the crickets, it was a good evening if he saw a possum or a squirrel. Carrots, tomatoes and herbs were growing in a long planter that Jack watched over as though he were tending his farm. Even though I had planted the seeds, I didn't fully enjoy the yard. Tired, worried and stressed, I was carrying clutter. The responsibility of looking after everyone was a great weight on my shoulders holding me back as if I were so overweight, I couldn't move. This hodgepodge kept me from finishing my book and delayed the healing of my body and mind.

This derangement was the distraction that kept me caged. It was an excuse for never finishing anything, a learned behavior that had returned with a vengeance.

Dealing with my mother's literal physical clutter—the amassed piles in the drawers, closets and corners of her house, I tossed out whatever I could. Thinking God had dealt her the wrong hand, she did not have the energy or the desire to clean out her house. She permitted the debris of her sadness over the war, my father's death, having to raise three children alone, and Billy and Allan's illnesses to permeate my life. My mother would try to keep me from doing anything that might move me forward. She would say, "Do you really hev to do dat today? Do you really neet to tek da kids to karate?"

"No, I don't need to, I want to. It's good exercise and they learn self-discipline."

I had great grades in high school and wanted the same opportunities as the other kids in my class. I knew my father would have wanted me to go to university. Many months went by as I cried to my mother begging for the chance to study and get away from the craziness. While my peers were supported at university, I felt like an ingrate from my family's reaction to me.

My mother gave my brothers anything they wanted if they stayed home, offering no emotional support if any of us wanted go out on our own. My family complained about me leaving home because they would have to spend money on me, letting me know I would never amount to anything anyway. Desperate to get out of that house and try to make it on my own, I applied to and was accepted by a major university. Elated, I was free at last!

The stress of having mentally ill relatives while trying to remain sane was as draining as though an entity, a negative energy, was pulling me down.

Allan yelled unintelligibly, Billy complained we would lose everything, and my mother changed her mind depending on who screamed the loudest. She had a way of avoiding conversations by seeming unavailable while she was cooking. She paid attention only when she was caught not stirring the soup pot. Having nothing to hold onto, nothing that made sense, I was confused as to what to do with my life.

Keeping my problems secret, I held in the pain and moved on by dressing well, sporting a brilliant smile and pretending life was perfect. Each day I ignored the truth of my struggle as I bustled across campus with my backpack, inspired by thought-provoking classes, professors pushing my buttons, and a mélange of great-looking guys. What I was missing was the backbone, the family to help me decide on my academic major and my life's direction. Inexperienced and saddled with a family that didn't care, I did my best to survive and learned to be my own support.

I remember one time when I was a university student and dialed my mother's phone number. Sweat beaded on my forehead as though the music from the "Psycho" shower scene were playing in my head. "Please God, let my mom be the one to answer the phone today."

"HELLO?" Allan answered.

I slammed the phone down hard. Allan's voice, hundreds of miles away, still scared me. As the school year progressed, this fear intensified.

My friend Seth Goldberg, a tall, skinny guy with curly black hair, had a large nose and a moustache he thought looked distinguished. His roommates called him "Jew back" because his back was covered with the same curly hair he had on his head. Seeing Seth outside one day, I asked him to come over.

"Seth, will you help me make a phone call?" I put the receiver in his hand and dialed my mother's number.

"If a male answers, hang up fast," I said. "And if it's a woman with an accent, pass the phone over."

"No! It's too weird," he said. "I'm leaving."

The family I had seemed worse than having no family at all. I needed a diversion from the chaos so I focused on my studies, exercise and men. I liked Seth's roommate, Nate. In fact, I wanted him. He was a muscular, blonde biology major with beaming blue eyes. He worked out four times a week, his dedication obvious by his pecs outlined beneath his T-shirt and his carved thighs revealed in cutoffs. I watched him walk as though he were a Belgian chocolate ice cream cone dripping in the warm sun and I was the tongue that would lick all that up.

I squirmed like a snake shedding its skin as I imagined how safe I would feel in his arms, my intuition telling me he wanted me, too. Fantasizing about him made my days easier.

One weekend while my roommates were out of town, there was a knock at the door. Through the peephole I saw Nate with an anxious look in his eyes. I tossed my hair forward and back and smoothed down my sundress before opening the door.

"Hi," I said.

"Hey. Thought if you weren't doing anything, you might want to share a bottle of wine?" he said, holding up the bottle.

"Yeah, sure. Come in."

I was amazed he appeared without warning, a voice in my head telling me I had manifested him just because I wanted him. He sat down on the couch, setting the bottle of cabernet on the coffee table.

"Hey, you know, we have some other alcohol here," I said. "How about a gin and tonic? That's my favorite."

"Sure, sounds good," he said.

I grabbed two short glasses from the cupboard, made the icy drinks and sat down next to Nate. Aware I was becoming warm, and noticing a tingle between my legs. I I realized I was excited by his nearness. I watched him sip the drink, my hormones raging with desire as I imagined how he would look naked, wanting to be pinned down hard by his lean body.

I took a few gulps of my gin and tonic, wanting to pounce on him like a wild animal, letting him know I was as strong as he was. While trying to remain cool and calm as though hot guys always showed up at my doorstep, I needed to bypass the small talk and get down to business. The scent of Coppertone coconut tanning oil mixed with his natural musk turned me on.

"I want to kiss you," he said.

"Mmmm," I said with a smile.

When he leaned over to kiss me, he stared into my eyes, my lips quivered and I felt warm all the way down to my toes and everywhere in between. He took my glass and set it on the coffee table before he moved me lower down on the couch so his body could rest on top of me. Listening to his breath, touching his muscles and soft skin, I was right where I wanted to be, letting him kiss me the way he wanted, the way I wanted.

Smiling, we both wobbled into the bedroom. I turned off the light switch and watched him move to the bed and lay waiting for me. I jumped on top of him straddling him, my dress hiking up to my waist. Leaning forward, I took his arms and forced them back behind his head. He laughed at my attempt to take charge. Looking into his beautiful blue eyes, I kissed him deep, engulfing him large and hard underneath me, his hands gripping the sides of my thighs, pulling me in closer. Never had I felt so sexy, so much the woman I wanted to be, the woman he desired.

Turning me over so he could be on top, he pushed my dress up and kissed my stomach. He removed my lace panties and went right there to my sweet spot, his soft tongue making me scream and dance, the moonlight coming in through the window igniting us further. He moved his hands across my back and caressed my hard nipples before he leaned in to taste them. Thrilled by the sensation, I arched my back, wanting more, my breasts tingling and dancing before him.

"You're beautiful," he said. As he reached for a condom, I pulled my dress and bra over my head as I waited for him. He slid his hand between my legs and lightly touched my most private place, moist and wet. I thought I might scream, holding in my pleasure while surrendering to him. My body went limp as energy shot

through me like lightening. He entered me slow and deep, divine and wonderful. In a magical place I had never before visited, I was one with Nate as though we rose above our bodies. Our souls met just as I was beginning to lose myself.

Nate flipped me over. He entered me from behind. I loved fighting back as hard as I could. No one had ever gone that deep with me physically or spiritually. His hard, repetitive motion became so intense I screamed until I cried tears of joy, because nothing in life could be better than this.

My life had always been a series of extremes, and Nate showing up out of the blue to make love to me was the most wonderful extreme. I believe God had given me this gift to counteract all the sadness and desperation. Finding myself engulfed in his arms was ecstasy, an escape that took me away, gave me freedom, and allowed me to discover—he was the antithesis of my reality.

Two weeks later, I called my mother.

"Oh, Alix, iz you, I didn't recognize it vas you."

Not being recognized by my own mother was a common occurrence, and a gut-wrenching stab, a phenomenon with which I never became comfortable.

"Na... talk to him," said my mother. With no chance to protest, I heard a rustling sound on the line. She had given the phone to Allan.

"Alix! How are you?"

"Fine."

"You know I used to carry you on my back and taught you how to read, Pooh Bear?"

As he told me more of what I did before I was six years old, my lunch came up in a disgusting taste that I pushed back down.

"Das enough!" my mother said. "Is expensif. Say goot bye to hair."

"Bye, bye, bye, Alix, bye."

"Oh, dat vas a niz conversation," my mother said. Forgetting I called to talk, she said, "I hev to go. Bye."

25
Eggs

When Billy and Allan were wreaking havoc, my mom would say, "Hev an egg," diverting the focus to a simple subject, a simple need—an egg. "Don talk," she said, "juz eat quiet d'egg." There was always an abundance of fresh, warm hard-boiled eggs on the breakfast table.

In my first year of university, I was afraid to see my brothers and avoided the house. Unable to remember everything that happened there, my instinct was to stay away from the war zone. I made regular appointments by phone to meet my mother. She was all I had.

I parked my white BMW a block away from the house, waiting for her to come out to meet me. We would have lunch at Nate 'n Al's Delicatessen and maybe do a little shopping. Our conversations were superficial and food focused. Every time I saw her, I hoped she would have some motherly advice to offer as the side dish. That never happened. Meeting her like this made me feel like an outcast, a scapegoat and the black sheep. She had made the choice to let her grown sons live in her home rent-free with food, utilities and laundry service provided. She pretended she had no control over the situation.

I came down from school one weekend to visit Noah. Now an assistant producer, he was one of those brilliant people, confident about what he wanted *in life, making it on his own. He wouldn't dream of asking his parents to pay for his university education so he went and got to work instead. Almost immediately when I saw him, I broke down into tears, unable to stop crying for hours, while assuring Noah I would be fine.*

I had no home. My foundation was gone, a fact which I kept secret from my friends. That day, I had reached the tipping point. I had cried for so long, I was too weak to drive back and too embarrassed to call anyone. Needing solid ground, I called my mother. This was a point of desperation because I had an aversion to her house.

This innate fear reminded me of what my mother once told me, "I didn go inside d howz in Ozerkov after d var, too meny memriz, too meny det. I juz valk back un fort. Dey vere all dead." (I didn't go inside my house in Ozerkov because I knew they were all dead. I just walked back and forth outside on the street.)

"Come over," my mother insisted with a tone that everything was fine and I shouldn't have a care in the world.

"De boys ven to San Diego. Dey won be home until tomorrow night."

I returned to the house after two years of being away. Dragging myself through the back door, I was raw, nervous, tense and cautious. I was starving and yet unable to swallow anything my mother offered. If I ate her food, I would have been sending a subconscious message all was forgiven. If I succumbed, she would think that she had been a good mother to me. Refusing her culinary offerings was my defense.

"I don't want your food," I said.

Ignoring my words, my mother reached for the bowl of hard-boiled eggs she had cooked and peeled. She pulled an egg out of a bowl with one hand, turning her palm upward, balancing the egg on her fingertips like a sculpture on a pedestal, a sacred sacrament and the cure to all that ailed me. Fulfilling the ultimate act of parenthood, as she understood it, my mother was doing the only thing she thought to do—feed me. Repulsed by the egg, I backed away. She made a lunge forward with the egg, refusing to give up.

"Iz goot. Tek it!"

She tried to shove the egg in my face. She was relentless. No longer a dependent child, I refused to eat this symbol of her dysfunction. Eating the egg was like admitting I was fine with the life she had given me. As hungry as I was, I refused to take one bite. Imagining Snow White's poison apple, I saw my childhood flash before me. She tempted me with a bite of the forbidden and pushed me deeper into the abyss. Backing away as if I were staring into the barrel of a loaded gun, I wanted to be back at my apartment where I was safe.

"I'm so hot and sweaty. I need a shower," I said.

"Uf curse, go tek a shower," my mother said.

Through the shadows of my past, I entered my mother's powder room and saw myself putting on her red lipstick, my face reflected in the silver hand mirror. I brushed my hair smooth with the silver hairbrush, thinking back to the time when I pretended I was a fairytale princess. I was four years old then, my father on the phone taking a business call in the adjacent bedroom, speaking in Polish, which I couldn't understand, the curly phone cord stretching across the floor.

My father had once blocked my mother's hand in mid-air with his forearm before she could slap me. I heard echoes of Allan's manic episodes ringing in my ears, and disturbing images of Billy appearing and disappearing. Overwhelmed, I stood in the powder room wondering why I had come.

After I undressed, I walked into the bathroom and opened the glass shower door hoping the memories would fade. I turned on the hot water and stood under the showerhead. The walls were closing in. I was sucked into the past, a dark place from which I wanted to escape. I heard distant voices turn to screams, tears of the past streaming forth, and the sounds of suffering. I held onto the shower walls, fearing I would faint. Sliding down into a kneeling position, I cried. Listening to the voices screaming up through the drain, the water pouring down, and feeling weakness wash over me. I feared I was going to die there.

I turned off the water and stepped out of the shower, my hot salty tears mixing with the cool water dripping from my hair. I needed to escape before it was too late, before I found out secrets that were kept from me. Something dark and scary lived in this house, or was it in me? The fierceness reminded me of when I grabbed the covers while watching "Rosemary's Baby" when Mia Farrow discovers that she is carrying the devil's child. "Don't stay to try and figure this out," my inner guidance insisted. "Leave now!"

"Vere are you goink?" my mother asked, surprised that I was heading for the door.

"I can't be here." I ran to my car and drove away.

26

Free Rein

This spring I went to Palm Desert, leaving the family to fend for themselves. The first evening, I sat at a small outdoor table enjoying a fresh crab salad with a glass of chilled chardonnay. I listened in to the quiet, into myself and opened to ideas beginning to filter in from God, the Source or whoever. The purpose of my trip was to flush thoughts onto paper without being interrupted with requests for grilled cheese sandwiches and tomato soup. Thinking, creating and writing, staying up late with reruns of the "Twilight Zone" in the background, I fell asleep in my hotel room at about 3 a.m.

With a view of a golf course and the endless desert, I wrote as soon as I awoke the next morning. Taking a break, I made coffee and turned on the TV to see Monica Seles, the tennis player, on a talk show. "Cutting through the fog of sadness, fear and frustration that made Seles overweight and unhappy, today she looks and feels better than ever and has created a life in balance."

Something had happened to her. She chose to keep the details private, while giving me confirmation that I was on the right track with my healing process. If she could heal herself, so could I. If she could do it, I could do it.

Trying to lose weight by dieting that spring, I noticed svelte moms by the pool sporting boob jobs, skin tightening treatments and the whole post-partum package. As enticing as it was to look that good, surgery scared me. If I ever went under the knife, I would start young like a famous blonde film actress. No one would be the wiser except, of course, my old friend Stella.

"I'm getting Restylane in my parentheses," Stella announced, referring to the natural lines around her mouth. "I'm going to the best Beverly Hills plastic surgeon. I'll give you his name."

"No thanks. Not my thing," I said.

"Last time I was at his office," Stella said, "I peeked into his black leather datebook. A famous blonde actress has regular appointments! She's smart! She does it gradually, that way no one notices. She gets older and never changes."

"Okay, I've got to go to the market and drop the kids off at karate by 4. Let's talk a little later!" I told her.

That afternoon Stella showed up at the karate studio, unannounced, to watch the kids have their lesson, an occurrence that was strange, since she lived on the other side of town.

"Hi, Stella," Jack said as he was picking up the kids. "What are you doing here?"

Without a word, she walked out the door. I spent a day or two trying to figure out why she ignored him.

Jack and I surmised that Stella needed more attention than I could give. She couldn't understand the time and responsibility I gave to my family and had a hard time being happy for me. Eventually I chose to let go of Stella's friendship as part of my healing process. Missing our shopping sprees and lunch dates very much, I had to do what was best for my family and me. Sometimes friendships were no longer a positive force. This was a time to move on and figure out what I wanted while attracting people that made me feel good.

I left the hotel room and drove to Chipotle for lunch. While I waited for a steak salad with extra lettuce, Pico de Gallo and medium-hot salsa, the loud, fast-paced music made me nervous, as if I had just ingested a bottle of amphetamines. Closing my eyes for a few seconds and listening to the boom of the bass, I was aware of the vibration moving from my feet up my body, in sync with the footsteps coming in and out the swinging glass door. I ate to the rhythm of the beat, as though I were a bongo drum, finishing the meal fast.

At Starbucks afterwards, I ordered a double Americano with dry foam, the fuel I needed to get me through another few hours of writing. As I waited, I thought about Jack and the kids blabbing to friends and synagogue members that I was writing a book. Not quite ready to announce it, I couldn't stop the progression of interest. "Now, I really do have to write this book!"

Jack had been telling his friends in Israel too. "The Israelis will be a tough crowd," I thought, remembering a woman in Tel Aviv stopping me on street. She told me I shouldn't be wearing white in winter. No one's opinions were off-limits.

When we lived in Israel, I was pregnant with Lola and wanted natural childbirth. The Israelis I knew trusted technology more than nature and considered natural childbirth primitive and something poor, uneducated women did. I opted for nature. The truth of the matter was the percentage of hospital and natural birth fatality rates were equal.
"Aren you afred? Don you tink e dat iz irresponsible?" (Aren't you afraid? Don't you think that's irresponsible?)

"No," I replied. "I am much more afraid to give birth in a hospital."

Muscular, with wide hips, I wanted to connect with the generations of women who had given birth before me, squatting in the woods, the way God intended. I pictured it a positive experience rather than a medical one. I wanted to depend on myself to give life and was not willing to pass on that privilege. Putting my wishes ahead of his Israeli friends' worries, Jack got on board with my way of thinking. When I went into labor Jack became my personal DJ, spinning the tunes of Peter Gabriel, Thievery Corporation and Miles Davis to relax me during the contractions, and African drums gave me a beat to push with as my sweet girl entered the world.

With no complications and full of energy, I made a quick recovery after Lola was born. The response from Jack's friends was, "You were lucky."

I thought to myself, "I thought I was intelligent."

Still waiting for my coffee at the Starbucks in Palm Desert, I recalled a family trip to Las Vegas when Jack and I celebrated our thirteenth wedding anniversary with the kids. Aidan was lying in bed running a fever of 102.

I felt a poking deep inside my uterus with pressing stings that would not let up, which began to irritate me. Wanting to connect with the pain, aware it was trying to tell me something, I laid down next to Aidan and using my iPod with head-phones in, I began breathwork. This practice became instinctive as the thing to do to get me to the next level of healing. Sharp pain rose to my throat. Crying loud and long, I relaxed, with tears settling in on my face when I saw Billy. His giant face lifting from between my legs, he was smiling. I released the energy of abuse connected to the prodding sensation in my uterus, an old trauma that my body held.

Not long after I had broken up with Noah, I drove up to my mother's house and waited outside. We had our bi-monthly lunch date, a secret well kept from my brothers. We often ate on Beverly drive or Rodeo. Sometimes when we had deli, we saw Cher, dripping in turquoise jewelry, ordering at the counter. If we ate early enough, we saw Larry King in a booth eating Matzo Brei, his favorite breakfast. Marveling at my six degrees of separation from celebrities, Mafia families and the rich and famous, I wondered how the rest of the world lived.

On this particular day as I waited by the side of the house with the engine running, I saw "them," my two brothers leaning on each other, walking up the sidewalk toward me. Allan was holding up Billy, who appeared sedated. Heat oozing out my pores, I could feel the sweat on my face and underarms. In a state of panic I went blank, forgetting to breathe, forgetting where or who I was, or where I was going.

Desperate to refocus while having a panic attack, I waited a few moments before driving away. My mother took a rain check.

This was an emotional pull from which I wanted to escape. Ever since I graduated from university, I treasured every "girls' night out" opportunity as valuable and necessary for my wellbeing!

Almost every Thursday night after work, I went out for dinner. One night, my old friend Susannah and I went to Café Sushi Beverly Hills. Having done a few lines of cocaine earlier that evening to curb my appetite, I was now famished. The sushi bar was dark, exotic and engaging. Enjoying the mélange of interesting people, I would often see movie stars, druggies, producers, directors, businessmen and even grandmas.

We sat at the sushi bar and reviewed the menu.

"A hot Saki to share, two yellowtail nigiri and one spicy tuna maki," I said to the sushi chef.

We heard the bells as the front door opened and looked up to see eye candy— tall, tan, lean and muscular, the kind of guy who spends hours doing weights in front of a mirror.

"Oh, my," Susannah slurped under her breath, like a Southern belle fanning herself on a hot, sweaty Louisiana afternoon.

"He's alone," I whispered.

His hair was as perfectly cut as his pecs underneath a green and white striped dress shirt and a grey-blue silk tie. He had just come from work, ready to let loose. Susannah stiffened as he turned and walked toward the sushi bar. He sat down next to her.

The waitress set the hot sake down and poured some into two small cups. Holding the cups high, we clanked them together.

"Kompai!"

Susannah's hands were shaking as she dipped her sushi into the soy and wasabi sauce. She stuffed the entire piece into her mouth at once and chewed with a vengeance as she glanced at the man to her right.

I looked at the specials up on a chalkboard and ordered, "Two salmon skin hand rolls please and the blue crab special."

Susannah was perspiring profusely. "Maybe she's not used to the sake," I thought.

"Hi," the man greeted Susannah.

"Well, hello," she responded in a low and sexy tone.

"What's fresh tonight?" he asked.

"Fresh, hmm. Oh, you mean the fish?" Susannah stammered. "Ha, this is my first time."

"A novice?"

"Well, yes, sort of. My friend Alix orders. I guess I could order for myself, but I don't."

His presence was making her hyper, with words blathering out of her mouth. I could tell she was picturing him in bed. Her desire was obvious. I poured us both another cup of sake. I kicked mine back. Attempting to rest her elbow down on the bar, Susannah hit the edge of her soy sauce dish and flipped it into the air, covering the man's dress shirt with a fine, brown mist. He turned bright red and jumped out of his seat.

She grabbed her napkin and drenched it in a glass of ice-water. She dabbed the man's arm and chest, making him cold and wet. His designer shirt was now a soaking rag.

"Stop, that's enough!" he shrieked.

She reached for a stack of white paper napkins and pressed them one by one onto his shirt, sopping up the water while enjoying the feel of his chest. I smiled as the napkins stuck to him as if he were an arts and crafts project.

"I'm fine," he said, backing away from Susannah. "That's enough! Really! Check please!" he yelled.

He paid his bill and kept his head down. Turning to leave the restaurant, he was silent, the bells sounding behind him as the door closed.

Susannah and I looked at each other and laughed. "Oh well," *she said.* "What a shame."

"Yep, damn shame."

"Two salmon skin hand rolls please and a yellowtail collar."

"Hai!"

27
Dead Week

I lived in a shared apartment near the university. It was Dead Week, an important time when students had the chance to ask questions and study in preparation for final exams. Monday morning, the energy I needed to get out of bed was lacking. Having stayed in bed for days, I was unable to hold my life together. The pressure of separating my family problems from the "me" people saw each day was bubbling up.

Friday was the first day I had the strength to drag myself to campus. I was on my way to biology when I saw Jacqueline Gilles, my French teacher. Petite and stylish, she threw together mismatched accessories, always pulling off an interesting look in a way that only the French can.

"Shit," I thought. "I don't want her to see me."

She walked toward me quickly, giving me no time to plot an escape route. "Hello, Alix," she said with an elegant French accent. "You weren't in class all week. What happened?"

I was silent. How could I explain what I didn't understand?

"Come to my office," she insisted.

I followed her to the language building, where she unlocked the door. "Have a seat," she said, gesturing for me to sit down on a cushy, faded red armchair. She *sat facing me as though intuiting what I thought I had successfully kept hidden. Quiet and lost, it was like I had beamed down from the Starship Enterprise, my mission not yet disclosed.*

"So," she said. "Where were you?"

"Home, sick."

Staring at me longer, waiting for me to say more, her patience was astounding.

"Okay," I said. "The truth is I was upset and couldn't get out of bed. I have some family problems. My brothers are in and out of hospitals. Sometimes they seem crazy, other times they seem like everyone else. It's hard. I think they do drugs."

"Where is your father?"

"Dead."

"And your mother?"

"She's a Holocaust survivor."

"My family was lucky. We escaped the war," she said.

"You're Jewish?" I asked.

"Yes, my parents were both dentists in Paris. All their money was invested in dental equipment. Afraid the Nazis would take it from them, they dug a big hole in the ground and buried their equipment, planting flowers on top. I was just a baby then. My parents went back to Paris after the war to dig up the equipment."

She paused for a moment and stared at me before speaking again.

"I want you to spend the weekend with us! We have a little house in the mountains. My daughter is thirteen and my husband is a professor of engineering. It will be good for you to relax. Come Friday after 4 when I get home from work."

I was surprised by her quick invitation. I agreed, my instincts telling me she was one of the good ones.

Friday after finals, I drove through a lush neighborhood before pulling up at Jacqueline's house in amazement. Her house was a giant golf ball.

She came out of the house and said, "Hello!"

"Hi! What a house!"

"It's a geodesic dome, the most efficient house ever made. They are common in New Mexico and Arizona," she said.

Inside, she poured me a glass of fresh lemonade and said, "Come, I will show you to your room."

We walked down the hallway on adobe floor tiles, surrounded by walnut furniture, French antiques and assorted souvenirs. After a short rest, I heard her family come home.

"Alix," Jacqueline called out.

Jumping up, I went into the hallway.

"This is my husband, Michael, and my daughter, Isabella."

"Hi," I said.

"Nice to meet you," Michael and Isabella said.

We went into the living room where Jacqueline turned on the antique lamps. A fire was already lit in the fireplace giving the room a warm glow. Books, artifacts and board games filled the room, along with an oversized set of hand-carved wooden chess pieces. Trying to make small talk with Michael and Isabella, I was uncomfortable, as I wondered what they thought of me. Not used to having family conversations that were not irrational or food-focused, I wasn't sure what to say or how to be myself. I was embarrassed to be there, not good enough to be in their presence.

"Alix? Please come help me in the kitchen." Jacqueline called out. She was draining boiled potatoes and asked, "Would you mash these, please?" She sensed my discomfort and plunged the masher deep into the soft potatoes, showing me how to proceed, and I took it from there.

She pan-fried white fish filets in butter until they were slightly brown and crisp on the edges before sprinkling them with dill and sea salt, then set them on plates with peas and mashed potatoes. Never having been taught how to cook,

I had missed out on bonding in the kitchen; my mother always ordered me out when she was cooking—especially odd since she was obsessed with food.

Everyone ate with appetite. Nervous and not saying much at the table, I was so insecure I couldn't speak. In my head, I expressed words of appreciation telling Jacqueline how scrumptious her meal was and how much I loved being there. I rested over the weekend, helping Jacqueline in the kitchen and the garden. Before I headed back to school on Monday, Jacqueline and I had coffee and toast with homemade apricot marmalade.

"I want to help you," she said. "Here are some names and phone numbers. Included is the number of a good friend of mine, Susan Neman. She is a psychologist I think you will like. I also know the head psychiatrist for the county. I hope this helps."

She reached out to give me a hug.

"Thank you for everything!" I said.

I made an appointment with Dr. Howard M. Luden, Head of Psychiatry for the county. When I arrived at his office, the shades were drawn. Across a dark green carpet, I caught a glimpse of him, his wrinkled face lit by a green glass banker's desk lamp. He was much older than I expected. He leaned forward onto his dark wood desk to look at me.

"What seems to be the problem?" he asked.

"I'm sad, having trouble getting out of bed and . . . ."

"All right," he said cutting me off mid-sentence as he scribbled on a notepad and pushed a piece of paper across the desk. "It's a prescription for anti-depressants. Have a nice day."

He was unprofessional because he never diagnosed me or asked any rudimentary questions before prescribing drugs. I was swept under the rug. The man professing to be a leader in the community was just a pill pusher. As I walked out of the building I crumpled up the prescription and threw it in the trash.

Next on Jacqueline's list was Susan Neman, a psychologist. Her office was large and flooded with natural light. We sat on a white couch and matching chair. I found her warm, friendly and nurturing, and possibly too empathetic for her own good—she probably worried about her clients after work. She wore knit pants, a colorful sweater and soft leather boots.

"You need to see me at least four times a week to start," she said.

"How much is that going to cost?"

"Don't worry about how you are going to pay me. I trust you. Pay me when you can."

"I'm going to send the bills to my mother," I said. "She's the reason I'm here." Susan absorbed my words and looked at me with compassion, connecting to my sadness. Sometimes she raised her eyebrows with an insight that she shared with me later. She taught me I could come into my own power and had the right to choose my destiny. She helped me understand that my mother, my family and their friends were part of a dysfunctional, self-feeding and self-gratifying system that tried to suck me in.

"Why would they want to do this to me?"

"Misery loves company. You have exposed them for what they are, and that is why they made you out to be the bad and evil one, because you are the one who no longer enables them. You are a threat to the status quo."

At our next meeting, Susan sat in her comfortable armchair with her shoes off and knees curled back, with a throw rug covering her feet. The more I spoke, the worse I felt as I turned into an enraged fountain, speaking my truth, with an angel listening. On the verge of falling apart, I now had a substitute mom to treat me well and give me healthy advice.

Eventually I became stronger and found a part-time job with a small ad agency. I wrote copy and designed newspaper layouts on the days I wasn't in therapy. School, therapy and working were distractions keeping me from feeling too much into my problems.

One day, my mother called out of the blue to announce she was coming to visit me while I was still a student in college. Nervously anticipating the train from Los Angeles, I was early at the station. Numb as I went through the motions of seeing her in my mind, I was certain that if I opened my heart, I would get hurt. The train arrived and through the window I watched her move toward the door. She peeked her head out and carefully stepped down onto the platform. She wore sensible navy blue stretch-pants with a matching scoop-necked shirt and a white jacket labeled "Members Only" on the pocket—one of three of these jackets she had purchased from a closeout sale on Rodeo Drive.

When she recognized me, she reached out to kiss my cheek. The tension between us was as thick as the Oslo Accords handshake between Yassir Arafat and Yitzhak Rabin. The whole scene was unfamiliar and perplexing, as she had never visited me before. She was the connection I wanted, mixed with detachment I despised.

She created undue anxiety for me, having only agreed to pay for my university education after weeks of hearing me sob. She then discussed the issue with Billy.

"You can go to UCLA if you live at home," Billy said, dropping a ton of bricks on my head.

I refused to live at home any longer than I had to, never even applying to UCLA because it was too close to home. Accepted to a comparable university up north, I left for school. Never once calling me to see how I was doing, my mother punished me for not living under her roof. Love was complying with or fitting into my mother's whims. She was saying, "If you don't dance to my tune, I'm going to shut you out!" She offered conditional love only to my brothers, who remained loyal by living with her.

Susan Neman explained that my mother and brothers felt safe within their system, feeding off each other. My brothers could have anything they wanted from her in terms of money, material goods and what they thought was love. She was content with them not working because she was happy to have them at home. The three of them were empowered and secure with each other. My striving to break out was a choice that threatened them.

As an eighteen-year-old university student, I should have had the time of my life; instead, I struggled to be normal, keeping my family problems a secret and focusing on my studies and social life, never relaxing enough to let myself feel. I kept quiet the way my mother kept quiet about the Holocaust, most people unable to relate to what she, and I, had been through.

As my mother and I walked to the car from the train, a fresh breeze blew, a simple pleasure after a long trip. In the car, her eyes widened with fascination as though she were a child on her first road trip.

"Oh vat a niz strit" (Oh what a nice street), my mother observed, as we drove up to the apartment I shared with three girls who happened to be away that weekend. The modest apartment had a living room, dining nook, kitchen, two bathrooms and two bedrooms, each with two single beds.

My mother sat, reserved with a cup of tea. Finally, she looked up and cleared her throat before speaking.

"Vay you neet a psychologist?" she asked. "I don understand. I van you stop."

"Is this why you came to visit me?"

"How she help you?" my mother inquired.

"She listens to me and gives me advice," I said. "Kind of like a mother should."

"Dial hair number, den gimme da fon. I van to talk to hair."

I called. "Hi, Susan, it's me, Alix. My mother is here at my apartment. Yes, really. She wants to stop our sessions."

I handed my mother the phone and watched her in awe as she tried to be assertive, her face stern and her body straight as she put the phone to her ear.

"Halo. Yes. Dis is da muder," she said. "Duz she rily nit to see you zo much?"

"Yes, she does," Susan answered.

"Tree to four times a veek?"

"Yes."

There was a moment of silence.

"Oh, okay. Tank you. Bye."

As she hung up the phone, her face was blank, as though she didn't understand what she had just done. Falling apart inside, I sucked in the anguish. As she did not ask Susan how I was doing or why I needed therapy, her concern was questionable. I wanted my mother to ask anything, to show me she cared. Because she didn't ask a thing, I surmised someone else must have convinced her to visit and make that call, someone in control.

"Billy!" I thought. Billy must have yelled until my mother gave in—the usual family dynamic.

"Mom, why did you really come here?" I asked.

"Billy tot you don nit it." (Billy thought you didn't need to see a psychologist.)

Continuing the conversation was pointless because she was silent, her mission having been completed. Since she was in town, I took her on a tour of the campus and showed her the student dives my friends and I frequented. We stopped at Tony's for a slice of New York pizza and sat at a wooden communal table in front of a bay window with a view of the road. "That's the mayor," I said, pointing to a slovenly guy lying on a bus bench across the street.

"De mayor?"

"That's what everyone calls him."

A former university student, he had taken too much acid before diving deep into his own world. He had long, matted, dirty blonde hair and a beard, and he hadn't brushed his hair or teeth in years. He wore silver-mirrored sunglasses and stared out into the universe with a broad grin that beamed against his tan, leathered skin. He sat on the same bus bench every day listening to a large boom box while drinking beer. Rumor had it his parents supplied him with a daily six-pack of Coors. Existing on that bench like a "say no to drugs" neon sign, he was a permanent fixture, a daily reminder of what can happen when you party too hard.

"Vat a shame," my mother said.

"Yes, what a shame," I answered, thinking the mayor was not much different from Allan, who may have taken too much acid or other drugs in the sixties.

From what I learned in a psychology class, drugs can bring on mental illness if one has a predisposition to it. I also concluded my mother fit the profile of a schizophrenogenic mother, a psychiatric term that described her as someone who thinks in black-and-white, emitting narrow and rigid parental guidance while creating mental illness in children. This was an "Aha" moment.

The mayor and my brother were probably in university around the same time, when partying meant taking a variety of drugs that might include marijuana, cocaine, mushrooms, heroin and acid, taken in different combinations and all washed down with alcohol, before, during or after wild sex, sometimes with strangers—all the bygone era of the '60s.

I returned my mother to the train station after breakfast on Monday morning, relieved she was leaving. She stood on the platform and gave me a kiss goodbye as somber and serious as the one she gave me when she arrived. Watching her walk up the steps to the train headed back to Los Angeles, I waited for the metallic squeal, listening as the sound of the moving train faded into the distance.

The empty space around me was eerie. Alone, confused and desperate, I consolidated my understanding that my family could not be trusted. Sucking in the raw emotion I was left with that day, I took the hurt into my body as if a butcher had wrapped me up in brown paper and tied me up with string.

As I enjoyed the comforts of my home with Jack and the kids, my current family, I thought of the empty space that was my heart the day my mother left on the train. As my mind wondered in silence, I heard my mother's voice in my head, singing the classic "How much is that doggie in the window?" by Patti Page. Remembering her singing songs to me when I was little, I couldn't recall her ever reading me a book, not even simple book, even though she could read.

I must have been married for ten years when I read *Lyle the Crocodile* and some classic Shel Silverstein poems to Aidan when he was six years old—the most blissful part of my day. He yawned and closed his eyes, signaling me to turn off the light. I snuggled with him until he fell asleep. Listening to his breath deepen and turn into a light snore, I closed my eyes and felt into to the incredible love I had for my little sweet boy. While enjoying this perfect moment, fear suddenly came over me. I was overwhelmed, a fight or flight situation in which my life was in danger. My breath slowed. Something bad was going to happen! In that moment, I remembered what fear looked like.

Backpacking through Europe with my friend Claire after graduating with a bachelor's degree in journalism with an emphasis on public relations, I stood on an old wooden dock in Lake Geneva, Switzerland, staring out over the water. Still shell-shocked from the visit to Dachau concentration camp a few days earlier, I couldn't forget the black-and-white photo display of medical experiments performed on prisoners without anesthesia.

In 1933, a few weeks after Adolf Hitler was appointed Reich Chancellor, a concentration camp for political prisoners was set up in Dachau, a model for later concentration camps. In the twelve years of its existence, over 200,000 people were imprisoned there and in nearby camps, and 41,500 were murdered. On April 29, 1945, American troops liberated the survivors.

I considered myself a tough person, prepared for anything, but I wasn't able to handle the photos, the physical evidence, the testimonials, the ovens and the total inhumanity. The Germans were so thorough at documenting everything in photos and film that the past became all too real. I thought about the family I never had a chance to meet and what my life would have been like if they had survived.

In the Bavarian Beer Gardens that afternoon, I got drunk fast as the smell of hops and the live music soothed me after Dachau. Garek, the son of a friend of Claire's father, had joined us with a bunch of his friends. When he saw me so emotional and heard what kind of a day I had, he told me he was Jewish, which I later found out was a lie. He was a Christian. Possibly he wanted to sleep with me, hoping his lie might increase his chances, or maybe he just wanted me to make me feel better. I have to admit that the idea of another Jew in the beer garden did make me feel better.

I travelled to Lake Geneva with Claire the next day with a hangover. When we arrived at the train station, I bought a pack of cigarettes at a kiosk for fun. Neither Claire nor I smoked, but being in Europe where everyone else did, we wanted to partake. I was self-destructive as we watched dusk turn to dark at a jazz festival. I smoked cigarette after cigarette until the pack was empty. A few minutes later, I was stunned. When I tried to speak to Claire I couldn't move the left side of my face. Paralyzed from the stress of Dachau and the nicotine from the cigarettes, I had inhibited the circulation in half my face. The festival physician said there was nothing he could do. Aghast my face would be stuck forever, I cried. God, let me off with just a warning this time! Fortunately, my face returned to normal the next morning.

I felt a sense of relief my face wasn't paralyzed anymore. I smiled as I focused on the present and on Aidan who was in a deep sleep. When I stood up to return *Lyle the Crocodile* to the bookshelf, I experienced a deep pain in my gut that connected to an ache in my lower back. The strain continued to entrap me, a force so strong, it made me want to press the juice out of my eye-sockets. The pain reached up from my back and squeezed my solar plexus, grabbing and hurting me, before moving to my throat. Constricted, I choked as it stretched to my eyeballs, pressing on them from the back of my head. I thought I was going to faint, but didn't. This was an extraordinary time when I had a beautiful family and my life was wonderful on the outside. But inside I was a mess; strange physical and spiritual happenings arose and my subconscious was getting ready to show me more.

The swirling pain coincided with my weight gain. No matter how much I exercised or which healthy foods I ingested, I gained weight. I wore big loose jeans with the bottoms rolled up, thinking pants with cool cuffs would distract from my expanding body—I looked like a cow-beast. I also cried at inopportune times, my emotions unpredictable. Of course, Fred was a regular intruder as well, providing surprise experiences so I wouldn't forget him.

An image of Neda, the flower essence healer, came to me, giving me the nudge to returned to her shop for a Polarity Therapy massage focusing on Fred.

"I'm going to touch certain points on your back, connecting the energy between them and bringing peace to the area," Neda said. "I will also move that same energy down your legs."

"This is never going to work," I thought, wishing I had never come. Too late for me to hop off the table, I surrendered to the situation. A few minutes after she began touching points on my back, my entire body was flushed with a tingling sensation. An image formed in my mind's eye.

While I sat on my bed in my university apartment, reading a book late at night while my roommates slept, the phone rang.

"Alix, it's me, Billy. I need your help. I'm in jail. Can you bail me out? Bring $400 cash."

Intrigued as if I were part of a spy novel, I decided to come to his rescue.

"I'm at the Oxnard Police Station," he said.

"Oxnard?"

"Uh, yeah, I was driving north to visit you."

It was strange he would come to see me, when he had neither visited nor called me in years.

Taking directions over the phone from an officer at the station, I drove the dark roads to the nearest ATM and took money out at 2:30 a.m., all alone. My breath was still as I jumped back into my car, locking the doors.

Exiting the freeway, I found the square white building with a green neon sign that read POLICE. The glass door opened easily as I walked into a large, empty room with three black chairs. An officer sitting behind a thick glass window motioned me to approach.

"I am here to bail out Billy Resnick." After signing a document, I handed over the $400.

"What did he do?" I asked.

"Let's just say he was erratic. That's all I can tell you."

Twenty minutes later a metal door opened and two officers escorted Billy out. He looked different than the last time I had seen him. He had a mustache and long, light brown, wavy hair just like Barry Manilow's. He wore a half smile I didn't recognize.

"Hi," I said. "What were you doing up here?"

"I was on my way to see you."

"Me? This late?"

"Uh, yeah. Um, I wanted to surprise you."

In my gut, I sensed his words were a lie; nonetheless I was so glad to see a familiar face. "Do you want to get something to eat and see my apartment?" I asked.

"No, I'm going home now."

I noticed his face was sweaty and puffy, and his eyes were crazed, dark and piercing.

"You came all the way to see me and you are going home now?" I asked.

"Yes. Thanks for getting me out. Don't tell Mom. Oh, and do you have a few extra bucks so I can get something to eat on the way home?"

After I handed him some cash, he got into his car and drove away. He left me alone in the empty parking lot, like the butt of a joke I didn't understand. Why had he really come north, and why had my mother come just a few weeks before that? I wondered if there was a connection.

Aware I was still on Neda's massage bed, I spoke. "I remember something! My brother came up north and he called me from jail to bail him out. He said he was coming to see me, but he never had before. He didn't want to come over afterwards."

"What do you think it means?" Neda asked.

"I don't know, but there is some reason I am remembering this." As I went over the details in my head, all of a sudden, the pieces fell into place.

"I got it! He didn't call me because he never wanted anyone to know he was coming. He wanted to do something bad to me. Really bad! I think he was coming to kill me!" I needed to figure out why.

28

Extracurricular Bliss

One Saturday, I was driving Lola back from her acting class.
"Mom, who was your first boyfriend?"
"Noah."
"How old were you?"
"I was seventeen when it started and twenty when it ended."
"What happened to him?"

Hillary and Noah's wedding was the culmination and downfall of the best relationship I had ever known. Even though Noah and I had stayed together for a year after my European fling and his consequential one-night stand, the relationship ended probably because I had to grow up and learn from the experience. Noah was now with someone else, leaving me alone and devastated as though I had been jilted and left at the altar because she was the better choice. He was my first love and the most exciting and intelligent man I had ever met. He treated me well, always putting me first.

The wedding took place at the Beverly Wilshire Hotel where "Pretty Woman" was filmed, starring Richard Gere and Julia Roberts. Everything reminded me of the movie: the elegance, the music and the décor. The private ceremony was reserved for close family, and the newlyweds greeted their waiting guests afterwards at the reception. Noah was dashing and gorgeous in his tux, while Hillary, in my resentful and begrudging mind, was a gigantic tent of faded off-white, shimmering window drapes—her face was a blur, and her body was not nearly as hot as mine. Dying inside of jealousy and envy, I was miserable. Even if she was the nicest, most beautiful woman on the planet, I still would have hated her.

Although I'd had my hair done at Umberto's Salon earlier that afternoon, and looked stunning in my taupe outfit, sadness and regret overpowered me. Loving Noah meant I had no choice but to set him free. I sat at the fancy white and silver table with our Beverly Hills High friends and some assorted Europeans who were invited to the wedding because they happened to be in town.

"Why did they even invite me?" I asked myself. "And why did I accept?"

It was because of Noah that I took that trip to Europe when I graduated from high school. He wanted me to travel with my friends and have my own adventures, as he had done. My mother had promised me the trip as a graduation present before going off to university. All my friends were planning something special that summer.

"I need to send the check in today, Mom," I said. "You just need to fill out the emergency forms."

She was silent.

"The check, Mom?"

"I am not writink da check," my mother disclosed.

"Why not?"

"I changt my mind."

"You don't need to go to Europe," Billy interrupted. "You're staying home."

Billy was behind my mom's change of heart and I was destroyed. Betrayed once again by my family, I left home that afternoon, my bags packed. I stayed with Noah and his roommate in an apartment near Culver City spending most of the week crying.

"Why does she always promise me things she doesn't mean?" I asked God. "Why did she let me think I could go to Europe?"

When my mother made promises to me I believed her, and when I asked why she changed her mind, she said, "Because."

In spite of all the broken promises of the past, I still couldn't believe that she reneged on the trip I had been planning with my friend for the last six months. Noah had a huge heart and took matters into his own hands. He pulled out all the stops to make things right by going to my house and talking with my mother in person. He convinced her to follow through with her original promise, never knowing his support of my adventure would result in me slipping away from him.

At the airport, about to leave for Europe that summer, I watched my mother cry, surprised she cared enough to cry. "Was she thinking about me?" I wondered. "Or was she thinking about some past experience during the war?"

Upon arrival in Germany with my school friend Nora Middleton, we met up with our tour group "Experimental Travelling." Free and exhilarated, we climbed into our luxury tour bus and met Sven, a Swedish driver who doubled as our security guard. After a cruise along the Rhine River, we headed to our next destination. Our tour guide, Clara, an English-speaking Austrian woman, gave us details about the country's history and statistics.

"Will we see a concentration camp?" Cynthia asked in her southern drawl. A Baptist from Alabama, she was smiley, plump and wealthy. I had never seen a girl of 18 eat as much as she did in one sitting.

"I always wanted to see one of them places from the Holocaust," she continued.
'No. We won't be doing that."

"Why the hell not?" Cynthia asked. "That's history, ain't it?"

"Many people believe the Holocaust never happened," said Clara, who must have been oblivious to the fact that at least half of our tour group was Jewish.

"That's like saying there was never slavery in the South," Cynthia laughed.
"Are you trying to tell us the war and the Holocaust never happened?" I asked.

"Yes," Clara answered.

"It happened. Both my parents were there," I said. "Where were your parents, Clara?"

"How can you say something like that?" Tim Goldstein's voice echoed from a few rows back.

"It's the truth," Clara said.

Never in my life had I met someone who denied the Holocaust, an eye-opening experience that gave me a lot to think about. Tim and I became comrades as soon as we stepped off the bus. Upset by our guide, he called the tour company when we arrived at the next hotel to complain about Clara's revision of European history.

Tim was a second year law student, smart and handsome, with a moustache. Our warm friendship suffused with sexual desire hooked its claws into me when he was near. Tim became something I wanted to acquire, a challenge of sorts. Not once did I think about the repercussions of cheating on Noah. Naïve about the proper way to behave, I let my young hormones guide me as I began my life's journey. Trying to figure out what was normal, I didn't have the instincts to know how to treat those who were most important to me.

Noah called my hotel when the group was touring through France. He spoke to Cynthia.

"Oh Hi," she said. "Alix isn't here."

"Where is she?"

"With Tim. They went to Paris. They should be back bright and early tomorrow."

I forgot about home, Beverly Hills and my family. I was flying by the seat of my pants, just wanting to have a good time. After an elegant dinner and a burlesque show in Paris, Tim and I got a hotel room.

"How could you do that to Noah?" Lola screamed. "You should have known better."

"You are right. I made a lot of mistakes until I got it right."

"I will never cheat!" Lola announced.

Upon hearing I was off with another man, Noah reacted by sleeping with Fiona, a set designer. When I returned home from Europe, Noah and I attended the opening of a new film. When Noah and Fiona saw each other there, I could tell by their body language they had slept together. Luckily, Fiona wasn't a priority because Noah was still with me. However, Noah wanted me to choose between him and Tim.

"Take your time to decide," Noah said. "But, I won't wait forever."

I loved the attention from both men and I didn't want to give it up. I kept them both on a long leash for as long as I could and always wondered why they stayed. I lived in a world of betrayal, not thinking twice about their response. Not that I wanted to hurt anyone, it was just that two wonderful men made me feel so worthwhile, after so many of years of worthlessness. With a false sense of security, I didn't realize Noah was losing interest. We had both been dishonest. The trust was gone.

Had I been older and wiser, raised with parental guidance, I may have gone on a different path. For years, I believed my cheating to be the biggest mistake of my life—hurting Noah, the one person who had my back. This was a lesson I had to learn. It taught me about loyalty and treating each other with respect, a standard I didn't learn at home. Home was the place where everyone lied.

On the other hand, breaking up with Noah had to happen. Otherwise, I would never have married Jack and had my angels, Lola and Aidan.

Before Noah proposed to Hillary, we had a talk.

"Your family," Noah said sincerely. "That would be difficult."

"I know," I said. "You don't need to take that on. It's my problem. You deserve better."

I left Noah's wedding with Alejandro, a hot Latin music producer I had met once or twice. I drowned myself in gin and tonics and chased them with cocaine, my torment and insecurity buried. Ending up in his bed, I numbed the pain with sex, which kept me afloat as my mind swam against the currents forcing me down to the darkest parts of the sea. My life looked beautiful on the surface, glorious and abundant, but when I dove down into the depths there was no light, only those frightening glow-in-the-dark fish.

"Mom!" Lola yelled. "How could you?"

"It's good luck for the bride and groom!"

"What do you mean?"

"Well, when your dad and I were married in the 150-year-old Renaissance-style mansion in Chicago, our best man, Daniel, and my friend, Ella, had sex in one of the upstairs dressing rooms."

"How do you know?" Lola asked.

"They were bright red and shiny as they returned down the staircase before the cake was served. It was obvious. They had gotten so hot and heavy having sex that they broke an antique lamp and a window shade in the dressing room."

"Oh my God," Lola said. "What did daddy say?"

"He smiled and said it was good luck!"

29
Hidden Threads

The brown dress came from Marshall Field's department store in Chicago. I first saw it on a rack among the new fall fashions. When I tried it on, it fit perfectly, exposing just a little skin here and there, remaining modest, yet attractive. Made in India from light gauzy cotton, with buttons all the way down the front, the dress hugged me on top and flowed gently from the waist to the middle of my shins. The soft fabric was lovely, trendy and hip, covered with tiny flowers in lavender and navy. I could have worn the brown dress at an ashram in India or on "Little House on the Prairie."

The girls on "Little House" would have worn the dress completely buttoned. I opened the top and bottom buttons just enough to be modest or sexy, depending on my mood. I could show my neck, but not my cleavage. And at the bottom of the skirt, I could open the buttons to show my boots and just a hint of leg. I felt comfortable, cute and sometimes a tease in this dress!

My new brown dress was chic everywhere—cool in Chicago where I was living at the time, and very cool in Beverly Hills when I went home to visit. It even held its own in New York where I found the perfect accent scarf at the Columbus Avenue flea market. The dress also encompassed the Seattle grunge look arising out of the bands of Kurt Cobain, Pearl Jam and the Counting

Crows. The dress was the height of fashion.

I found the perfect low-heeled, dark chocolate, knee-high lace-up boots, adding another identity to the magic brown dress. Designed by Kenneth Cole and costing $350—the most expensive I had ever purchased—the boots had metal brackets that looked tough and military.

Wearing the brown dress and boots I was anonymous, incognito and unattainable, an enigmatic mystery with my long brown hair blown straight, framing my face and cascading down my back.

As I stood in front of my 100-year-old West Rogers Park building in Chicago, I raised my arm for a cab to the airport. In the ivy-covered, three-story, mansion-like apartment building, Jack and I rented the second floor apartment from an artsy, retired couple. We had three bedrooms, a guest room, breakfast room, sunroom, kitchen and a den; a living room with an elaborate family crest on the fireplace, a dining room and two bathrooms, all connected to an oval hallway that made the square building seem round.

When my job took me to New York on business, I walked into the airport terminal pulling my suitcase along. The gauzy fabric against my skin made me smile. A soft breeze nestled the dress against my body.

I had moved to Chicago to live with Jack, and was fortunate to find a great design job. This was an adventure, living in another state, the windy city and starting life anew. Driving two hours to work in the snow, I loved the change of seasons and a culture rich with music, food and festivals. And yet a subconscious, existential cord tugged at me to return home to Beverly Hills for a visit, an awareness I listened to even though the pilgrimage would be complicated.

Home meant anxiety and fear, and for that reason, while in L.A., I kept my social life separate. I was anxious to return to L.A. to feel its energy, see my friends and my familiar restaurants and shops. A car and my credit cards were all I needed to be free in the town that had held me as a psychological hostage. I was independent now, with a successful career, a boyfriend who loved me, and abundant drive and energy.

Open to all energies that took me to a better place, I saw no cap on happiness, figuring out, one layer at a time, that I could free myself from the ropes that bound me. No longer was I struggling in that fast-moving river, my head pulled under by the current toward an empty, sordid black hole. Instead, I safely walked alongside that river, careful not to get wet.

"Beverly Hills couldn't be that bad a place to grow up," Jack said, and he was right. If it weren't for all my wealthy friends, their over-the-top desires and quality drugs, I would not have been able to escape my absurd home life. Cocaine helped me shine on the outside while forgetting the nightmare I called home. It was a crutch that worked. When I was able to love myself more, the need for the crutch and my craving for it subsided. I was lucky that my coke experimentation didn't lead to addiction. I do not encourage people to use drugs as a means of escape, as they only hinder the healing.

I was on my way home to see my family, like an abused wife coming back home to her husband one more time. I decided to go home, crazy as it was, in hopes the situation would have evolved and changed.

Driving from LAX like a robot, emotions buried, I pretended a family was waiting to heal the holes in my soul. I went home to Beverly Hills with childlike faith that things would be different. Faith was what kept my mom going during the war and faith was what motivated me to keep trying to have a healthy family. Finally, I drove up the stone driveway to the picture-perfect house surrounded by trees and blooming flowers.

I had to believe everything would be okay. I got out of the car, grabbed my luggage and stopped to take a breath, preparing myself for what might be in store for me on the other side of the front door.

"Mom! I'm hungry! Bring me some food," I heard Allan yell as I walked inside. "Ve all go for diner," my mother said. Billy chose a restaurant thirty minutes away in the Palms area. Although I didn't want to travel so far for dinner, I agreed to drive, not wanting to see either Billy or Allan go into a rage.

Any conversation with my brothers kept me on the defensive, an accepted *family trait from which I needed to escape. In those days when I felt trapped, I used cocaine, sniffing a few lines to feel better. It cost about $120 a gram and seemed worth every penny to rid myself of the negativity in exchange for the illusion of normalcy. An appreciated side effect of cocaine was that it made me feel full and I lost weight.*

"This restaurant is cheap," Billy bragged.

"How's the food?" I asked.

"Oh, I'm sure iz very goot" my mother said.

"You're so cheap, Billy, I want to throw up," Allan yelled.

"F*** you! Who do you think you are? You're nothing special. What do you do for the family?"

The banter went on like static on a broken radio. I blocked them out to focus on the road.

"Oh vat a beautiful vide strit," my mother exclaimed, acting as though she were on a sightseeing tour.

"It's so empty for a Friday night," I said pulling up in front of the restaurant.

Once inside, we all ordered the special. The waitress set down the warm plates. I thought the worst had passed until I tasted the food. As bland as the décor, the soggy pasta was covered with what looked like canned tomato sauce topped with orange, oily melted cheese. The overcooked vegetables were accompanied by a dry, chewy chicken breast. As I attempted to swallow, I thought about Valentino, the Italian waiter with whom I had lived. He would bring home dinner from Toni's Italian Kitchen—al dente pasta and crisp, grilled veggies with a hint of extra virgin olive oil and herbs.

As we left the restaurant, I noticed Allan and Billy's eyes were glossy and watery as though they were medicated, trying to walk upright. Their potbellies rested on their thin legs as they balanced themselves like "Weebles" and hobbled to the car.

I drove home and passed the women's gym where, many nights a week, I worked out as a teenager so I wouldn't have to go home. I blinked to refocus as dusk turned dark, my life force seeming to drain out the car like a bad oil leak, leaving a trail that stained the road.

The constant arguing from the back seat was nothing out of the ordinary. Billy and Allan sounded like white trash druggies who had forgotten their grammar. Allan fumbled over his words, with spit flying out his mouth. After having smoked crack for too many years, Billy spouted attitude and little else.

"He is not the same," I remembered my mother uttering under her breath after Billy stole the rest of her jewelry and the vacuum cleaner. The streetlights blurred as they reflected off the glossy windows of Saks Fifth Avenue and Neiman Marcus on Wilshire Boulevard. The remainder of the ride home was uneventful and I collapsed into bed.

"The apple doesn't fall far from the tree" was a phrase I hated, because I was a different color apple from anyone in my family. I was like my father, a go-getter. I must have a lot of him in me—inspired ideas, family first, building for the future. I could forgive our dog for peeing on the carpet, Jack for forgetting to take out the trash, Aidan for watching "Family Guy" instead of reading, Lola for using my makeup without asking, but I didn't know how to forgive my father for dying and leaving me to deal with a mess.

30
Soulful Secrets

*V*alentino, my Italian boyfriend, was the rebound relationship after Noah. When we first met, he was the headwaiter at Mange, a popular Italian restaurant in downtown Los Angeles where his twin, Enio, bused tables. Celebrating his new employment, he hosted a late-night party at his West Hollywood apartment. An array of beautiful people, artists and designers, chefs, models and entertainment executives, many of whom had foreign accents, gathered to enjoy a variety of homemade pastas and fine wine. As the party began to dissolve late that Saturday night, I put on my coat and said my good-byes. The brightly colored lights were shining through the rain as I headed home.

Wired from the accoutrements, cocaine and marijuana joints that had been served after dinner, I watched the windshield wipers slide across the glass as the rain poured down. The streetlights shined white and yellow as my hands moved the steering wheel back and forth as though I were someone else driving somewhere else. Sidetracked, I found myself off course and in an older neighborhood with smaller, Spanish- and Craftsman-style homes. Browsing the homes as if window-shopping I had déjà vu, remembering my mother bringing me to this neighborhood when I was small.

A car crept around the corner toward me as the rain fell harder. The tires *plowed through the water, forcing it up the sides of the vehicle into a misty frame for the devil himself.*

"Shit, it's him." I forced myself to exhale. It was Billy in his dark blue jeep.

He slowed down as if he were looking for a house number. Dim figures moved toward his car like hungry cockroaches in the dark.

"He's looking for a prostitute," I acknowledged in disgust.

Speeding up to get away, I made the next right turn.

I hightailed it to Dr. Marie's office first thing the next morning hoping to release the negative emotion this jam jar full of new memories was bringing up. Her light touches on my back turned the light gray of my mind's eye to lavender. The six men and eight women in my writers' group came to mind, the sounds of their voices, a symphony as I marveled at our connection and determination to spread trust, love and creativity.

"Turn over," Dr. Marie said.

She touched the points on the tops of my feet before lifting my back from underneath, pressing points on the sides of my spine before gently letting me down. She brushed the sides of my head and shoulders in a swift motion. I jumped and shivered, reaching a different level in my healing, a shift in my being, a spiritual promotion.

"Okay, we are done for today," she said. "How are you feeling?"

"Uncomfortable," I said. "It's like I've been sliced in half, and two different sides of me are competing."

"I want to show you something," Dr. Marie said.

She opened a book to a marked page of caveman drawings; a line was connecting their minds to each other's hearts. "This represents the higher-mind of love and friendship," she said. She then turned to the next page of similar cavemen, a line connecting their minds to each other's groins. "This represents the lower-minded places of rules and taboos." Suddenly, it became clear as to why I was dropping friends that didn't mesh with the new more heart-centered me. They were no longer on my spiritual path. I had become a different person.

You have a choice of which world you want to live in, hence, the two different sides you are feeling right now."

At home at 12:30 a.m., I couldn't fall asleep. I put in my meditation CD and began the breathwork. Spirits appeared in my mind's eye, small images of all ages from different time periods in agony were trying to tell me something. An image of me at seven years old came into view. I was sitting in a chair with my mouth covered with black duct tape. Billy came toward me with a blindfold. He put it over my eyes and tied it in the back. The image disappeared.

The next morning as I went about my day disturbed by the image from the night before. I was aware of the two sides of myself, clear and distinct, needing to fuse together. Having re-experienced so much of what had been hiding deep inside my body and mind, I wanted to integrate those parts with the rest of me; my childhood was now ready to mesh with my current life. At the same time Fred grew larger, a big black spot protruding from my lower back, radiating down the side of my left leg.

Then, a strange thing happened. My pelvis would spontaneously move back and forth throughout the day as though I were dancing with the pain, moving my hips from side to side, forwards and backwards, and in a circular rotation. These movements occurred while sitting, standing and driving. I went deeper within the hurt, until it hurt "so good." The energy within me was changing.

"Fred, are you ready to move on and allow me to become one with you?" I asked.

There were brief moments I didn't feel Fred and luxuriated in the emptiness of my sacrum. But just when I tapped into that euphoria, Fred would show up again, fierce and swollen, radiating a current so strong I wanted to vomit.

Instinctively, I began the breathwork. Sending my breath toward his core like a spear, I punctured Fred, energy releasing as if he were a balloon popped by a pin, his blood spilling fast. I sat up in horror as my body convulsed, the energy rising up into my throat. A vision came in through the darkness.

Billy's form materialized in my mother's bedroom. I was sitting in a chair, a young child in the darkness, with a scarf tied around my eyes. Able to see through the thin material of the blindfold, I saw Billy ripping a piece of duct tape. He covered my mouth. I struggled and screamed with all my might, with no one to hear me.

I sat up in horror wanting to throw myself against a wall.

"It's okay Alix, it's just a memory. It's not real. You're okay," I told myself.

At the time I was working in Jack's office in the accounting department. While plugging in numbers, I became an emotional wreck, crying off and on for days, the tears gifting me an energetic release. Then, something strange happened. Fred began to change in shape and texture, becoming solid and sharp, while the universe gave me signals through dreams, heightened intuition and body sensations that a new realm was opening up for me. I was connected to spirit.

Dr. Marie touched my feet, underneath my back and brushed my sides. A few minutes later the energy in my mind's eye changed shape. Fluffy balls of yellow and orange swirled and formed a vortex. This vortex grew out of me into a supersized funnel. A black blob with crinkly edges appeared at the top of the funnel and rolled around the top like a ball on a roulette wheel going round and round, then began to transform into a headless man in a black cape, a sinister creature reminiscent of the "Dementor" who tried to kill Harry Potter by taking his breath away.

Flying round and round the funnel, the headless man descended. He looked like a court judge in his black leather shoes and classic attire. Then, as if a toilet flushed, he was sucked into a black hole at the bottom. Beautiful streams of yellow and orange oozed out of the black hole and turned into flower petals. A large human hand full of light and energy came forth and touched me.

Had I been I touched by the hand of God? Thinking about the headless man for days, I went to see Loretta, the EFT therapist, to ask what she thought.

"You have just released yourself from male judgment," she revealed.

Surprised, I felt free.

The next day, my mother was scheduled for a small surgical procedure at Cedars Sinai hospital. As I drove her to the appointment, the image of Billy having tied me up to shut me up was clear in my mind. Wanting to tell her everything, the timing wasn't right. Pressing on, we walked into the hospital admiring the original artwork exhibited on every wall when we happened upon a woman sitting at the admissions desk—Lewanda, an overweight and jolly African American woman with a luscious head of wavy hair. She was wearing a black cotton dress with an orange honeysuckle print.

"Have a seat," she said, pointing to the chairs in front of her desk.

"Name, please?" she asked.

"Nahama Resnick," my mother said.

"Wow, Nahama? That's a hot name, girl. I could say that name all day long. Nahama, Nahama," she said, making my mother smile.

As I sat there, I thought about the conversation my mother and I had that morning.

"Zo, vat you dit on de veekend?" my mother asked.

"I've been doing work on myself, trying to get rid of the pain in my back."

"Like a medication?"

"No, no drugs. It's mostly a breathwork meditation. I can remember things I couldn't remember before."

"Vat kind of tinks?"

"Shocking things I had locked up in my body. Don't you still have memories that are all locked up?"

"Vell, before de Nazis took us avay dat day, my muder med sure I vas vearing a sveater. Imagine, she vas vorried if I hed a sveater. Vell, she was a muder. Of course.... ... a sveater ... I remember dat." (Well, before the Nazis took us away that day, my mother reminded me to take my sweater. Imagine, she was worried that I didn't have a sweater.)

I pictured my grandmother, whom I had never met, handing her that sweater. They would never see each other again.

"I worked on my book, too," I told my mother.

"Vell, if I wrote a book dere vould be no paper left. Who vanz to reat abat tragedy?"

"Are you kidding me? There are libraries filled with books about the Holocaust. Everyone's story is important. Steven Speilberg even sponsored a research project to save all the history. You didn't want to be part of that, remember?"

"I dunno. I couldn't."

"You did something just as good. You let us video you speaking about your life, which couldn't have been very easy."

"No, it vas hart. Very, very hart."

"Any valuables you would like the hospital to hold for you, Nahama?" Lewanda asked.

Putting her hand on my leg, my mother said, "She is my only valuable."

A shiver went through my body, a spiraling back into all I had been through up to that point, grief mixed with relief.

"Is she all you have left?" Lewanda asked.

"Yes."

When I returned home, it was late. I sat down on the couch and began the breathwork, inhaling into my stomach and upper chest, letting the air out before remembering more.

When I was twenty-nine years old, single, living and working in Chicago, I visited my mother in Beverly Hills and stayed in the Spanish house. As I sat in the powder room of the master bathroom applying make-up and brushing my hair, the vibrations, memories and fears within the house swirled around me once again. The longer I stayed inside, the worse I felt.

Before going out with Stella, my girlfriend of ten years, I locked the bathroom doors, closed the two tiny windows, and pulled down the lace shades. I pulled a small paper package out of my make-up bag and opened it. Using the edge of my Gap credit card, I lifted a little cocaine to prepare a line on a lavender-colored tile. Turning on the faucet to block out the sound, I inhaled the powder with a rolled-up hundred-dollar bill. It was just enough to take the edge off, give me energy and help me forget.

I was dressed in flared black pants and a sleeveless vest that showed off my lean, tan arms. Underneath I wore a sleeveless white T-shirt, turning the sexiness down a notch, covering up my cleavage, leaving something to the imagination. Jack bought me that outfit while we were dating, something I never would have bought for myself.

Glistening in the light, my brown hair accented my dark features as I put on red and black platform shoes and grabbed my purse. At the front door, Billy walked up and stood in front of me.

"Wow," he said. "You look great."

As though my breath had been caught in a zipper, I was made uncomfortable by his presence. Walking past him without getting too close, I wanted to shove him into the wall along with that creepy look he was giving me, that look that men give women sometimes when they imagine them naked. "You are not supposed to look at me that way, big brother," I thought.

One night after dinner, Jack and I were watching the thriller series "24" on television when I felt a heaviness pinning me down, forcing me to remain on the couch. As I tried to act normal and enjoy the program, I began to cough and gag over and over again. An energy was stuck in my throat and getting larger.

"Are you okay?" Jack asked.

"I don't know. Something's happening to me."

"You've been coughing and hacking like crazy. What's going on?"

"This is worse, strong now. Can't stop it. Need to be alone. Get out, please, get out!"

Jack walked out of the den and moved to the living room, giving me the space I needed.

As I tried to free my throat, I was struggling as if an invisible man were choking me, squeezing hard and refusing to let go. Afraid of what was happening, I had no choice but to give in and choke. A power kept me sitting upright, and in my mind's eye, I felt a scarf being tied around my eyes. A large, long object was going in and out of my mouth in a repetitive motion, a grown man's penis, large and veiny, the tip of which was jarring the back of my throat causing me to choke, my neck thrusting hard backward.

"Please stop," I gasped in my head. "I'm going to die if you don't stop."

Not knowing what was going on, I thought someone was trying to kill me. My breath had been taken away.

In my mind's eye, as though I were above and looking down, I saw David Elliott's dog, Buffy, jump up on her doggie bed. She looked up at me as though she were trying to connect, comforting me, before I had to endure anymore.

My mind went back. I was sitting on my bed in my mom's room alone, having a nice time laughing and playing dress-up with her clothes. Someone came in and spun me around while I was laughing. Usually playing alone, I was so happy to have someone there, someone familiar, spinning me toward him. Finally, I was up against him and a scarf was wrapped around my head, covering my eyes. Tricking me into thinking it was all part of a dress-up game, Billy had caught me, blindfolded me and scared me by not letting me see. Suddenly, I was gagging and couldn't breathe.

"Get this thing out of my mouth," I yelled in my head.

"HELP! Why won't someone help me?"

Despite probing my memory, I couldn't remember what happened next.

31
Off Cloud 9

The days following were like no other days, as I was a walking contradiction. On the one hand, my body was light, open and flexible, a heavy weight having been lifted. On the other hand, I was in shock from staring the inexcusable in the face. Feeling disgusting and unworthy on an emotionally level, I wanted to disappear. I even wondered why Jack wanted to stay married to me, a woman who had at one time been thought of as just the bottom of the barrel, the crap no one cared about.

The more I tried to forget, the more often the memory returned. Shortness of breath, pain in my chest and fear I would die were all symptoms I was experiencing, the shock of what I thought could never have happened. "Incest!" echoed in my head. Sick to my stomach, I needed to overcome these haunting thoughts. I went to see Loretta hoping EFT would help.

Over a period of a few weeks, Loretta honed in on the associations of worthlessness I had made about myself. Visualizing the most negative moments, while little by little bringing in better feeling thoughts, I tapped a sequence on my hand, face, chest and body with the fingers of my right hand. Afterward, the debilitating emotional charge became distant. I could recall what happened without feeling bad about myself. Major relief was achieved.

When I returned home from my EFT session, Jack, Lola and Aidan were in the den looking at a spider in a web spun between the staircase and the CD cabinet. The magnificent spider had a fuzzy head, and a large white spot that looked like a third eye in the center of his forehead. In awe of its presence, we admired his marvelous body and unique shade of brown. The spider was still. He stared back at us when Lola, who was futzing with Aidan's Nerf gun, without warning, shot off a pellet. We gasped as we saw the spider hang limp from his web.

Our innocent curiosity that evening ended in a violent jolt. The entire incident made me wonder about violence, and if I had inadvertently passed on negative energies to my children, who started having scary feelings like the ones I used to have. They felt scared when they were happy. As a result, I took them to Dr. Ruth to get a few NSA entrainments until the scary feelings cleared. Then I treated myself to a session and remembered more.

Lying in bed in my West Hollywood apartment when I was twenty-six, I couldn't move. I had just returned from a trip to Mexico, where I caught a virus that depleted my energy. Dizzy, sweaty and weak, I called my mother as a last resort, her love only materializing when I was sick.

Still afraid to hear Allan and Billy's voices, my body tensed as I anticipated who would answer the phone. I was relieved it was my mother.

"I'm really sick," I said. "I can barely move. I can't go to the store."

"I vill come right avay," she said.

She arrived within the hour, straightened up my apartment, made me tea and toast, and walked to the grocery store. Bringing me fresh fruits, she also cut up vegetables and served them along with a fresh piece of broiled salmon. She made a hearty meal, and my body was grateful for the nutrients. She always made sure I had food. Whatever else happened to me didn't really matter.

"Mom? Did either of your sons ever do anything to me that they shouldn't have?" I asked her as we were driving to my house.

"Vel," she said "It vas always lout (loud) in da home. It vas like a var (war) dere." As she thought back, she cracked a strange, endearing half-smile as if she were missing the good old days, an expression that made me shiver.

Later, we were sitting at the seven-foot long wooden dining table where my mother was perusing Time magazine. On the opposite end of table, I was engrossed in thought and typing on my computer. She looked up and asked, "Doink billz? You hev lot of pepers der." (Doing bills? You have lots of papers there.)

"No, I'm typing a book about growing up in your house. You know, Mom, I would feel better about everything if you would apologize."

"Apoligiz? For vat?"

"Letting your sons abuse me."

"Vell, der vas a var going on in dat house," (Well there was a war going on in that house,) she said. "Lotz of d screamin."

I remembered all the screaming when I was about eight years old.

I was wearing a frilly nightgown and afraid Billy was going to hurt me. Instead of punishing him, my mother slapped me for crying.

"I still deserve an apology."

"I diden know."

"So you say. Ignorance is not an excuse for sin."

"Okay, Mom, this is what a normal mother might say to me: 'I am sorry for letting Allan terrify you day and night. I am sorry that I didn't look for better options like a boarding school. I'm sorry I didn't protect you."

I looked straight at her, pinning her into a corner with my eyes, waiting for my truth to be acknowledged by the person who could have prevented it.

"Okay," she said. "I apilgiz."

As though the rats underneath the house were standing on their hind legs playing trumpets, I was satisfied.

"I accept your apology."

32
Fragrant Fedora

Worried about being late to Dan's funeral, my mother made me nervous, pacing back and forth. Once in the car, I kicked my Mario Andretti-like driving skills into gear. We arrived an hour early.

The Orthodox rabbi dressed in black wore a fedora. The tassels of his white, cape-like prayer shawl fluttered as he began his sermon.

My Polish great-grandfather must have looked like this rabbi, gray hair and a long beard, dressed in a black suit, with a black hat covering his head to honor God.

I remember my mother describing him. She said, "Mine granfader didn hev to do anytink. He hed d bakery unda buildingz. Mine granmoder did all d biznis. He drank vudka after dinner, spiritus, and vent out to davin (pray). He was always davinin, davinin...." (My grandfather didn't do anything except drink Vodka and pray. My grandmother did all the work at the bakery and the buildings.)

As I stared at the Rabbi who had similar dark features as me, I imagined the past from stories I had heard over the years.

"Go buy da flour from da mill," my great-grandmother yelled. *"Ve nit to mek*

da dough!"

A frustrated, introverted scholar hiding behind his long white beard, my great-grandfather was annoyed. He sat at the table in the far corner of the room while his twelve grandchildren played outside his window. He looked up from his book. "Im readink! Leaf me alon, vife!" (I'm reading. Leave me alone wife.)

"Go, now! Odervise ve vill hev no bred. Ven you finish, you nit to chop de vood for de fire."

When her back was turned, my great-grandfather grabbed his books from the table—the Talmud (central text of rabbinic Judaism) in its many interpretations. He carried the books with both hands as he walked toward the village square, his back bent over, until he reached the jail. When he opened the jail door, he saw his best friend, Yehuda, sitting at an old wooden desk.

"Ah, Lazer! Vat brinks you here?"

"Yehuda! Lock me up vit da key zo I hev quiet vit da books. My vife, she von leaf me alon. I can stant da houz noizy mit de kinder." (Lock me up with my books. My wife won't leave me alone. I can't stand the noise in the house with all the children.)

A good friend and a religious man himself, Yehuda opened the first jail cell and in walked my great-grandfather.

"Tank you very much, Yehuda!"

Locking the gate behind him, Yehuda walked away, carrying the key.

"You are velcome, my friend!"

"If you see mine vife, tell hair I vas arrested!"

As I listened to the rabbi's funeral words about Dan's last days, I remembered the last time I saw Dan. It all started with Reuben.

One summer afternoon when I was nine years old, I walked to Thrifty's Drug Store with Reuben, my neighbor from a few doors down. Reuben and I tried out gadgets, goo, gels, toys and eyeglasses before chasing each other down the aisles.

While Reuben ran off to sporting goods, I sampled the perfumes in cosmetics, loving the shapes of the bottles. My favorite was the old-fashioned squeeze ball kind the actresses in the old black-and-white movies kept on their dressers. I tested one of the bottles, sniffing my wrist afterward, which made my nose itch. The pungent scent had given me a brilliant idea.

"When Reuben comes around the corner, I'll spritz him!"

I hid the perfume bottle behind my back and watched Reuben in the convex mirror in the corner of the store. Boiling over with anticipation, I waited. "Hey, where have you been?" he yelled. "I just spilled slime on aisle five."

I whipped out the perfume bottle, aimed the small nozzle at Reuben, and squeezed the ball quick and firm over and over as if I were firing a machine gun, spreading a fine mist over him. Losing his balance, he fell back against the WD40 cans, his eyes wide with disbelief.

As I ran back to the perfume aisle, a well-powdered and stiff saleswoman with her hair pulled back in a bun stood behind the perfume counter, dressed in a black woven suit with large gold buttons. Her blood-red lips and matching long nails looked eerie, like lobster claws, as she rang up a customer.

As I caught my breath, I returned the perfume bottle to its rightful place. Satisfied and elated, I had one-upped my friend, the same friend who once locked me in his tree house before throwing in smoke bombs. Gasping for air, I was lucky to have made it out alive!

I walked the aisles and looked for Reuben, hoping he wasn't too angry. Turning the corner, I ran smack dab into someone. Startled, I looked up at Dan, Emilia's husband, who was staring down at me with a wide smile, his teeth so white they reflected the metal frame of his eyeglasses. He was tall with dark hair and pale white skin, the kind of skin that would tan if he would ever lie out in the sun. Even though he was handsome and had a gentle demeanor, he scared the hell out of me.

"Hi there!" he said. "How are you?"

I stood frozen wanting to run away. I didn't trust him.

Dan and Emilia dined at our house numerous times, expressing their sympathies to my mother for being a Holocaust survivor and having sons with mental illness. Like most of my mother's friends, they disregarded me, a fact that made me hate them. Never did I understand why no one had the courage to ask about me. I wasn't an issue. This way they couldn't be held accountable for sweeping me under the rug, a fact that reminded me some Polish people looked away when the Nazis took their Jewish neighbors.

I saw Reuben at the far end of the store near the pharmacy and ran toward him. "Bye, Dan. Gotta go!"

We walked to Beverly Drive skipping over the cracks in the concrete, and joking about anything that came to mind. We happened upon a little shop with a green awning. The sign read "Beverly Hills Cheese Shoppe".

"Wow, what a yummy smell!" I exclaimed. "It's making me hungry."

The sales lady saw us standing outside. "Would you two like a sample?" she asked.

"Sure!" I said.

Following her inside, she led us to a refrigerated display featuring cheeses of all shapes, sizes and textures.

"What kind of cheese would you like?"

"That one," I said, pointing to a white cheese that looked like something my mother would buy.

"Ah, the hard white goat cheese. Good choice," she said.

"And you, sir?"

"I'd like a slice of your stinkiest cheese. I always wanted to know how the most stinky cheese in the world would taste."

"Well, the stinkiest cheese would probably be this imported yellow Limburger."

The sales woman sliced off a piece of each with a sharp knife. She then wrapped the Limburger and goat cheese in thin white paper.

"Here you go," she said, handing us the samples.

Once out of the store, I tasted my cheese. "Yum! This is good."

While I was enjoying the flavor, Reuben grabbed my arm tight, pinning me back as he rubbed the Limburger cheese all over my shirt, pants, and hair with all his might, making sure the stench was absorbed.

Standing tall even though he was short, Reuben, also quite stinky, felt wicked and satisfied he had one-upped me. We both laughed.

"We'd better go home," I said. "We smell!"

33
Fetus and Fins

B illy and Allan saw a female psychologist, Sheri Wagner, who told them she
wanted to give her old clothes to charity. Billy brought them home in brown
paper bags and gave them to my mother, as though he were doing her a favor.
When I came to visit, my mother would dip into her bag as though she were
pulling a rabbit out of her hat.

"Here, dis iz for you," she said.

"No, thank you."

I hated the idea she was hoarding someone's old clothes and wondered if my
family could get any weirder. In Poland before the war, my mother had a large,
extended family that passed down clothes. A young girl would be thrilled to
receive a hand-me-down from an older cousin. Never mind we lived in Beverly
Hills, California. I watched my mother behave as if she was still poor. The
older she got, the farther back she regressed, until she acted as though she was
back in a Polish shtetl. She often reminded me of an article I had read entitled
"Manhattan Mystery," in which a bag lady, a Jewish Holocaust survivor, hid
the fact that she was loaded. When she died she had over $200,000 dollars in the
bank, which she willed to the Hebrew University in Israel. She and my mother
probably shared survivor guilt. They lived when others died and for this reason

didn't deserve their wealth. They also may have feared if they showed their wealth, it would be taken away.

When Jack and I were living in Israel, we went to the Red Sea near the Eilat for a weekend. On this bright sunny day, we wore wet suits and swam alongside the dolphins. One dolphin swam up and bit down on my arm, holding tight. Then he loosened his grip and swam away. When I came out of the water, our guide said dolphins only hold onto people when the person is pregnant. They can hear the small heart beat.

"That's funny," I said. "I wish I were pregnant. The dolphin probably just heard my stomach growl."

I earned a masters degree in Science Management from Boston University at the Tel Aviv campus while running the family business from abroad. I had hired a competent manager in Los Angeles. Everything seemed to be fine until Billy hired a lawyer, Mr. Eric Orin, in an attempt to acquire everything.

He convinced Mr. Orin he should manage the family business, bringing Allan and my mother on board with his plan. The lawyer asked me to give up control and relinquish all documents. His letter had a signature that looked like my mother's. When I called her, she said she couldn't talk. She sounded under duress. Concerned, I booked the next flight out to L.A.

As soon as I landed, I drove to Beverly Hills in a rental car. No one answered the doorbell so I tried my house key. The locks had been changed.

"We are not letting you in," Billy yelled from the other side of the door. "You don't belong here anymore. We decided you are not part of this family."

I took a few steps back and looked up at the breakfast room window where my mother was standing, dressed in a frilly, flowered housedress in front of my brothers with only a window screen between us. Billy, Allan and my mother stared out at me like a weird version of the painting "American Gothic." Allan and Billy turned around to walk away.

"Mom, what is going on?" I yelled looking up at her.

"It has to be like dis," she said. "I can talk." (can't.)

For some reason my mother couldn't say "can't" so she always said "can," no matter what.

Whatever system the three of them had in place enraged me, fanning the flames of courage. Determined to take charge, I found a reasonably priced hotel room. From the hotel room, I called friends and acquaintances for suggestions of a good lawyer until I found Seth Bergman in Century City. He immediately understood my predicament and encouraged me to tell him every gory, crazy detail.

An hour before meeting him in person, I was nauseated. My period was late. I purchased a pregnancy test kit and opened it in a public restroom. I peed on the stick and soon pink lines appeared pointing to YES! Ecstatic, I ran to a phone booth and called Jack long distance.

"I can't talk long," I said. "I'm meeting the lawyer. I peed on a stick. It says I'm pregnant! The dolphin in the Red Sea was right!"

Happy as could be, Jack encouraged me to make a doctor's appointment so we would be sure.

At Seth Bergman's office, the pregnancy results lingering in my head, I answered his questions as he grilled me for two hours as though I were on the witness stand. He made sure I was for real and not out for myself. When he was satisfied, he had his secretary bring me papers to sign, stating he would represent me.

I went back to my mother's house, thinking the news of a grandchild might change the spirit of things. Ringing the doorbell, I saw my mother's brown eye through the peephole.

"I can open the door," she said. (can't)

"I'm pregnant," I said.

She was silent, the eye still staring.

"Why should I tell you I am pregnant?" I said. "I never mattered to you, did I?"

I returned to the hotel and called Lucy.

"You're pregnant? Do you have a doctor?"

"No."

"Tomorrow after breakfast, you are staying with us! I insist. I'll find an obstetrician. You need rest!"

Staying with Lucy, I nourished myself and worked with my lawyer by phone. The first part of the plan was to have a meeting with my lawyer and Billy's, my mother and me. That way we could state our grievances and reach a decision. Scared and anxious on the meeting day, I called my mother to make sure she was coming.

"I tek a cab now," she said.

"What about Billy?"

"He say he vill come."

We waited in a large conference room with a panoramic view. My mother was happy to see me, as though we were just getting together for coffee and cake. Billy had not arrived. My mother called him. There was no answer. Almost an hour later, with him a no-show, both lawyers witnessed the wacky side of Billy—the unreliable, unstable and confused person who liked to pull a fast one. Both lawyers and my mother discussed whether I would continue helping my mother or if Billy would take over. After going over the relevant documentation, including years of Billy's threatening faxes and psychiatric medications, they decided no modifications were necessary.

"What about you?" Billy's lawyer asked me as we were standing at the elevator.

"What about me?"

"Well, the apple doesn't fall far from the tree."

"I'm not the one who took Billy Resnick's case, am I? What does that say about you, Mr. Oren?"

When I drove my mom home, Billy's car was gone. In his room, my mother saw things were not quite right. Banana peels were strewn on the bathroom floor and toothpaste smeared on the walls. His bedroom looked like it had been ransacked, with clothes hanging over the sides of open drawers, the lamp tipped over, and black paint spilled on the grey carpet.

"Something happened to him," my mother said.

Just then the phone rang. Thalian's Mental Health Institute at Cedars Sinai told my mother Billy had checked himself in that afternoon. Being sick was a good reason for behaving any which way in our family. Illness was his excuse for not showing up to the meeting.

Upon hearing the news my mother looked tired and frail.

"It vasn supposed to be like dis," my mother said. "Da two of dem livin inda home vit me, shouldn be like dis."

She needed a break, an irony I would never forget, having endured their nonsense all my life. She wanted me to save her. She looked straight into my eyes, putting it all on my shoulders. She begged me to change her situation.

I seized the moment and came up with a plan, got her approval and began the execution. She asked for an apartment small enough her sons would never be able to move in and stay with her. I found her a new place to live near her friends, shopping and favorite delis.

The next day I found a board and care specializing in Allan's health problems. He would be monitored round the clock. I would send him spending money. My mother promised she would visit him often.

While she and Allan prepared to move, I hired a real estate agent, who rented out the house within two weeks. The synchronicity of everything falling into place was miraculous.

Billy was discharged from the hospital and found new place to live. When everyone was settled, I flew back to Israel to enjoy my pregnancy. Jack and I were happy about having a baby. Our elation out-weighed any crazy stuff my mother or brothers could ever have done to me. The happiness of having a child and a loving family was so much stronger than any negative energies that fate could deliver. My pregnancy was the fuel that could move mountains up to heaven.

34
My Third Eye

The breathwork became the backbone of my daily existence, catapulting me further into my healing process so much so that for the first time in years, good energy surpassed the pain; Fred had moved on! This was a tipping point, and my intuition told me to see David Elliott for a private session. Something big was coming.

Energy rose from my upper back to my neck like a mutating golf ball stuck in my throat, growing larger. My upper body moved back and forth as though God were using dental floss to clear the debris between the discs of my spine.

"What do you see right now?" David asked.

"Nothing. But something big is stuck in my neck." The large golf ball was pushing upward.

"Wait, wait. I see it. I've seen this before," I exclaimed. "How strange. I see a group of young children on lush green grass running in circles, yelping with joy. In the background I see an old, brownish building immense against the blue sky like a Magritte painting where everything is familiar, yet odd. The building was round like the Coliseum in Rome or the Parthenon in Athens. The children have small facial features, strikingly opposite of mine, their lips thin and noses tiny. Their hair is a beautiful strawberry blonde, a brilliant color I have never before seen. They are wearing bright primary colors. Their play clothes are elegant and expensive, as if the children are from the past, pampered and loved. The girls are wearing patterned skirts that resemble Catholic schoolgirl uniforms. I am zooming in on one of the girls. She is wearing a bright red sweater. She recognizes me and smiles. How can this be?"

"You were there," David said. "You need to do some research and figure out who those children are."

The dynamic sounded crazy. And I didn't care, my gut telling me to take this ride no matter how wild.

"How am I supposed to research an image in my head?" I asked.

"Watch Eva Braun movies and see what you come up with," he said.

"Eva Braun? Hitler's mistress?" And then it hit me like a ton of bricks. The children were German. They looked so Aryan, so opposite of me.

"Google it," David said. "You need to do the research. Find the girl in your vision and take a photocopy to your mom. See if she recognizes her."

The prospect of researching my vision was intriguing. Full of energy, a bat out of hell, I was embarking through a spiritual portal into a new universe.

Having had this vision before, I had written it down and kept it in my files.

Journal entry (May 26, 2009)

I meditated, going deep. I had a flash of the bright green grass growing next to a stone structure that looked like the Coliseum. Lots of children were playing, dressed in bright primary colors and their hair was shoulder-length strawberry blonde, glistening in the sun. I remember this image from before. I dismissed it. I can't place the faces with names.

Watching movies and reading articles about Eva Braun for the next two days, I jotted down the information that spoke to me. Hitler had given his girlfriend, Eva, a camera for her nineteenth birthday. Through her films and photographs, she presented a slice of Nazi life often filming Hitler receiving his guests on their balcony at Berghof. A tremendous view of the Alps behind him, Hitler was respectful and civilized toward his guests, most of them in the upper echelons of the Nazi regime. The films did not show the evil that was his true self.

SS officers wanting to visit with Hitler had to prove their Aryan ancestry dated back to 1750. Families, especially those with little girls, were often invited. Hitler adored one young guest, Rosa Bernile, who was photographed with him when she was about six years old. When it was discovered that Rosa's maternal grandmother was Jewish, and that she had two uncles in the Dachau concentration camp, she was never invited to return and was probably killed.

Joseph Goebbels was the German propaganda minister responsible for producing uplifting photos of the Nazi regime, such as ones of Hitler surrounded by smiling children and portrayed as a warm and likable leader. Goebbels also devised the anti-Semitic propaganda that was distributed throughout Europe, aimed at brainwashing European and German youth.

In an old photo of the Goebbels family, I found the children in my vision on the Internet. The beautiful strawberry blonde girl who had recognized me was posing with her six brothers and sisters. She was Helga Goebbels, the daughter of Joseph and Magda Goebbels. The old building that stood behind them as they were playing on the grass was featured in many films aggrandizing Germany before the 1936 Olympics. That same building was bombed out at the end of the war and partially destroyed.

This was the first time in my life I could focus on the actual historic details of WWII. Searching for the strawberry blonde mystery girl made it easier for me to deal with the technical, strategic and gory details. It wasn't easy, but I was able to handle reading about my relatives killed in such a gruesome manner along with gypsies, gays and the Germans opposed to the Nazi regime. Watching Eva Braun movies, seeing the other side of German life, I was able to take in more as I separated out the details.

The Germans wanted to win the war and take over the world. Hitler followed the motto "Divide and Conquer." Counting on rivalries to keep him in supreme command, he depended on Goebbels' relentless propaganda to make it easier for Germany to murder Jews. Germans went into battle easily and homeland soldiers systematically destroyed a race of people. Meanwhile, Eva Braun filmed herself with Hitler's favorite dog, a German shepherd named Blondie, on the balcony at Berghof. She also played with the white rabbit Hitler had given her. Oddly, Himmler, the mastermind behind the Holocaust, happened to have been a rabbit breeder. The same man who brought cute soft rabbits into this world conjured up the plan to exterminate masses of humans.

My visions and my research led me to believe in past lives. Seeing the Goebbels children playing right in front of me, with Helga staring into my eyes and smiling, I think I may have been alive at the same time. I may have been German in the 1930s and Helga recognized me as she played on the bright green grass, while Europe went up in flames.

Printing the Goebbels family photo, I took it with me when I visited my mother.

"Do you know who these people are?" I asked her.

"Of course I do," she said. "Dey vere da famoz children. Da Nazi children. Dey ver killed by da suicide ven da Russians came."

Magda Goebbels and her husband committed suicide after poisoning their six children with a cocktail of cyanide and morphine, believing dying would be less painful than the rape and torture the Russians would inflict. Photos of the entire family lying dead on the ground in a line was a surreal image I didn't expect to see.

Dressed in his Nazi uniform complete with warm coat and hat, Dr. Mengele stood in the snow in his sturdy black leather boots. My mother described him, "He vas a tall man, Mengele, finger like dis. Links, rechts, (left, right,) tick, tok.

Den da people. It vas like a beauty pageant, dem valkin naked. Da goot lookin un dhealty vones stayed. Da rest vere taken avay."

Keeping his forearm upright, his palm facing out, he used his notorious index finger to systematically separate my mother from her family. He looked at each person, individually pointing each one to his or her final destination. Her father and uncles were sent to one group, her mother, aunts and cousins to another. My mother and her Aunt Golda were the only survivors in her family. My mother remembered Dr. Mengele's index finger and his horrifying voice, as though it happened just yesterday. That brief moment was charred into her memory. It was the end of the life she had known. When she was eighteen and the war ended, my mother walked out into the street, soon discovering everyone was dead. Her family had been killed soon after Dr. Mengele had separated them seven years earlier.

Mengele was a predator, known for his fertility treatments on women and twins. His goal was to figure out the best way to produce more Aryan babies. I had to wonder if my mother had any part of an experiment for the Master Race. Was she used in hormone-related experiments? Were her eggs were taken?

My mother was about fifteen when she first stood in front of Dr. Mengele. Her beautiful features and good looks may have attracted someone in the higher ranks who could get away with sexual abuse. Was she forced into a brothel as in "House of Dolls?" A 1955 novella by Ka-tzetnik 135633, the novella describes "Joy Divisions," groups of Jewish women in the concentration camps during World War II who were kept for the sexual pleasure of Nazi soldiers.

As David Elliott writes in his book *The Reluctant Healer*, "A predator is an energy, a person, a family or group that takes from others or destroys others for gain. A sexual predator uses dark sexual energy to accomplish this. Predators are skilled and often aggressive, determined and persistent about their intent to abuse. With this skill and focus, the second chakra—Love of Power—is the easiest way for the predator to enter into a person's energy field."

35
Spirit Portal

I woke up in the middle of the night in a panic, a cold thick sweat beading over my body. I opened my eyes with a sense my anxiety meant something important, but I didn't know what.

A few days later, I got a phone message: "This is lieutenant Brigit Collins-Hutchens from the Los Angeles Police Department. Please call me as soon as possible."

This had to be bad. Calling the lieutenant back, I anticipated the worst. "This is Alix Weisman. You called me this afternoon?"

"Do you know an Allan Resnick?" She asked.

"Yes, he's my brother."

"Has anyone contacted you yet to inform you?"

"No."

"Mr. Resnick passed away. We have his body here at the police station. We identified him by his fingerprints. He went into cardiac arrest in the ambulance on his way home from the hospital."

Thank you," I murmured. A heavy burden had been lifted off my shoulders.

My head was spinning. I walked down the hallway and fell flat on Lola's bed. Grabbing onto the bedspread so as not to slip off, I cried in one long emotional burst. Sniffing and wiping my tears away, I tried to make sense of it. My tears weren't so much about Allan as they were about what could have been. I mourned what I never had, the whole sibling thing.

I had to turn this suffering around and make it positive in my head. So I thought, "I love everyone and everyone loves me. If there is anywhere to be free, it's with my true friends and family. And no matter how difficult, here I am and here it is. Yes, it's sad. It's tragic, it's deep, it's mental and it makes me feel like shit. But somehow shit turns to fertilizer, and then the beautiful flowers pop out of the ground and smell so sweet and that's me on the other side of it. That's the real me. The orange-yellow flower warming her leaves in the sun."

After convincing myself I had a wonderful life, I got back to business. I called Hillside Mortuary where my father was buried and gave the pleasant woman on the phone the details, making an appointment to pick out the burial site the next morning.

"How do I say your favorite son has died?" I wondered. With a weak heart at almost eighty-six, she had already outlived most of her friends. The next morning before I left for Hillside, I called her.

"Hi," I said.

"Oh, who iz dis?" she asked, not recognizing my voice.

"It's Alix. Would you like to have lunch today?"

"Okay, any time. I am here!"

But first, at the mortuary, I chose the burial site and decided what accoutrements to purchase. Signing the contract, I was amazed how expensively one could decorate a lifeless body. It was as though I were in ancient Egypt deciding how to mummify. The rain came down when I picked my mother up for lunch. We went to Fiddler's Café and had a pleasant conversation over split pea soup and tuna salad.

She wore a bright pink and lavender shawl she had knitted herself. Smiling, she was happy I had come to visit.

"You know," she said. "I het a drim dis veek. About d grandmoder. It vas like she vas here inda front of me, big un clear." (I had a clear dream about my grandmother.)

Revitalized from the dream as though she had gone back in time, my mother described her grandmother, the one who had run the bakery in Poland.

"In da dream, I saw all da children in da family and from da neighborhood making matzos for Passover in da bakery. Dey ver havink zo much fun. It vas azoy (so) real!"

As my mother spoke, I wondered if there was a connection between her dream and Allan's death. Maybe the dream was meant to ease the pain of what she was about to hear, her grandmother helping her cope. My mother's skin looked younger as she spoke, her eyes bright with delight.

Driving her home, I still hadn't told her about Allan. "I'll come up for a minute," I said.

I sat on the couch. "Mom, I didn't want to tell you this over the phone. And I couldn't tell you in the restaurant. I . . . I have some news. Allan has passed away."

Her face dropped, her mouth hanging open. "How?"

"Heart attack."

"When?'

"March 23."

Standing up, she paced around the living room. "Da Tata, your fader, diet on the 19th of March. Dat vas a veek before de Passover."

"Jack's mom died a week before Passover," I said.

"Dat mus be vy my grandma came," she said. "She knew!"

Staring out the window, she asked, "Vat are ve goink to do?"

"I took care of everything this morning. It's all set. We just have to show up at Hillside Mortuary at 2:30 on Tuesday."

She said, "I hef to go out. I neet some air."

She put on her "Members Only" white parachute jacket.

"I'll go with you," I said.

"De dream," she said again, as she locked the door. "It vas like I vas dere or dey were here. It vas zo real."

"Mom, they are with you. They always have been."

"He didn't hate you," she said.

"What the hell does that mean?" I said. "Are you going to try to blame me for this too, for him hating me?"

I arrived home tired and hungry after walking home from school. I entered through the back, placed my backpack on the laundry room floor and tiptoed into the kitchen. Opening the refrigerator door, I pulled out the challah bread and cold cuts. My mouth was parched, as I smelled the veal bologna my mother had purchased from the Polish deli in Santa Monica. I took a plate from the cabinet and assembled my sandwich, finishing off the bologna. Lifting the top slice of bread, I spread on yellow mustard.

Just then, Allan came down the hallway from his bedroom. He walked into the kitchen wearing only his boxer shorts, having just woken up, even though it was mid-afternoon. I tensed at the sight of him. His face was angry and sleepy, his hair a mangled mess, his potbelly hanging over his boxers.

Returning the challah and mustard to the refrigerator, I started to clean up when Allan saw my sandwich sitting on the counter. Looking like a cheetah hunched over the day's prey, he grabbed my sandwich and turned to leave.

"Hey, wait a minute! That's mine!"

"Tough shit bitch," he screamed. "Why can't you make me a sandwich?"

He threw my sandwich on the floor and stomped on it, flattening it into an inedible paste. I ran into to my room. Sobbing, I locked my door and crawled into bed. Living in fear every day, I always misinterpreted how Allan would act. Expecting everything be done for him, he had changed from my favorite person in the world into the monster who smashed my sandwich.

"He didn't hate me?" I said. "So you think the way he treated me was love?"

We stared at each other for a few seconds.

"The way he treated me was not love. The way you let him treat me was not love either."

Worried that she had upset the only person left in the world that would care of her, she reached her arms out trying to hug me. "I didn min to upset you."

Backing away, I turned toward my car. It was the way she said "he didn't hate you" that brought back the memories, insinuations that everything my brothers did to me was acceptable and anything I did was not.

Meeting my mother and Allan at the California Pizza Kitchen in Santa Monica, Jack, Aidan, Lola and I sat in a booth. Lola was six and Aidan was four. My mother demanded that we include Allan in our lives. I agreed under the condition that if he acted in any way that reminded me of my childhood, in an abusive or hurtful manner, it would be the last time we would ever see him. After we ordered, Allan began screaming at the tip of his lungs.

"I don't have any money! Damn it!"

"Why not?" I asked. "You have money sent every month."

"I don't have any frickin' money!" Pulling out his wallet, he opened it wide and tuned it upside down, shaking it violently. Nothing fell out.

"Don't talk that way in front of my children," I said. His loud voice was also disturbing the table next to us.

"I'm leaving," I said, trying to stand up.

"Sit down, Alix. It will be all right," Jack said.

"No! I told you if he acted this way, this would be the last time."

I walked over to the cashier. "Please," I said, pointing to Allan. "That man is going crazy. Could we please have our meals to go? I'll pay for it right now," I said, handing her my credit card.

"Sure," said the cashier.

"Should I call the police?" she asked.

"I would."

Waiting for the food to be packed up, I walked over to the family seated behind us.

"I'm sorry that we disturbed your lunch."

"Oh, honey, we are sorry for you. Don't worry about us."

I saw our orders ready on the counter and grabbed the bags of food in one hand and Aidan's hand in the other. I walked out of the restaurant, brushing against the policeman who was entering. Jack followed and met us at the corner. We watched Allan come out of the restaurant, turn right and walk away. My mother came out after him.

"Come on, Mom," Allan yelled.

Confused, she looked at him and then at me standing on the corner.

"It's your choice, Mom," I said. "We are leaving."

I was walking to the car, sure she would go with Allan. Instead, she turned toward me, walked fast and caught up with us. We ate lunch at home and never saw Allan again.

"Are you ready to view the body?" the funeral director asked.

"What? No!" I said. "Do you want to do it, Mom?"

"I can't," she said, looking down at the ground.

"I'm sure it's him, sir. Please don't make us look at his corpse. He's been dead for more than three days," I said.

"Okay, I'll take responsibility. Just sign here."

As I signed the document releasing the body, I felt giddy as we drove to the burial site. Relieved, having one less asshole to fear, it was all I could do to keep a straight face as I sat down in a blue chair while a few friends gathered.

The mortuary men carried out the gray wooden casket. As Jack read the Kiddush, my mother grabbed my arm. Turning to look at her, I saw a lone tear

BEVERLY HILLS CONCENTRATION CAMP

roll down her face. I hadn't seen her cry since she was mugged walking home from the hairdresser one afternoon when I was in high school. We walked through the cemetery grounds afterward looking at the nameplates of all the famous people that Allan was buried near; Jack Benny and Michael Landon to name a few.

"How are you doing?" Emilia asked me, as I noticed how close my brothers name plate was to Max Factor, Sr.

"Fine."

"What are you feeling?"

"Not much."

She was dying for me to spill my guts, pressing me to speak. Not about to break down and say things I would regret, I wasn't going to give her ammunition to use against me.

Later, a week after the funeral, we had the usual Passover Seder at my house, the subject of Allan's death on our minds yet never mentioned. The next morning, the sun shone through the batik drapes in our bedroom. The smell of Matzo Brie and fresh coffee permeated the air. I snuggled deeper into my warm blankets. I was hungry as I pictured Jack in the kitchen happily preparing breakfast. I was comfortable and secure. I sat down at the table with my family to eat.

After breakfast, I held my second mug of coffee, warming both hands, sinking deep into the couch, staring into the garden through the open glass doors where lavender wisteria cascaded over the trellis, its petals dancing in the ocean breeze. Satisfied my house was organized and clean, I took a deep breath, grateful that this Passover, I stayed healthy! Even Fred had disappeared.

I recalled a list I had scribbled on a pad, the last set of questions I wanted to ask my mother. Jack and I had made videotapes of her experiences in WWII.

We filmed it every weekend until she had a sudden heart attack, from which she had now recovered.

"Hey Jack, I have more questions to ask my mom," I said. "Maybe we could do that now?"

Jack set up his camera in the garden a few feet back from the white trellis. I sat on a cushioned café chair with my notes in my lap. I could smell the white roses and bluish-purple hydrangeas behind me.

Sam, Jack's older brother, took a seat at the far end of the table. He was hunched over, his elbows on his knees, a filmmaker making history. Just then a sense of unworthiness flowed through me as though my beautiful surroundings were too good for me. Why is it sometimes I still feel like I don't deserve what I have?

In front of the camera, wearing black this morning, my mother looked good against a backdrop of bright green leaves, her short brown hair coiffed to perfection. She was thinner and weaker than she had been the last time we filmed, her presence was stoic, her attitude serious and mindful.

Clearing my throat, I looked at the camera and then down at my notes. The remaining questions were about my father.

"Rolling!" Jack announced.

"I'd like to move in a different direction today if that's okay with everyone," I said. "My remaining questions are an effort to get to know my father."

"Vat you vant to know?" my mother asked.

"I want to know about what life was like for you and my father in California. Also, I wonder if I was anything like him?"

"No," she said. "I don't tink you vere like him."

"Where did you two like to go out to eat?" I asked.

"Mostly ve ate at home."

"Did you ever go to Langer's?" Jack asked. He was curious because in his opinion, Langer's deli served the best pastrami sandwich in Los Angeles.

"Oh yez," she said. "It vas sometink back den. No von vould ever vear tennis shoez dere. Ve vere dressed. Dressed nice!" Pursing her lips, she nodded her head as she remembered.

"What were your husband's favorite foods?" I asked.

She had a faraway look. "Soup," she said. "He liked soup."

"What kind of soup?"

"He like da chickin soup. And he liked vegetable, too."

"What did he read?" I asked.

"De Yiddish paper."

"I don't think I am like you, so I am wondering if I am like my father. Isn't there anything I have in common with him?"

"No."

Not believing her, I sat silent as she stared at me deep in thought.

"You were both intelligent," she said. "You turned out to be the smart one in the family," she said sadly, the concept obviously having blown her mind.

"What else did you guys like to do together?" I asked.

Her eyes widened. "You mean sex?"

We all looked at each other and laughed. She had never discussed sex, boys, love, menstruation or pregnancy with me. The comment came out of nowhere.

"Let's move on to dessert. Did he like dessert?"

"Vell, yes. He liked Éclairs," she said, "da little puff pastry vit cream and chocolate." She used her hands to describe the layers.

"Ve vent out for dessert after dinner mit friends," she said. "Ve went to a bakery owned by Kapulsky. You know Kapulsky. He vas Polish. He made da best cakes and den von day he moved to Israel to open up more bakeries."

"Mom, but how was my father like me? There must something!"

"Intelligence," she said. "You were both intelligent."

As the interview was running out of steam, a reaction came over me, an intuition telling me I had to do more. Manifesting heightened consciousness, I perceived this was my chance to be witnessed. Because even though nothing could compare to my mother's history, I went through something, too.

"Okay everyone, I want to be in the spotlight for a second. A lot happened to you, Mom, and it was terrible. Something happened to me, too, in our house. I want to know why."

I took a deep breath. "Why did you leave me in that house with two men who were abusing me, one of them sexually, and I think you knew? You also made me live with a mentally ill man who screamed, manipulated and frightened me everyday, a life I used to consider my own hell. Living there was like walking through a mine field."

Finally, I had said it. After all these years, I put the truth out there, a slice of the past. Sam, who was busy filming, hadn't been privy to this information, now witnessed by him and by those who would later view the video and read the book.

My mother shut down the way she always had when there was the slightest bit of stress. She had no answer, her silence confirming the truth.

"Well?" I said

"I diden know," she answered.

"You didn't know? You were there. You had options. You had money. If you wanted to be with them, you could have sent me to a boarding school. Why did you make me live in that house? Why did you allow me to go through the torture?"

"I diden know," she said again.

It was in this moment I forgave her. She was incapable of more. The war skewed her vision and left her damaged. Her denial was so great she believed our home had been normal. In her mind, she remained in the Polish shtetl, in the ammunition factory, and in the death camp, all while going through the motions of being a Beverly Hills matriarch. She had created a version of her childhood in my childhood home. Triggers of the past held her hostage. The war made her the way she was, although one might argue many strong and successful people emerged from the Holocaust.

Was she a "baby soul" who did not have the spiritual maturity to become a fulfilled, loving parent? In The Michael Handbook by Simon

Warwick-Smith, the five evolutionary stages of the soul are explained, and somewhere in this continuum is my mother.

1. Infant – barely coping in society
2. Baby – dependent on structure and rules; fearful, narrow and rigid
3. Young – the drive for power and having power
4. Mature soul – adding in relationships and emotions
5. Old Soul – adding in spirituality, grasping the big picture of existence

I attended a Healer Training summer retreat in New Mexico; the emphasis was on developing a spiritual practice for personal healing, guidance on self-love, exchange, value, worth and money.

I met my flip-side, Jürgen Furst, the German son of a Nazi, who was randomly assigned to be my healing partner. Looking into his clear blue eyes after I told him the hellish history of my mother in Auschwitz and my abusive brothers, I wasn't sure how he would react. His jaw dropped. We stared at each other. We both felt it, all the history, craziness and pain between us, our parents born less than a year apart. What are the odds that we would be sharing a yoga mat, in an afternoon that would move us both forward as we embarked on healing? The universe was providing us with each other, what we needed to heal ourselves.

His energy was like none I had ever experienced before except in myself. He was sensitive yet volatile, deep and hidden yet so desperate to come out, to change and be set free. His fear of abandonment was so engrained that he kept reaching out to touch me. He even grabbed me making sure I was still there for him, projecting onto me his fear.

Jürgen Furst's father was a soldier for the Nazi party at age seventeen. That lasted for two years until the Russians came and took most of the soldiers to Siberia; they took his father to a prison camp because he was of a higher rank. He stayed there being starved and abused until the war ended.

As strange and awesome as it all was, I reminded myself I was at the retreat to help heal, and I tried not to make any judgments. He was another soul, like me, wanting to be free and happy. After breathing a while and a few instinctive touches and healing oil placements from me, he let loose in a way I was not expecting, going deep, seeing his parents and finally mentally traveling to Auschwitz.

He cried and screamed and his whole body flailed around, knocking over everything, sending my oil bottles flying. I was careful to stay away from the stones in his hands I thought he might inadvertently throw. At one point, he grabbed my arms and pulled my hands to his chest, needing me to press on his heart chakra as hard as I could. I reminded myself that afternoon my most important job was to heal him no matter our history. I was his coach, persuading him it wasn't going to be easy, but he could do it!

I told him, "Keep doing the breathwork, choose life and open your heart, change the energy of your lineage because if you have kids, you are not going to want them to receive what you had received."

Something wonderful happened. The shakiness that scared him was what would save him. Raw and vulnerable, he had gone deep into a place I had visited years earlier, seeing the suffering and experiencing it all, paving the way for healing.

He grabbed my neck in sort of a headlock and pulled me down to the mat, hugging me very hard. The energy was intense and I was afraid he was crossing a line between healer and healee.

"I feel there is a lot of healing here for both of us," he said.

He hugged me even harder before letting go. We both had an energy release. It was an opening where spirit had entered during breathwork, a shift, a connection made before moving forward. This happens to me almost every time I do the pranayama breathwork, whether alone or in groups.

Nobody had told me where to sit that day in the circle or that I would be facing someone with a mirror image of my issues, the most interesting reflection I had ever seen. I had no idea it would complete a circle for me, too.

Filled with emotion, I wished I could have expressed more to him that day about how grateful and happy I was for the experience.

I cried all morning after our experience together, having so much respect and love for my partner. He and I both lived with what was done to our parents and in turn what was done to us; the evil still coursed through us, the next generation of victims of war.

He did a lot for me just by being there and telling me his truth when I told him mine. We shared a deep understanding, something so rare, a conflict and a heart I could feel, and a person like me who just wanted to be free. Afterwards I was different, having a sense that all human beings are one, wanting to be seen, heard and loved. All the separations we have created based on religion and nationality, that we thought made us better than someone else, are just a farce.

This deep healing nudged me to sign up for another event the next winter. So a year later, I stood outside, chilled by the air, at David Elliot's New Year's retreat in Albuquerque, New Mexico. We gathered wood pieces and twigs, placing them in a teepee-like circle.

As I stared at the conglomeration of love and nature that would soon be a roaring fire, I remembered my mother telling me about the train from Lodz to Auschwitz. The Nazis forced her family to pile into a filthy cattle car for two days, with no water, no windows, no restrooms, no seats, and thrown together with the sick and dying. Docile and weak from starvation, they were told there would be more food. She said, "Ven Ve came to Auschwitz, I saw d fire. Ve didn know."

My relationship to fire was easy. Getting a minor burn in the kitchen while cooking, I was warned by the universe to be careful. I watched Aidan make scrambled eggs and saw him touch the hot frying pan, a good lesson he learned. When my clothes dryer blew up with flames shooting out, my house did not burn down. Instead, I learned an important lesson about cleaning the lint screen and vacuuming inside the dryer.

On all the camping trips I had been on, someone other than me maintained the big warm fire, a roaring blaze, so I never got cold. The most I ever did was pick up kindling twigs and carry wood. Fire has never scared me.

At the retreat, dressed in a blue and gray flannel shirt and black wool cap, Alexandre, a brilliant engineer, breathwork healer and ballroom dancer, began to start the fire with two pieces of wood. Using a bow drill, he created a notch and spun a cottonwood spindle stick on a piece of cedar fireboard. Dust collected in the notch, becoming compact and heated until smoke appeared. The friction generated enough heat to ignite the dust, creating an ember. He tapped the ember into a ball of tinder, and blowing on it, he watched it burst into a flame that he put at the base of the woodpile. We watched in amazement as a blaze emerged.

I stood alongside experienced healers and those eager to be healed. Everyone was focused on the fire, the sacred flames heating the coals we would later be walking on.

"I am just not getting it," I thought. I reflected on how my ability to have visions has grown in the last few years, noticing that I must be receptive for it to happen.

I listened to others divulge deep moments of expression, connecting the flames to nature. I got nothing, a blank page. I waited to see what would come up, if anything. I remained still, letting myself feel into the flames, my skin toasting, and my mind wandering.

When I was about to give up, a baby wrapped in a tiny blanket emerged in my mind's eye. It was my father's baby with his first wife. The baby girl who appeared now in the orange flames had died along with the old woman holding her after the Nazi soldier grabbed them, the baby having been passed around like a football between protective females. That was my half sister. If the war had never happened and those two souls had lived, I would never have been born from my particular set of parents.

The baby was in my heart as though she were a part of me. Soon, everyone killed in the Holocaust was in my heart, their souls swimming through the flames. As I stared, voices came through, layers of sound telling me that they were ready to let me go. They wanted me to go on with my life because I had paid my dues, had written enough about it, and would finish this book, a fact that would set their souls free.

Emotion rose up from my belly, through my throat, and my eyes watered. I thought I might cry like a baby so I went inside and made myself a chai tea. I tried to make sense of what I was experiencing, while I stood in the kitchen staring out the window at my friends who were still focused on the fire.

Later as the dusk turned to night, a twenty-foot area of ground was cleared, surrounded by a thick frame of snow. Some of the stronger men loaded a wheelbarrow with hot coals and they laid them out on that piece of cleared ground atop seeds, needles and pebbles. Everyone stood around the rectangle with hands held straight up, pointing toward the sky.

I heard the word freedom in my head and chose that word to be my mantra for the evening. Jogging in place in front of the hot coals, I was enthusiastic, warm on the inside and chilled on the outside like a jet engine raring to go. David held me firm at the waist to keep me from taking off too soon.

"Will you be free to finish your book?" David asked.

"Yes," I yelled.

"Will you be free to go on with your life?"

"Yes."

"What's your word?"

"Freedom!"

I yelled out the word 'freedom' as I stared up at a star in the night sky. I heard the voices of my peers encouraging me, yelling freedom with me until as if in a trance, I walked quickly across the burning coals. My ancestors set me free this night from the guilt, shame and negative energy that came through the umbilical chord of my lineage. As I walked, I saw the past behind me, and the future up for grabs in front of me. I was in the happiest place I had ever been. Still in a trance, I walked off the coals onto the snow where Borut caught me with a bear hug.

In those moments on the coals, I had an instant vision of the next complete draft of my book. I was ready to flesh out those stories, as though my ancestors had set me and future generations free during this fire walk, the energy of my family and friends supporting me through all the chapters, rewrites and crumpled-up yellow legal pad pages. With this freedom, I felt certain more freedoms would come, the law of attraction at its best.

Holocaust energies had held me back throughout my life, a fog causing me fear of leaving my comfort zone. Maya, my healer partner that day, described me as someone with "much fire in my heart." It was true. I had so much passion and energy, I wanted to fly. The fire walk helped me muster up the courage to allow myself the freedom to do, be and write whatever I wanted as long as it fulfilled me, no forces holding me back from satisfying my true desire.

God had typecast me as a child of Holocaust survivors, and I am. Yet this is only one part of me. I am a writer, a healer, a manager, a mom, a wife, a friend, a lover, a traveler and one who enjoys futzing with the ukulele and trying new things. I look forward to finding out who else I can be, without limits as I move forward, without the baggage I carried all my life, without the fear and entities my mother carried.

As my mother aged and became weaker, I felt the entity, the negative energy she had carried for a lifetime, present itself as strong-willed and aggressive, wanting me to lie down, rest and do nothing. Compared to my mother's dose of this energy, I believe I inherited less of it than my brothers did. Sensing intuitively I needed to escape from it, I didn't understand what it was or why it was.

When I visited my mother in the hospital, she was sitting in a chair. She wanted me to lie down in her bed while she wasn't using it. The idea she was determined to see me in a hospital bed was scary enough, but when I would not comply, her voice became loud. "Juz lie down!" she said.

Mustering up the strength to resist her strange request was difficult. This happened after a long day of carpooling children, running errands and navigating traffic. Most of my life she had wanted me to lie down and stay in bed. I saw Allan lying in bed most of the day, depressed and doing nothing. I would jump up and refuse to copy that behavior even when I was tired. It seemed all my mother cared about besides my eating was that I lie down, a behavior that could have stemmed from the fact Nazis shot prisoners who weren't sleeping flat in their bunks.

Weeks after having had heart surgery, my mother was driving to a movie with Emilia, who was missing her husband, Dan. Emilia was looking for comfort, and seeking out new social connections, hopeful about her future. In the passenger seat while Emilia drove, my mother said, "We are finished. We are old and done! It's the end."

She told her friend that they were on death's door, encouraging Emilia to give up on life. Then, in her early 60s, Emilia looked younger than she was.

"It was like she was a stranger!" Emilia told me, describing how my mother had upset her. "I was afraid." She and my mother didn't speak for a year after that.

Jack, Lola, Aidan and I headed for a much-needed summer vacation on the island of Kauai before the kids returned to school. Having a great adventure on the island, we explored the beaches, snorkeled and tasted the local cuisine. Chickens with blue feathers strutted casually down the main roads. We took a speedboat out to the Na Pali coastline early one morning; Aidan, Lola and Jack sat at the front of the boat. The wind was blowing in their hair and smiles were on their faces. I turned white and went downstairs to throw up.

The next day was the perfect tropical afternoon of sun and rain. Setting out to explore the coastline, we hiked up the trail, sloshing in the muddy red ground, squishing between the thick roots that formed a natural staircase leading up. We hopped over sharp, black lava rocks, making our ascent, without looking down. We peeked through the wild greenery to Hanalei Bay, which fused with the next bay over. We took large, long steps to avoid the slippery spots where we could have rolled down the side of the cliff.

Aidan's tiny, skinny little legs maneuvered over the rocks as Lola led us with fearless speed and courage. Never once had they shown any fear of tripping, slipping or getting stuck in the rain. We reached the top of the cliff and were awed at the view. We sat on a rock staring out at the water having a quiet moment and lost track of time. A strong wind came without warning, the kind that steals away baseball hats and lens caps, sending them out to sea.

Afraid we might be blown off the cliff, we began our hike down.

"We made it!" Lola screamed, a climactic moment as we high-fived each other when we reached the bottom.

"Let's get the snorkeling gear," I urged.

We walked up a road lined with so many trees we couldn't see the sky through the branches. We headed toward Ke'e Beach beneath the cliffs we had just climbed, intrigued by stories of Ke'e's shallow reef abundant with fish and corals. As we came closer to the beach, I saw locals sawing coconuts off the tall palms to sell to thirsty beachgoers and lifeguards as we came out into hot, bright sun to a beautiful bay shimmering blue-green, royal blue and dark green. Snorkelers and swimmers were scattered in the water. The kids dropped their things on the sand and ran ahead into the cool water. Jack ran in after them.

Heightened awareness came over me as if we were all part of a painting, a perfect picture of the most beautiful beach in the world. Amazed by the spectacle, I stood there as a sudden warm breeze burst through, and I held my breath.

"Oh my God. I'm having déjà vu."

Embracing the moment for a few seconds longer, warm and tingly with this ever-present heightened awareness, a deep sense of joy and being universally connected, I felt my father! His spirit was in the breeze, surrounding me, something I hadn't felt since I was four years old.

I sat motionless accepting, absorbing and appreciative of this magical and spiritual presence reminding me of when my parents had taken me to Santa Monica Beach over forty years before. Relaxing on beach towels, their love was mine as they watched me play on the sand with my plastic shovel and bucket. This was my time of joy and innocence when I didn't have a care in the world.

My father's graceful presence was now real. Reminding myself to breathe, I embraced him, and the universe flowing over him and my family in perfect harmony. Reliving joy, clarity and a memory I wanted to keep forever and extend to my children, I was part of something larger than I could see with my eyes, and my children were part of that purpose.

I saw life in a new light, a new beginning. I found the culmination of what I had been searching for all my life here and now on Ke'e Beach; the purpose of my existence was clear. I sifted the fine white granules of sand through my fingers. I was grateful to have encountered my father's spirit here, my father who I missed so much.

Paradise for all, I thought. This was only the beginning.

EPILOGUE

I began this book angry toward those connected to my past, with judgment about how they behaved. I saw my tale as something so "out there" no one would believe it. As you have read, traumas and emotions from my past that I thought were gone were instead lodged in different compartments in my body. These invisible, stuck areas created an energy blockage so intense, it caused physical pain. My solution was to look for alternatives.

As I wrote about the past, I discovered I was healing my lineage, gaining a deep understanding of who I really was, and becoming spiritual in all aspects of my life now. I want to teach others to find their true selves, sharing ways to connect, release and transform energy through breathwork, writing, creativity and positive expression of all kinds.

Through sheer determination, not wanting to be a victim, having the guts and the inner strength to find healers, resources and support to tackle a problem that was bigger than me, I healed myself.

Deep issues offered tears of healing; the aim was to revisit each trauma again and again until finally the tears were gone. While I wrote this book, I was teary, often with a sinus infection, wanting sugar and other compensations for the hurt. The only viable option was to go through it and feel the pain enough times, until the emotion had burned out and passed. The result was I became healed and whole.

I believe my mother has lived with negative thought forms and entities since the Nazis invaded her shtetl (village) in 1939 and, of course, when she faced Dr. Mengele. She passed those energies onto her children. I chose to clear that energy and keep it from transferring further. When I began writing, I had a vision of vast numbers of faceless people coming towards me. I believed I was perhaps meant to help bring healing to the next generation by writing this book. When I saw all those people, they were sending me a message without words, and it was quite clear to me.

I could see that Dr. Mengele had all the power. When he pointed to my mother, something evil was launched down through generations.

Today, my body and mind are free. I can barely remember the entrapment, the pain that would not let me move, or the constriction that kept me from speaking my truth and living life. Naming my pain Fred and having a relationship with him was very effective, eventually resulting in his complete disappearance. There was a tipping point when I saw Fred in my mind's eye and kept trying to pierce him with my breath, desperately wanting to break in and connect with his gooey black form. In that moment of self-discovery, I felt into my heart and became one with him. A huge impact in making this transition was the fact the disc in my neck had further lifted off the nerve from the traction exercises, corrective chiropractic adjustments, neck and back stretches, my healing assisted by hydration, fish oil and other positive changes. I am more than 90 percent better than I was when I walked through Dr. Grace's door so many years ago. Now I'm exercising, walking on the beach and enjoying life much more. No surgery, no medication—just me. The curve in my neck is going in the proper direction. I have full use of my left arm. I have no drugs in my system. I feel GREAT! I continue to heal in many ways and my energy flow is beyond belief.

Much tension had been released though the breathwork and Network Spinal Analysis on a physical and emotional level. Emotional Freedom Technique (EFT) helped me lessen the emotional triggers associated with my traumas. All the modalities working together were a gift from God I had gradually found through trial and error. My nervous system was responding in positive ways.

During all this, there were scary, bewildering and frightening times, as I checked out in pain, crying or screaming. My family learned this release was a positive reaction. They watched me became a better wife, mother and friend. While my metamorphosis was happening no one knew where it would lead. My husband calmed the kids down, reassuring them often that we would get through these tough times. He knew I wanted more than the conventional methods of surgery and pills. A side effect of my healing was Jack began writing a screenplay, my daughter excelled in creative writing, and my son found his voice journaling each morning before school. Many of Jack's friends, other husbands, might not have put up with their wives going through this intense alternative healing regimen. The love and connection between all of us grew and remains strong.

War and other types of human suffering can create appalling effects that ripple down through generations. It's important that we as a people do not ignore atrocities of any kind, such as the genocide of the American Indians, the Armenian genocide of 1915 and more recently ethnic cleansing in Bosnia, Africa, parts of the Middle East and anywhere injustice exists. The generations following genocide don't understand the nature of the burden they carry. The first stage of healing is acknowledgement.

The light of my mother's life had been her family in Poland before age eleven. The experience of subsisting in the hell of the concentration camp destroyed her hopes and created a wound impossible to heal. Conscious of this darkness, raw and scary, while growing up, I was fortunate friends pulled me out, gave me good advice, and invited me to their family celebrations. Having my own children and the chance to create the family I always wanted, I am blessed.

Another healing gift I received was the understanding that I was not to blame for Allan's illness. If I had understood that what was happening to Allan was not my fault, and the family's turmoil had nothing to do with me personally, maybe I would have been able to separate myself emotionally. Instead I felt worthless and full of blame for having been born.

Nonetheless, I found even though I was happy in my current family life, I wanted to be heard and accepted, having purpose. I found what I was seeking in my spiritual community of breathworkers and healers where I was able to speak my truth and be accepted for who I was. They are the extended family I have chosen. Levi allowed me to tell his story in order to help others. Depression is so prevalent among young people that I believe it is important that our society spot the symptoms before they become fatal. Levi's story exemplifies the importance of finding solutions to emotional problems early and, if possible, trying to solve them without the awful side effects of prescribed medications.

When I met Levi that day at Starbucks, I could tell he was holding in trauma that imprisoned him and kept him from joy. He was stuck in the past where he no longer belonged. My intuition was that the breathwork would help to release stuck memories, his symptoms would lessen, and he would find joy. He in fact followed up with this and benefited from it.

Focusing on what feels good is important. For the last four years, I have listened to Abraham discs and read the books, learning to take just the next easy step. For example, as I am writing this book, my next best feeling thought is finishing the section and deepening the process. As I am proofing the book, my next best thought is holding the finished book and people wanting to read it. At this point in my healing, I find that I can wish for things, think about them and they manifest, sometimes too quickly, to the point that I have to be careful what I wish for. Focused intent is a skill one can develop.

Children of Holocaust survivors suffer in their own ways. Enduring tremendous guilt, we are still connected to our ancestors, experiencing the hunger, pain, loss and devastation of our parents, as we try to protect our own children from those same nightmares.

If I could tell my friends and loved ones anything I learned from this experience, it would be to listen to our inner voice, the psychic place that tells us to invest in ourselves. We are strong enough to overcome anything. We have the power to change by controlling our words and thoughts. Whatever upbringing we were dealt, we can heal it, and walk a path that empowers. That voice is more important than what any practitioner or doctor tells us to do. We are in charge. Healing takes time and is worth it.

I've learned over the years I can take any issue or block in my body and condense it into an image, ramp it up with my breath and resolve it, a practice that is very helpful for healing. Having witnessed my transformation over several years, friends, acquaintances and neighbors began asking me for breathwork sessions and private coaching, wanting to experience the secret that helped me heal. I was also asked to lead breathwork classes, a challenge for which I thought I was not ready, convinced I would be a disappointment and fumble over my words. This insecurity was necessary. I sat with it, and accepted it until the energy changed. Happy now, I was able to manifest my desires and teach others based on my experience; others who have the courage and will to make major changes that just might reinvent their lives.

I watched my role as a teacher positively shift week after week until it was easy to hold a nurturing and helpful space for others. Now I teach and facilitate breathwork group classes and hold private sessions in Los Angeles and nearby beach cities, teaching others to break unwanted chains of behavior. Before I began journaling and doing breathwork, I couldn't remember details of my childhood. The stream of consciousness writing, jotting down anything that came to mind, led me to ideas and solutions I would never otherwise have reached. Journaling is an invaluable practice.

Today, my mother is comfortable and lives independently in a diverse community where she hosts her grandchildren and friends. Even though she has suffered heart attacks and a stroke, she remains with a strong will to live. Often, when she delves into the past to tell us more, she can't believe that she, herself, had gone through the nightmare of the Holocaust....

GLOSSARY

Abraham - A group consciousness from the non-physical dimension that deliver a message of joy. They are known for catch phrases such as: "You are what you think about; be easy about it; you will never get it (all) done; it's how you feel about them that's important, not how they feel about you."

Abraham describe themselves as "a group consciousness" from the non-physical dimension. They have also said, "We are that which you are. You are the leading edge of that which we are. We are that which is at the heart of all religions."

Abraham have told us through Esther Hicks that whenever we feel moments of great love, exhilaration, pure joy, stoned-out bliss, and even the energy of sexual orgasm, when we feel Energy Flow rushing through our bodies, that is the energy of Source, and that is who Abraham "is." Abraham's teachings are as follows:

1. You are a physical extension of that which is non-physical.

2. You are here in this body because you chose to be here.

3. The basis of your life is freedom; the purpose of your life is joy.

4. You are a creator; you create with your every thought.

5. Anything that you can imagine is yours to be or do or have.

6. As you are choosing your thoughts, your emotions are guiding you.

7. The universe adores you for it knows your broadest intentions. (I think that this means that the universe loves us because it knows who we are. It's something that I feel into, rather than use words to describe.)

8. Relax into your natural wellbeing. All is well. ("Really, it is!")

9. You are a creator of thought ways on your unique path of joy.

10. Actions to be taken and professions to be exchanged are by-products of your focus on joy.

11. You may appropriately depart your body without illness or pain.

12. You cannot die; you are everlasting life.

Breathwork – Ancient two-stage practice based on Pranayama Yoga that can generate amazing feelings and insights. During this active meditation, inhale through the mouth taking air first into the belly, then the upper chest and let the air release. During the resting stage, breathe through the nose.

Chiropractic – A form of alternative medicine focusing on the diagnosis and treatment of mechanical disorders of the musculoskeletal system, especially the spine. These disorders are believed to affect a person's general health.

Coccyx - The very bottom portion of the spine. It represents a vestigial tail (hence the common term "tailbone") and consists of three or more very small bones fused together. The coccyx is made up of between three and five separate or fused vertebrae.

Corrective Chiropractic - Chiropractic Corrective Care is a process by which using diagnostic x-rays, specific chiropractic adjustments and active therapeutic spinal exercises can improve the function of the nervous system, change curves, and alter structural changes like reducing bone spurs, improving disc health, improving joint motion and restoring muscular balance. In addition to the physical corrections, patients are given an education in proper lifestyle and nutrition to enhance and support the structural and physiological changes that can ultimately improve one's quality of life long term.

Dr. Donny Epstein – The founder of Network Spinal Analysis (NSA) and a genuine alchemist of growth, human potential and body/mind healing. He teaches strategies for living, from adapting to stress, dissipating tension from the spine and nerves, connecting with the body's natural rhythms and experiencing greater wellness. Healing is relative to a person's experience and is growing into new areas. His technologies on the energetics of change are being presented in corporate training programs.

Emotional Freedom Technique (EFT) – is a healing aid, based acupuncture principles. EFT rebalances the body's energy system with respect to unresolved emotional issues. By gently tapping on key acupuncture (meridian) points on the head, torso and hands, EFT is able to rebalance, relieve and resolve blocked energy meridians which compromise our emotional well-being as well as our natural healing potential. For more information: selfcarepower.com

Entrainment – A Network Spinal Analysis session is called an "entrainment," a term that means to get "in sync." During an entrainment a wave-like deepening of your breath will spontaneously occur and various regions of your spine will begin to gently move in sync with each other as tension releases.

Epigenetics – The study of changes in gene activity not caused by changes in the DNA sequence. It is the study of gene expression and the way genes bring about their phenotypic (physical or biochemical characteristics) effects. Epigenetic change is a regular and natural occurrence but can also be influenced by several factors including age, the environment/lifestyle, and disease. New and ongoing research is continuously uncovering the role of epigenetics in a variety of human disorders and fatal diseases.

Gate – A community educational experiential weekend open to members of Network Spinal Analysis practices and led by Dr. Donny Epstein.

Genocide - The systematic destruction of all or a significant part of a racial, ethnic, religious or national group. Well-known examples of genocide include the Holocaust, the American Indians, the Armenian Genocide, and more recently the Rwandan Genocide and the Bosnian Genocide.

Ghetto – A part of a city in which members of a minority group live, especially because of social, legal, or economic pressure. The term was originally used in Venice to describe the part of the city to which Jews were restricted and segregated.

Gluten – A protein composite found in wheat and related grains, including barley and rye. Gluten gives elasticity to dough, helping it rise and keep its shape and often gives the product a chewy texture. Gluten is also used in cosmetics, hair products and other dermatological preparations.

Gluten Intolerance – An allergic reaction triggered by gluten. Symptoms include bloating, abdominal discomfort or pain, diarrhea, constipation, muscular disturbances, headaches, migraines, severe acne, fatigue, and bone or joint pain.

Holocaust – Genocide of approximately six million Jews killed by the Nazi regime and its collaborators. Some historians use a definition of the Holocaust that includes the additional five million non-Jewish victims of Nazi mass murders, bringing the total to approximately eleven million. Killings took place throughout Nazi Germany and German-occupied territories.

Merkabah – (also spelled Merkaba) Image seen in the cover art and described in the artist's comments. The divine light vehicle used by ascended masters to connect with and reach those in tune with the higher realms. "Mer" means Light. "Ka" means Spirit. "Ba" means Body.

Network Spinal Analysis (NSA) – Academic research at major universities has demonstrated that NSA promotes coherency in the central nervous system. NSA consists of gentle, precise touches to the spine called entrainments that cue the brain to create new wellness-promoting strategies. Each entrainment improves the spine toward further healing. The result can be a spontaneous release of spinal and life tension and greater knowledge of the relationships between one's body, mind, emotion, and expression of spirit.

Sacrum - A large wedge-shaped vertebra at the inferior end of the spine. It forms the solid base of the spinal column where it intersects with the hipbones, forming the pelvis. The sacrum is a very strong bone that supports the weight of the upper body.

Shtetl - Small towns with predominantly Jewish populations existing in central and Eastern Europe before the Holocaust.

Somato Respiratory Integration (SRI) - A set of breathing exercises designed to connect isolated traumas and memories locked away in the body. It is another modality of personal healing focusing on body rhythms through close attention, gentle breath, movement and touch.

Soul – The incorporeal and immortal essence of a human being.

Spirit Guides – Incorporeal beings that are assigned to us before we are born that help nudge and guide us through life. They're responsible for helping us fulfill the spiritual contract we make with ourselves before we incarnate. Our higher self helps select these guides, who help through insights, signals and messages while we are living out our incarnation.

ABOUT THE COVER

Artist Cher Lyn creates mystic art medicine: one of a kind, individualized artwork designed to promote healing.

In 2014, I commissioned Cher Lyn to paint the cover of *Beverly Hills Concentration Camp*, my soul painting, asking her to paint a vision I doodled years earlier while writing the book. The vision was a beautiful naked woman with long hair jumping through a tree, dark energy falling off her. Cher Lyn took my idea way beyond what I imagined, creating a powerful image rich with symbols and meaning.

A note from the artist

"SAVIOR SOUL"
As a "Savior Soul" you make the world whole.

The painting "Savior Soul" depicts an Angel in a woman's body, powerful and graceful. Emerging through the center of her heart is the "Merkabah," a six-pointed three-dimensional Star that is a vehicle to higher realms. She is the Tree of Life, her body, mind and soul lifting from iron shackles and offering Transcendence. Her consciousness rises to the whole of her lineage, the "human holocaust," before it returns to the Light in Love. Cognizant of the dark, the White Owl assists in bringing the light through while understanding the Angel's true Nature.

The foundation of the tree is strong. Fed with light, it represents the past, present and future time continuum, holding the power of protection. This "now" offers forgiveness for the atrocities. The Hummingbird-like wings of the Angel through the Tree of Life send high vibrations into the corrupted iron minds riddled with evil thoughts that created deeds too low to mention. Through this portal, the evil is brought to the Light.

ACKNOWLEDGEMENTS

My special thanks to the following people
for their emotional support, time and contribution
to this creative process:

Tok Braun, Hyla Cass MD, Marie E. Cavanaugh, D.C.,
Nadine Dakema, David Elliott, Dr. Donny Epstein,
Sandy Factor, Ann Faison, Charlie Griak, Juliette Huck,
Kevin Kwan, Cher Lyn, Levi M, River Lark Madison,
Adam Maggid, Benjamin Maggid, Liana Maggid,
Audrey Marco, Loretta Sparks LMFT, Simon Warwick-Smith,
Dr. Talat Halman, Vickie Cgenari, Gemma Rose,
Rabbi Steven Silver, Alaric Smeets, Grazyna Sniatkiewicz,
Dr. Grace Syn, The writers' group, Debra Vaupen,
Drew Vaupen, Samuel L. Weiss R.I.P, Dr. Ruth Ziemba,
and Felice Zoota-Lucero.

ABOUT THE AUTHOR

Randi Maggid is an author, breathwork facilitator and healer having studied with renowned clairaudient, David Elliott. She offers group classes and private sessions in Pranayama Yoga breathing, a two-stage technique that helps move energy in the body and invite ease while releasing fears and blocks. This conscious breathing brings about a meditative state of calm, relaxation and joy while illuminating truth and awakening spirituality. Healing through breath can be an astonishing experience and also provide healing breakthroughs.

Randi attended UC Santa Barbara, received her BA in Journalism from the University of Southern California and her Masters of Science Management degree from Boston University. She worked as an Art Director in Los Angeles and Chicago and owned an Art and Frame Gallery in Israel. She is a married mother of two and lives in Los Angeles, California. For more information about this book and related articles and subjects or to sign up for breathwork classes, workshops and private sessions, go to www.randimaggid.com.